Microsoft® Office for Teachers

Third Edition

William J. Gibbs
DUQUESNE UNIVERSITY

Patricia J. Fewell
EASTERN ILLINOIS UNIVERSITY

Allyn & Bacon
is an imprint of

Boston   New York   San Francisco
Mexico City   Montreal   Toronto   London   Madrid   Munich   Paris
Hong Kong   Singapore   Tokyo   Cape Town   Sydney

Acquisitions Editors: Kelly Villella Canton and Darcy Betts Prybella
Editorial Assistants: Annalea Manalili and Nancy J. Holstein
Project Manager: Sarah N. Kenoyer
Production Coordinator: Carol Singer, GGS Book Services PMG
Design Coordinator: Diane C. Lorenzo
Cover Design: Jeff Vanik
Cover Image: Corbis
Operations Specialist: Susan W. Hannahs
Director of Marketing: Quinn Perkson
Marketing Coordinator: Brian Mounts

For related titles and support materials, visit our online catalog at www.pearsonhighered.com.

Between the time website information is gathered and then published, it is not unusual for some sites to have closed. Also, the transcription of URLs can result in typographical errors. The publisher would appreciate notification where these errors occur so that they may be corrected in subsequent editions.

Library of Congress Cataloging-in-Publication Data

Gibbs, William J.
    Microsoft office for teachers / William J. Gibbs, Patricia J. Fewell. — 3rd ed.
        p. cm.
    Fewell's name appears first on the earlier edition.
    Includes bibliographical references and index.
    ISBN-13: 978-0-13-158970-4
    ISBN-10: 0-13-158970-9
    1. Microsoft Office. 2. Microsoft Excel (Computer file) 3. Microsoft Word. 4. Microsoft
PowerPoint (Computer file) 5. Microsoft Access. 6. Teachers—In-service training.
I. Fewell, Patricia J. II. Title.

    HF5548.4.M525F49 2009
    005.5024′37—dc22

                                                                2008005340

Printed in the United States of America
10 9 8 7 6 5 4 3 2 1   **BRR** 12 11 10 09 08

Allyn & Bacon
is an imprint of

This book is dedicated to our families:
Earl and Joy Longman and the Longman gang; Annette,
Lauren, and Liam Gibbs; and James and Helen Gibbs.

ABOUT THE AUTHORS

William J. Gibbs

William is an associate professor at Duquesne University. He holds a Ph.D. and a Masters degree in Instructional Systems from The Pennsylvania State University. Dr. Gibbs teaches courses in instructional design, e-Learning, human computer interaction, interface design, and digital multimedia. Prior to his present position at Duquesne University, he served as head of a media and technology center where he assisted faculty with the design and development of instructional materials, learning resources, and technology-based courses. Dr. Gibbs has given numerous technology training seminars and workshops on Microsoft Office, Web development, and interactive multimedia applications for faculty and K-12 educators.

Dr. Gibbs has been actively involved in original research projects that resulted in scholarly publications and conference presentations. He has given presentations at state, national, and international conferences on numerous topics related to the use of technology for teaching and learning. In addition, Dr. Gibbs published a number of research articles on topics ranging from technology-based learning, developing e-Learning applications, online learning, computer-mediated communication, and human-technology interaction.

Patricia J. Fewell

Patricia is currently a professor and chair of the Department of Secondary Education and Foundations at Eastern Illinois University, where she teaches courses in technology application, curriculum development. She received her Ed.D. in 1988 from Illinois State University. She has been certified as a K-12 media specialist within the state of Illinois. She is involved in teacher certification serving on numerous accreditation teams within the state and nationally. She gives presentations on technology applications in the classroom at state, national, and international conferences.

When away from the university, Patricia enjoys the two dogs, two cats, and two horses that live with her and help her in her garden and "mini farm" at the end of a dead-end road out of town.

PREFACE

Conceptual Framework

In this book, computers and associated software are presented as tools or means to accomplish tasks in instruction, learning, and classroom management. From this perspective, we examine various types of computer software, including word processing, presentation, database, spreadsheet, and telecommunication applications. Each category is presented as part of the Microsoft Office suite comprised of Word, PowerPoint, Access, Excel, Outlook, and Publisher as well as through a combination or integration of the Office products. We offer specific instructions and recommendations for using these products in the classroom and provide teachers with a starting point to develop their technological knowledge and integrate technology into the curriculum.

Teachers are busy and often do not have time to learn new software applications. Word processing, databases, and spreadsheets can improve work efficiency, expand the range of tasks performed, improve accuracy and effectiveness, and reduce the amount of time needed to perform routine tasks. However, the initial time needed to learn these applications can be an obstacle for some teachers. We address this issue in three ways. First, we present a visually illustrated and nontechnical approach to learning the Microsoft Office 2007 suite. The book includes screen captures supplemented with text descriptions, work templates, and exercises to help teachers learn and use these applications without the frustration often experienced when studying intensive technical manuals. Second, we believe it is useful to build on the suggestions and work of others, so we have created work templates (e.g., sample newsletter, grade book, and so on) and exercises that demonstrate the usefulness of the Microsoft Office suite and the diversity of its applications. Teachers can quickly and easily tailor these templates and exercises to meet their specific needs. Third, the book focuses on various tasks—such as creating grade books, newsletters, and posters or making presentations to parent groups or the school board—as a catalyst for learning the Microsoft Office suite.

For example, many preservice teachers need to know how to create a class newsletter, store student records, calculate test scores, and help students create an electronic presentation: Word processing, database, spreadsheet, and presentation development skills are fundamental to these tasks. The activities in this book focus on these tasks to cultivate basic computer proficiency. Using nontechnical and graphically illustrated "how-to" procedures, teachers and students accomplish real-world, computer-based tasks and develop skills in word processing, database management, using spreadsheets, and making presentations.

This book is written for in-service and preservice teachers with very basic computing skills, such as opening, creating, and closing files and operating a mouse. The activities described in the book require a computer capable of running Microsoft Office 2007.

Organization of the Text

Chapter 1 introduces the text and offers information on state and national technology standards for teachers and students related to integrating technology in the classroom.

Chapter 2 addresses the Microsoft Office 2007 interface, including taskbars, menu options, and the Ribbon. It also presents information about using the Quick Access Toolbar.

Chapter 3 discusses word processing, including creating a new Microsoft Word document and modifying an existing one. It focuses on creating a book report, a Web page document, and a newsletter. Using the chapter activities, students create word processing documents. They use the copy, cut, paste, and formatting options as well as Word Art and Clip Art to create a document with columns resembling a newsletter.

Chapter 4 introduces Microsoft PowerPoint. It focuses on the fundamentals and how they apply to developing a presentation. Using the example of a student research team reporting on weather conditions, the chapter outlines the steps in creating a presentation. It discusses slide layout, design, importing graphics and clip art, and printing a presentation and saving it as a Web page.

Chapter 5 focuses on Excel fundamentals and their application to classroom learning activities. It presents step-by-step instructions for creating workbooks and editing and manipulating data in worksheets. Activities include creating a workbook; entering data into a worksheet; editing, calculating, and charting data; and using Pivot tables.

Chapter 6 presents detailed instructions for creating and entering information and searching a database using Access. It also shows how to save files, prepare mail, merge documents, and print reports.

Chapter 7 presents basic e-mail concepts and presents procedures for composing, sending, reviewing, receiving, organizing, and deleting e-mail in Microsoft Outlook as well as using contacts, journals, and calendars.

Chapter 8 discusses preparing brochures, postcards, and flyers with Publisher software using many of the same processes used in Word.

Chapter 9 builds on the previous chapters and presents readers with ideas on integrating the various Office products to increase work efficiency and enhance the quality of materials created.

Although the chapters are related, they can be used independently and out of sequence. Teachers who want students to create a monthly newsletter will find chapters 3 and 8 useful; teachers who want students to create book report presentations or perform analyses on data will find chapters 4, 5, and 9 informative.

Accompanying CD

The accompanying CD contains new material providing all the examples presented in the book and other materials that may be created using the Office suite. You will find examples and exercises in the Examples folder and the Let Me Try folder. Referring to the example on the CD as you follow the text helps facilitate your understanding of the topic being presented. All exercises, activities, and examples in the text that have a corresponding file on the accompanying CD are called out in the text with an instruction line and are identified by the CD icon. Readers are encouraged to refer to the CD as they read the section.

Features of the Book

Advance Organizers

Each chapter begins with a set of advance organizers to prepare readers for the main topics. They include the following:

- Chapter outline
- Learning objectives
- Technical terms
- Overview, which provides the rationale for the topics and discusses their use

Show Me

Each chapter presents step-by-step instructions for manipulating the technical aspects of various applications, such as writing a letter in Microsoft Word. Using text and graphics, the steps necessary to accomplish this task as well as the rationale for performing specific software functions are illustrated.

Let Me Try

Let Me Try exercises are embedded throughout the chapters so that readers can practice the concepts learned. These exercises (a) offer guided practice for operating the software; and (b) produce outcomes, such as a database field, a Word document, and a PowerPoint presentation, which teachers can use. The Let Me Try exercises are based on daily instructional and managerial tasks, which include creating grade books with Excel, class newsletters with Word or Publisher, and/or student research reports with PowerPoint presentations. In some cases, templates and examples to support the Let Me Try exercises are provided on the accompanying CD.

New to This Edition

- *Revised Chapters for Office 2007.* Office 2007 has a much different interface from previous versions. You will find that the way in which you interact with the Office programs and conduct your work has changed substantially. Because of the new Office interface, all chapters have been revised and updated.

- *Expanded Let Me Try Exercises and Examples.* Additional Let Me Try exercises and examples have been added to the chapters and to the CD. Throughout the text, references to materials on the CD have been added to direct the reader to additional digital resources.

- *Windows Vista:* At the time of this writing, Windows Vista is the most current Windows operating system. Appendix A has been revised to reflect the new features of the Vista operating system, and appropriate revisions have been made in the chapters.

Acknowledgments

A number of the ideas within this text were conceived of or provided by classroom teachers to whom we are most grateful. We would like to especially thank the teachers at Prairieland Elementary School for their ideas. Bridgette Belasli graciously provided work samples that proved most useful and helped us develop practical examples. Terry Hyder spent many hours reviewing drafts of the text. Her suggestions were invaluable, and we greatly appreciate her efforts. We also thank Darcy Betts Prybella and Nancy Holstein for their support of our ideas and the insights they provided along the way.

The following reviewers also provided invaluable advice: David L. Bolton, West Chester University of Pennsylvania; Ann Boyer, private consultant and KEDCO; and Jan Dickinson, University of Arkansas, Fort Smith.

Mostly, we thank our families for their understanding and support as we developed this book. Earl Longman, Joy Longman, and Suzanne Schertz; and Annette Gibbs, Lauren Gibbs, Liam Gibbs, and James and Helen Gibbs, your encouragement made this book possible.

Brief Contents

CONTENTS

CHAPTER 5 EXCEL 2007   88

CHAPTER 6 ACCESS 2007   144

CHAPTER 7 OUTLOOK 2007   173

Note: Every effort has been made to provide accurate and current Internet information in this book. However, the Internet and information posted on it are constantly changing, so it is inevitable that some of the Internet addresses listed in this textbook will change.

1 TECHNOLOGY AND THE CLASSROOM

CHAPTER OUTLINE

1. LEARNING OBJECTIVES
2. CHAPTER OVERVIEW
3. ABOUT THIS BOOK AND USING TECHNOLOGY
4. EXPECTATIONS OF TEACHERS
5. EXPECTATIONS OF STUDENTS
6. COPYRIGHT IN THE CLASSROOM
7. ACCEPTABLE USE POLICIES
8. TEACHER PRODUCTION OF MATERIALS
9. TYING IT ALL TOGETHER
10. REFERENCES

LEARNING OBJECTIVES

At the completion of this chapter you will be able to:

- Identify the ISTE standards for teachers
- Note technology standards for students
- Be aware of copyright issues
- Be aware of acceptable use policies (AUPs) in school districts
- Identify teacher production activities
- Identify student production activities
- Identify how Microsoft Office products help teachers integrate technology

CHAPTER OVERVIEW

This chapter discusses the contents of this text and provides an overview of its structure and scope. It offers information regarding technology standards for teachers and students that can serve to establish a context for integrating technology in the classroom. In addition, the chapter presents an overview of acceptable use policies and copyright law.

About This Book and Using Technology

In order to comply with the International Society for Technology in Education (ISTE) and the National Council for the Accreditation of Teacher Education (NCATE) standards, teachers, including preservice teachers, must possess computer skills beyond the basics. In today's educational environment, there is constant pressure for teachers to become technologically competent because of increased access to computing, networking, and communications technologies, among other reasons.

The effective use and integration of technology into teaching and learning is a complex process. Teachers, not technology, should direct this integration. The acquisition and configuration of sophisticated computing and networking systems is essential for technology integration. It is shortsighted, however, to perceive hardware and software as the only requisites to successful integration and utilization. As Earle (2002) points out, it is comparatively straightforward to situate computing hardware in physical locations. However, it is another matter to integrate technology into teaching, learning, and the curriculum, which should be at the heart of all technology integration efforts. Schools must invest in technology training and development for teachers. Teachers need a fundamental understanding of technology and its uses prior to successful implementation or integration of that technology in the classroom. They must have the opportunity to learn about appropriate and effective uses of technology and practice using computers, software, and other communication devices. Additionally, schools and teachers must seek innovative ways to foster teachers' willingness to invest the time and energy needed to use technology effectively.

This book serves as supplement to computer application texts used in colleges of education for preservice and kindergarten through grade 12 teachers interested in enhancing their computer skills. Using examples and exercises based on the work teachers and students routinely perform each day in the classroom, it provides a technological foundation for beginning students (preservice teachers) to guide them to more advanced skill levels. This introduction to technology should serve as an initial step for teachers as they begin using and integrating technology in their classes.

Expectations of Teachers

Many teachers struggle with how to effectively use computers and software not merely as tools to facilitate the presentation of information but also as conduits with which students can construct their own knowledge. The expectations for teachers to integrate technology into the classroom are high. Teachers are expected to use technology not only for class management but also to facilitate and support the curriculum, which can be challenging.

Each state has specific standards for teachers to follow when implementing technology in the curriculum. Many states have adopted or adapted the standards of the ISTE, which has been a leader in the field for establishing technology standards. As teachers begin to integrate technology into their classes, the standards provide an invaluable resource to guide their efforts.

Addressing the development of student knowledge and skills to meet these standards is beyond the scope of this book. However, the text gives specific illustrations for using and integrating the Office products in the classroom environment, which will provide you with the knowledge and skills to meet many of the standards. The ISTE standards for teachers focus on the following areas:

1. Technology Operations and Concepts
2. Planning and Designing Learning Environments and Experiences

3. Teaching, Learning, and the Curriculum
4. Assessment and Evaluation
5. Productivity and Professional Practice
6. Social, Ethical, Legal, and Human Issues (ISTE, 2000)

The ISTE National Educational Technology Standards (NETS) and Performance Indicators for Teachers are found on the inside cover of this text for your review.

ISTE has also developed educational technology standards for administrators. In many states, these standards are also integrated into the standards for individuals to become administrators in school districts. The technology standards for administrators provide a view of how technology can effectively assist in the optimizing of school capacity to provide a successful school environment. The ISTE standards for administrators focus on the following areas:

1. Leadership and Vision
2. Learning and Teaching
3. Productivity and Professional Practice
4. Support, Management, and Operations
5. Assessment and Evaluation
6. Social, Legal, and Ethical Issues (ISTE, 2002)

Expectations of Students

Because technology is now an integral part of the curriculum, learning standards have been developed throughout the nation to provide a basis of expectations for what students should know and be able to do utilizing technology. For instance, ISTE developed technology standards for students that focus on the following areas:

1. Creativity and Innovation
2. Communication and Collaboration
3. Research and Information Fluency
4. Critical Thinking, Problem-Solving, and Decision-Making
5. Digital Citizenship
6. Technology Operations and Concepts (ISTE, 2007)

The ISTE NETS and Performance Indicators for Students are found on the inside cover of this text for your review. The standards for students were released in 2007, and many states are reexamining their expectations for students based on these standards.

Microsoft Office suite offers many tools with which to create innovative assignments, activities, and exercises that engage students as they use and apply technology. As you become familiar with the concepts presented in this book, you will be able to utilize the standards to cultivate your own technical proficiency.

Copyright in the Classroom

As noted in the ISTE standards for teachers, administrators, and students, ethical issues are addressed within the Digital Citizenship standard for students and within the Social, Ethical, Legal, and Human Issues for administrators and teachers. Teachers are expected to "model and teach legal and ethical practice related to technology use" (ISTE, 2002). Central to modeling expectations is appropriate respect for and use of copyright laws. Copyright law is a set of federal laws pertaining to the legal right to use original works. These laws set forth rights and conditions regarding how an individual may use or copy materials. The Copyright Act covers eight broad categories:

1. Literary works
2. Musical works
3. Dramatic works, including any accompanying music
4. Pantomimes and choreographic works
5. Pictorial, graphic, and sculptural works
6. Motion pictures and other audiovisual works
7. Sound recordings
8. Architectural works.

A copyrighted work may be used or copied under certain conditions:

- Public domain—Work belonging to the public as a whole, such as government documents and works with an expired copyright or no existing protection.
- Permission—Permission has been given for the proposed use by the copyright owner.
- Legal exemption—Use constitutes an exemption, such as a parody.
- Fair use—Use for educational purposes according to certain restrictions (Newsome, 1997).

Public domain work is a creative work that is not protected by copyright and may be freely used by all. Works created after 1978 have a copyright life of the life of the producer plus 70 years (or if the work is of a corporate authorship, the shorter of 95 years from publication or 120 years from creation). If works were published before 1923, they are in the public domain.

The Copyright Act of 1976 established fair use, or guidelines that allow educators to use and copy certain copyrighted materials for nonprofit educational purposes (Section 107 of the U.S. Copyright Law defines fair use). Copyright issues can be convoluted, particularly when materials are for use on the Web or other computer-based media. School districts provide teachers with specific guidelines for using copyrighted materials in their classes. It is in your best interest to ascertain and adhere to the policies advocated by your school.

When discussing "fair use," the law sets out four factors to be considered in determining fair use:

1. The purpose and character of the use, including whether such use is of commercial nature or is for nonprofit educational purposes;
2. The nature of the copyrighted works;
3. Amount and substantiality of the portion used in relation to the copyrighted work as a whole; and
4. The effect of the use upon the potential market for or value of the copyrighted work (U.S. Copyright Office, 2006)

The distinction between "fair use" and infringement may be unclear. There is no specific number of words, lines, and so on that may be safely taken without permission. Acknowledgment of the source does not substitute for obtaining permission. In addition, ownership of a book, image, software program, or other work does not confer copyright ownership. The right to copy, display, or otherwise use must be specifically granted.

The following items are general recommendations to follow when contemplating using copyrighted materials:

- When computer software is intended for one computer, it should be used on only one computer.
- If the picture, video, audio, text you would like to use does not belong to you (you did not create it), ask permission from the individual or entity that produced the materials.
- Never download material from the Internet unless it specifically says "copyright free." Even if the material is copyright free, you must cite the source when you reuse it.

Acceptable Use Policies

To further address the issue of ethical use of computers, computer software, the Internet, and the World Wide Web, many schools have acceptable use policies (AUPs). These are agreements among students, parents/guardians, teachers, administrators, and staff that govern the use of school and school district computers, networks, and the Internet. AUPs vary greatly from school district to school district. Some schools have separate AUPs for students, teachers, and staff personnel. AUPs generally address access to and transmission of data and information within the school and any technology-based device in the school or personal device brought into the school. Generally, AUPs include the following key elements:

- A preamble—Explains why the policy is needed and that the school's code of conduct also applies to online activity.
- A definition section—Defines the key words used in the policy.
- A policy statement—Describes what technology-based devices are covered under the AUP and under what circumstances students can use those devices.
- An acceptable use section—Defines appropriate student use of the technology found in the school. This would include the parameters of student use of network technology.
- An unacceptable use section—Gives clear examples of what constitutes unacceptable student use.
- The violation/sanctions section—Explains to a student how to report violators and to whom to address questions about the AUP. Some AUPs note that violations will be handled in accordance with the general student disciplinary code for the school.

A typical AUP has a section where students and parents sign the document, acknowledging they are aware of the information contained in the policy, and their intentions of abiding by the policies outlined in the document. As a teacher, it is your responsibility to monitor student use of the computers in your classroom and school. Also, you have a responsibility for abiding by the AUPs set out by your school district.

Teacher Production of Materials

Throughout this text, examples are provided for how your students can use the Office products. Office can be used by teachers for many classroom management tasks (e.g., grading, materials inventory, and so on). The lists given in Figure 1.1 and 1.2 are organized according to Office products and present some examples of how to use Office to increase effectiveness and productivity.

Instruction/Learning	Classroom Management
Word	**Word**
Create lesson plans	Worksheets
Make activity flyers	Field trip permission letters
Develop Testing materials	School reports
PowerPoint	**PowerPoint**
Teacher presentations	Teacher in-service
Graphic handouts	Parent teacher conference overview
Presentations saved to the World Wide Web	Conference presentations
Excel	**Excel**
Graph special project incomes	Assessment checklists
Represent data in graphical form	Attendance chart
Testing hypotheses	Grade book
Data analysis	Attendance chart
Access	**Access**
Keep records of readings, related notes, and citations	Monitor classroom books
List curriculum content objectives	Student and parent/guardian information
Thematic units support material database	Classroom inventory
Store teaching activities and strategies	Monitor classroom DVDs
Outlook	**Outlook**
Cross-cultural e-mail exchanges	Maintain a to-do list using Tasks
Personal journals	Send/receive e-mails to/from parents and students
Set calendar to help with lesson plans	Use Contacts list to send e-mails or start letters
Correspond with experts	Calendar sets teacher/parent/student appointments

Figure 1.1
Teacher activity chart

Word	
Write book reports	Create Web pages
Creative writing: stories and poetry that can be illustrated	Writing process: notes, outline, rough draft, editing, final copy
Create story problems for math	Design letterhead and stationary
Keep a journal of science experiments	Develop newsletters about historical topics
PowerPoint	
Present a research project	Post a presentation on the Web
Create a picture book by printing individual slides	Team teach researched concepts
Create book reports	Create hyperlinks to other reports or Web pages
Use presentation outline to start a written report	Create science experiment reports
Excel	
Chart local rainfall	Project grades
Answer "what-if" questions	Create budgets for fictitious business
Create time lines	Analyze data using estimation and prediction
Compare and chart fast-food calorie counts	Create daylight hour chart
Access	
Create a state information database	Create a database of local trees
Create a "books read" database	Create a database of addresses
Create a database of resources for a report	Create a U.S. presidents database
Outlook	
Create a time line of what happened on this date in history	Set calendar with assignments and due dates
Keep a journal of reading done by the month	Keep a to-do list of class activities
Using e-mail, as scientists or physicians about research projects	Using contacts, create a list of local senators and representatives

Figure 1.2
Student production of materials

TYING IT ALL TOGETHER

This chapter provides an overview of the book and presents standards that set expectations for how teachers should integrate technology into their classroom, how students should use technology, and an overview of technology standards for school administrators. As you work through the book, you will likely find many useful opportunities to use the Office products to enhance your teaching and learning activities while at the same time identifying ways to help your students meet established technology standards.

REFERENCES

Earle, R. S. (2002). The integration of instructional technology into public education: Promises and challenges. *Educational Technology, 42*(1), 5–13. Retrieved November, 2004, from http://www.electroniccampus.org/student/srecinfo/publications/Principles_2000.pdf

International Society for Technology in Education NETS Project. (2002). *National educational technology standards and performance indicators for teachers.* Retrieved September 21, 2007, from http://cnets.iste.org/teachers/pdf/page09.pdf

International Society for Technology in Education NETS Project. (2002). *National educational technology standards and performance indicators for administrators.* Retrieved September 21, 2007, from http://cnets.iste.org/administrators/a_stands.html

International Society for Technology in Education NETS Project. (2007). *National educational technology standards for students: The next generation.* Retrieved September 21, 2007, from http://cnets.iste.rg/students/s_standards.html

Newsome, C. (1997). *A teacher's guide to fair use and copyright.* Retrieved September 21, 2007, from http://home.earthlink.net~cnew/research.htm

U.S. Copyright Office. (2006, July). *Fair use.* Retrieved September 21, 2007, from http://www.copyright.gov/fls/fl102.html

2 GETTING STARTED WITH OFFICE

CHAPTER OUTLINE

1. LEARNING OBJECTIVES
2. CHAPTER OVERVIEW
3. WORKING WITH MICROSOFT OFFICE SUITE
   a. Opening Office Applications
   b. The Ribbon in Microsoft Office
   c. The Quick Access Toolbar
   d. The Office Button
   e. The Help Function in Microsoft Office
   f. Inserting a Hyperlink
   g. Inserting Clip Art
4. TYING IT ALL TOGETHER

LEARNING OBJECTIVES

At the completion of this chapter you will be able to:
- Open the Microsoft Office suite
- Use the icons on the Ribbon
- Use the Office button and the actions associated with it
- Modify the Quick Access Toolbar
- Add a hyperlink to a document

CHAPTER OVERVIEW

This chapter provides an introduction to the ribbons, menus, and functions that are available in the Microsoft Office suite. Each Office application has additional components in the ribbons and menus unique to that program. After studying this chapter, you will be able to customize your Quick Access Toolbar and use basic commands common to all the Office products.

Working with Microsoft Office Suite

The Microsoft Office suite may include any or all of the following products: Word, Excel, PowerPoint, Access, Publisher, and Outlook. Most standard professional Office editions for Windows include these products. All the toolbars or ribbons, menus, and help information function similarly from product to product. This compatibility makes working with the Office applications easier with less of a learning curve. To view ribbons, menu items, and help information, the Office program (e.g., Word) must be open.

Opening Office Applications

To open any of the Office applications, click *Start* on the Windows taskbar. On the Start menu, move the mouse pointer to *All Programs*, and the Programs submenu will appear. Move the mouse pointer to *Microsoft Office*, and the Microsoft Office submenu appears. Click the Microsoft application that you want to open. *Note:* Depending on how you installed Office 2007, the menu items for the applications may be placed in various locations on the Start menu. In most cases, they can be found under *All Programs* or under *Programs* within the Microsoft Office folder (see Figure 2.1).

Figure 2.1
Opening Microsoft Office

To see examples of some of the similarities between the programs, open Microsoft Office Word 2007 by clicking the icon in the menu noted in Figure 2.1. You will be able to see the Ribbon and other components that are similar throughout the Microsoft Office suite (see Figure 2.2).

Office Button menu—Displays a menu of file commands, such as New, Open, and, Save As, as well as listing of recent documents. This takes the place of File on the old-version toolbars.
Quick Access Toolbar—Displays quick access buttons such as Undo and Save commands.
Ribbon—Displays groups of related commands in tabs.
Title bar—Displays the name of the open file and the program that is open.
Program window controls—Buttons used to minimize the program window, restore to full size, or close the window.
Help—Displays the Help screen to get assistance using Microsoft Office (this replaces the Office assistant).
Scroll bars—Using the horizontal and vertical scroll bars, different work areas will be displayed within a document.
Zoom controls—These features allow you to zoom the view of the document.
Document window controls—These buttons minimize or restore the current document.
Status bar—Displays the information about the current file.

The Ribbon in Microsoft Office

The menus and toolbars in Word, Excel, Access, and PowerPoint have been replaced with a new Ribbon feature. The Ribbon is organized in groupings, or categories of commands, that relate to a function. The Ribbon is arranged in tabs, and each tab holds related commands (see Figure 2.3).

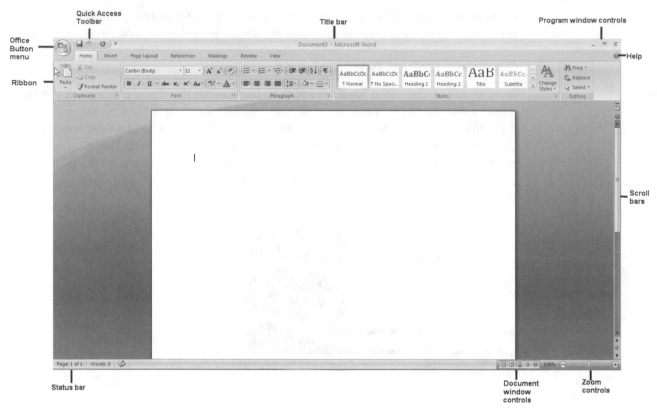

Figure 2.2
Screen components

Figure 2.3
Word Ribbon

As you make changes in documents, such as changing the size or style of lettering if you have the text highlighted, the program will preview what the type or style would look like prior to applying it to the document.

The Quick Access Toolbar

The Quick Access Toolbar is not available in Publisher or Outlook. The functions that automatically appear on the toolbar are Save, Undo, and Redo. You can add commands and customized the toolbar by choosing commands from the pull-down menu (see Figure 2.4).

The Office Button

The Office Button lists functions related to an overall document. Like the Ribbon, the Office button also has arrows next to some of the functions indicating that another layer of function is available, such as Save As (see Figure 2.5).

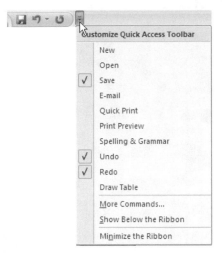

Figure 2.4
Quick Access Toolbar

The Help Function in Microsoft Office

The Help button has replaced the Office Assistant of previous Office editions. The Help button allows you to type a word or phrase that you would like to learn about. To utilize Help online, you must be connected to the Internet. You can also browse the Help screen. To activate the Help window, click the question mark at the top right-hand corner of the screen (see Figure 2.6).

Inserting a Hyperlink

A hyperlink is a reference or navigational element in a document that allows you to go to another section in the same document, another document, or (if connected to the Internet) a separate Web page. To apply hyperlinks in a document, select the text or

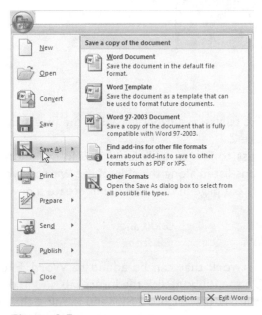

Figure 2.5
Office button

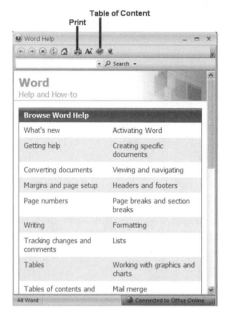

Figure 2.6
Help Window

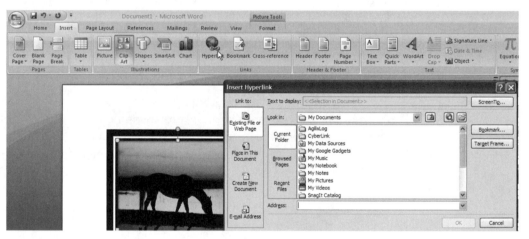

Figure 2.7
Hyperlink

image that you would like to use as a hyperlink. Click the Insert tab on the Ribbon, then click *Hyperlink* (see Figure 2.7).

Type the URL address to link to, including *http://* in the address, then click *OK*. As you can see with the icons listed along the side of the window, you can insert a link to an existing Web page or to a page in this document, create a new document, or link to an e-mail address.

Inserting Clip Art

Clip art is predrawn artwork that can be added to Word, Excel, PowerPoint, and Publisher documents. On the Ribbon, click the Insert tab, and in the Illustrations grouping will be an icon for clip art (see Figure 2.8). Keep in mind that wherever the curser is placed on a document is where the clip art will be placed. Clip art can also include such things as photographs, sounds, and movies.

Figure 2.8
Clip art

Once the Clip Art icon is clicked, a Clip Art pane will appear. This allows you to search for a particular subject area of clip art from a variety of media types. If you are connected to the Internet, you can search for clip art on Office Online as well as other clip art sources (see Figure 2.9).

To select the particular clip art, use the mouse pointer to move over the image, and a pull-down menu will appear, allowing you to insert the clip art into your document.

Figure 2.9
Selecting clip art

TYING IT ALL TOGETHER

This chapter gives an overview of the toolbars and options that are available in most Office products. As you open the Office products, you will see that the applications have some of the same options no matter what program you are using. This commonality gives you an interface for using Office and makes learning the programs easy.

3 WORD 2007

CHAPTER OUTLINE

LEARNING OBJECTIVES

At the completion of this chapter you will be able to:

- Start Word and create a new word processing document
- Navigate the Word workspace
- Spell-check a document
- Add clip art to a document
- Format a document
- Insert a hyperlink into a document
- Create a table in a document
- Preview a document for printing
- Undo and redo
- Save material as a Web page
- Create a diagram

CHAPTER OVERVIEW

This chapter provides an introduction to Word 2007. The content focuses on Word fundamentals and how to apply them to a variety of learning activities. Using the examples of writing a book report, the chapter's Show Me section presents instructions on how to use many of Word 2007's tools for creating, editing, and manipulating information within a word processing document. The Let Me Try student-oriented exercises provide specific examples with step-by-step instructions for using Word 2007 in learning activities. In addition to the Let Me Try activities, the Challenge using Word section provides stimulating projects for practicing Word 2007. Each illustration in this chapter may be found within the Word folder under Examples on the CD accompanying the book. You may follow along with the document as you go through the text by pulling it up from the CD. Other examples using Word may be found on the CD.

How Teachers and Students Can Use Word

Microsoft Word can be used in a variety of activities by both students and teachers in the classroom. When examining Bloom's taxonomy of cognitive levels in conjunction with the National Educational Technology Standards for Students: The Next Generation, teachers can utilize Word to accomplish instruction and, it is hoped, learn at a variety of levels and addressing multiple standards. Some examples of using Word by students could include the following:

- *Knowledge*—Students can create their own worksheets to practice material and create flash cards to use in practicing such things as vocabulary.
- *Comprehension*—Students can create book reports on recently read trade books, find more information about a topic and create a Web page about the topic, and use Word to explain a lab experiment and interpret the results.
- *Application*—After reading *My Side of the Mountain* by Jean Craighead George and further research, the students can create a brochure for other students who want to investigate beginning falconry; after reading *Sarah, Plain and Tall*, students will research and make a chart that classifies the characteristics of the two geographical regions Sarah lived in during the story.
- *Analysis*—After reading *Charlotte's Web*, students will compare and contrast the characteristics of Templeton the rat and Charlotte the spider, creating a report about the differences; after reading *Hatchet*, students will create a résumé for Brian Robeson to use for his job next summer, organizing the skills he had acquired during his adventure.
- *Synthesis*—After reading *My Side of the Mountain*, students are to invent a survival kit for any situation; after reading *A Year Down Yonder*, students will imagine 70 years from now and write a book reflecting on "now."
- *Evaluation*—Students will establish the criteria and write a critique of a video presented in class; after reading *Hatchet* and *My Side of the Mountain*, students will select which novel they preferred and which novel was plausible and provide justification for their selection.

NETS for Students[*]

Apply Word to activities to address the following standards:

- *Creativity and innovation*—Students demonstrate creative thinking, construct knowledge, and develop innovative products and processes using technology.

---

*Reprinted with permission from *National Educational Technology Standards for Students, Second Edition*, © 2007, ISTE® (International Society for Technology in Education), www.iste.org. All rights reserved.

- *Communication and collaboration*—Students use digital media and environments to communicate and work collaboratively, including at a distance, to support individual learning and contribute to the learning of others.
- *Research and information fluency*—Students apply digital tools to gather, evaluate, and use information
- *Critical thinking, problem solving, and decision making*—Students use critical thinking skills to plan and conduct research, manage projects, solve problems, and make informed decisions using appropriate digital tools and resources.
- *Technology operations and concepts*—Students demonstrate a sound understanding of technology concepts, systems, and operations.

What Is New in Word 2007

As with the entire Microsoft Office suite, the Ribbon replaces the menu and toolbars of the previous versions of Word. As with other versions of Word, you can create short documents, newsletters, and Web pages. In this version you can post on weblogs. Word 2007 has added some features that were not as readily available in the past. Table styles may be selected to design a look for a table in a document. Themes may be used to provide a look to a document, including colors, theme fonts (such as heading on body text fonts), and effects, such as fills and shadings for charts, objects, and flowcharts. Styles allow you to apply multiple formatting settings at one time by using a Quick Styles gallery. Building blocks are reusable pieces of content or other document parts that are stored in galleries. You can compare two documents side by side. There is a document inspector that looks at any changes or editing, comments, and revisions, and finalizes a document for publication.

About Word

Microsoft Word is the word processing component of the Microsoft Office suite. It is a productivity tool for you and your students to use. In many ways, Word is the electronic typewriter of the computer, but it has many more features than a typewriter or word processor. When you open Word, you are literally rolling an "electronic piece of paper" on the screen. With the click of a mouse, you can easily manipulate text material, add graphics to text, check spelling and grammar, and place words in a column or table format. The finished product may be saved on a memory device, printed on paper, or even saved as a Web page for posting to the World Wide Web. As a teacher who knows how to use Word, you can produce all types of interesting materials and facilitate student production of materials.

Working with Word

The primary purpose of this chapter is to introduce fundamental components and features of Word so that you may use them in productive ways. To accomplish this objective, we present several examples throughout the chapter. Although the examples are specific, the steps and procedures they present for developing Word documents, tables, and Web pages are generic and applicable to a variety of classroom management tasks and learning activities. As you work through the chapter's contents, substitute our examples with your own. *In addition, you can locate files that correspond to the chapter activities on the CD in the Word folder under* Examples. *Additional Let Me Try activities can be found on the CD in the Let Me Try Exercises folder.*

Opening Word 2007

To create a Word document, you need to open Word 2007 (see Figure 3.1). Click *Start* on the Windows taskbar; move the mouse pointer over All *Programs*, and the Programs submenu appears. Move the mouse pointer over *Microsoft Office*, and the Microsoft Office submenu appears. Click *Microsoft Word*, and Word 2007 opens (see

Figure 3.1
Starting Word

Figure 3.2). The Word workspace will appear (see Figure 3.3). The Ribbon on the Word workspace is delineated by tabs at the top of the Ribbon that are activated when selected, allowing the user to utilize the tools that are located on each tab. There are certain menus that appear when the user will need them, such as Table Tools when a table is created or selected within a document. As you go through creating a document, the tabs will be utilized.

Show Me

1. Open Word as described in the previous section.
2. The Home tab automatically is selected when Word is opened. Within the Home tab are the general word processing tools that are generally used with basic word processing (see Figure 3.4).

Figure 3.2
Selecting Word 2007

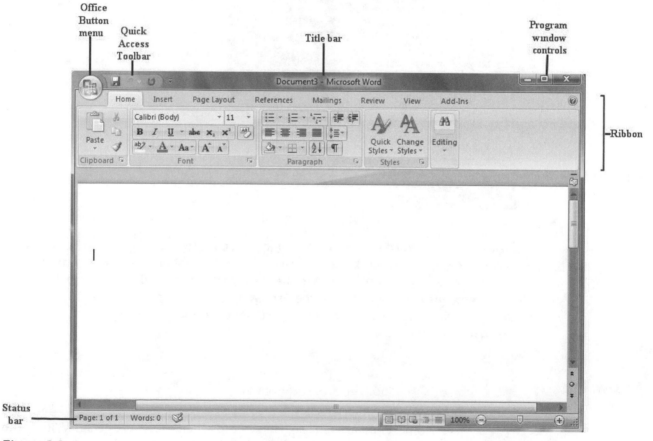

Figure 3.3
Word workspace

Figure 3.4
Home tab of the Ribbon

The sections of the Home tab are divided into Clipboard, Font, Paragraph, Styles, and Editing. By clicking the arrow next to the label, such as *Font*, the Font dialog box will appear (see Figure 3.5). A similar dialog box will appear for each section as the arrow is clicked.

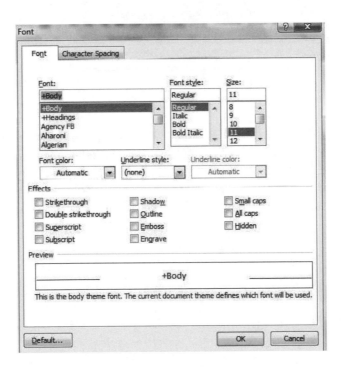

Figure 3.5
Font dialog box

As an example of the type of project that a student could develop, you will create a book report on *Sarah, Plain and Tall* by Patricia MacLachlan. For an example of the completed project, see "Sara Book report" on the CD.

3. To create a professional looking book report, type the document first without doing any formatting or spell checking (there will be red squiggle lines under those words that are of question, but you will address those as you spell-check the entire document). At the top of the page, type the title of the book, the author, and the byline (your name) on separate lines (press Enter after each item).

4. As you type, the words will wrap to the next line. To leave an extra line of space between the paragraphs, press Enter. You will type the book report and then format the document (see Figure 3.6).

5. Once text has been typed in, you may select words, lines, or paragraphs by doing the following:

   a. Dragging the cursor over sections of type and holding the mouse button down

   b. Double clicking anywhere inside a word you want to select

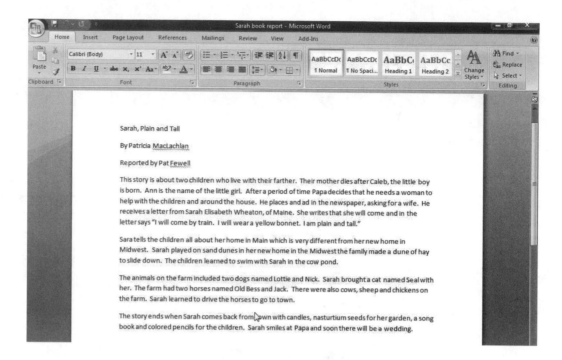

Figure 3.6
Entering text

  c. Clicking inside the left margin to select the entire line of text
  d. Double-clicking inside the left margin to select a paragraph (see Figure 3.7)
 6. After highlighting (or selecting) the title of the book, you want to make the text bold. With the text highlighted, click on the Bold icon. The text highlighted will become bold (see Figure 3.8).

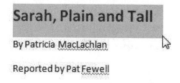

Figure 3.7
Selecting text

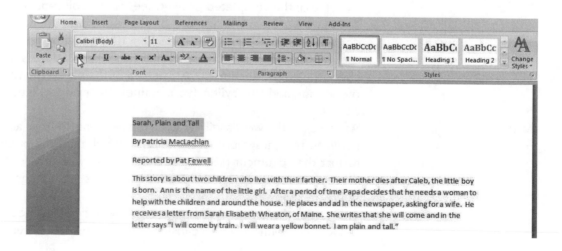

Figure 3.8
Bold text

7. Beyond bolding of text, the font formatting section of the Ribbon allows you to make changes to the text (see Figure 3.9).

8. To increase the font size of the title of the book, click on the arrow next to the font size. As the mouse is moved over the different font sizes, the change is reflected on the document to give a "live preview" of the changes. Select 18-point font for the title of the book (see Figure 3.10).

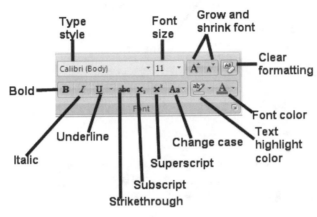

Figure 3.9
Font formatting

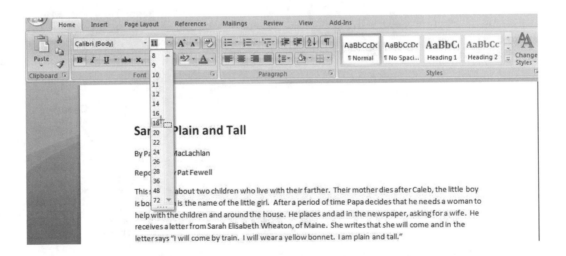

Figure 3.10
Font size

9. The paragraph section of the Ribbon allows for bulleted lists, alignment of paragraphs, and spacing changes within a document (see Figure 3.11).

10. By using the mouse pointer, highlight the title, author, and byline of the document. Select center alignment from the paragraph formatting (see Figure 3.12).

11. The Styles formatting on the Ribbon allows you to apply multiple formatting settings at one time by using styles. You can select from a number of styles. There is a slide bar that allows you to see additional styles besides the ones displayed on the Ribbon. Also, Change Styles allows you to modify style set, color, and fonts (see Figure 3.13).

12. Highlighting the title *Sarah, Plain and Tall,* select the style. The text highlighted will reflect the style on which you have the mouse pointer prior to clicking the

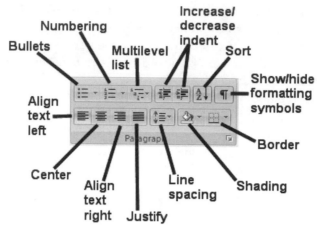

Figure 3.11
Paragraph formatting

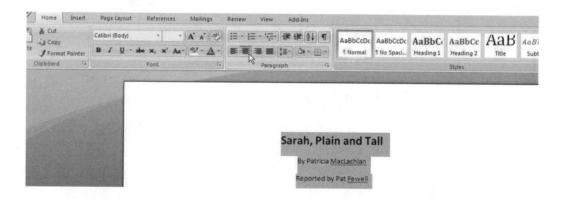

Figure 3.12
Centering text

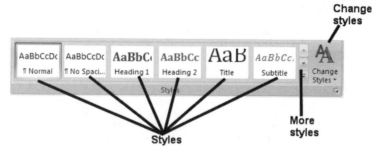

Figure 3.13
Styles Ribbon

mouse so that you have a "real-time" idea of what the selection will look like before committing to that style. Select the *Title* style (see Figure 3.14).

13. Highlight *By Patricia MacLachlan* and *Reported by Pat Fewell* and select *Headings 2* for this selection.

14. The next tab on the Ribbon is the Insert tab. As the Ribbon indicates, items that you would insert within a document are found on this ribbon (see Figure 3.15). New to this version of Office is the opportunity to add equations and symbols from a drop-down menu when selected. Also, SmartArt provides the opportunity to add visual representations of communication information, such as organizational charts and diagrams.

Figure 3.14
Changing styles

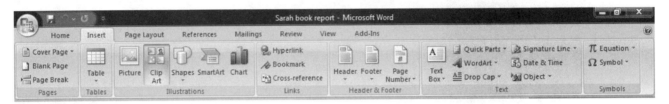

Figure 3.15
Insert Ribbon

Figure 3.17
Clip Art task pane

15. In any document, a visual can add interest. To place clip art into your document, place the cursor next to the title *Sarah, Plain and Tall*, on the right side of the title, and from the Insert ribbon select the Clip Art icon (see Figure 3.16).

16. Once the Clip Art icon has been clicked, a Clip Art task pane appears on the right side of the Word workspace (see Figure 3.17). Type in *woman* in the *Search for:* pane. Because this illustration is drawn from a computer that has access to the World Wide Web, you are able to access the clip art from Clip Art on Office

Figure 3.16
Selecting clip art

Online, which adds to the selection possibilities. The clip art will appear where the cursor is positioned in the Word document (see Figure 3.18).

17. Once the clip art has been placed in the document, a new ribbon appears that deals with the manipulation of clip art. This ribbon appears only when a picture or clip art has been selected by clicking on the object. In this case, select the dropped shadow rectangle format (the fourth icon from the left of the picture styles) (see Figure 3.19).

18. In addition to picture styles, this ribbon allows users to adjust the picture, arrange the picture in the document in relationship to other items in the Word document, and adjust the size of the document.

Figure 3.18
Clip art in document

Sarah, Plain and Tall

Figure 3.19
Picture Tools Ribbon

19. Place the cursor at the beginning of the first paragraph prior to clicking on the Insert tab. Click back on the Insert tab and select the Text Box icon. You want to add a quotation as a special effect to the book report. This will allow for a predetermined graphic layout for the document that will allow for a more professional look. Select the Alphabet Sidebar text box. The text box will appear on the page (see Figure 3.20). Type in the text box the following quote: *I will come by train. I will wear a yellow bonnet. I am plain and tall. . . . Tell them I sing.* (see Figure 3.21).

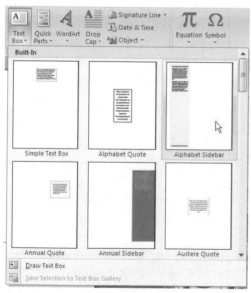

Figure 3.20
Text box

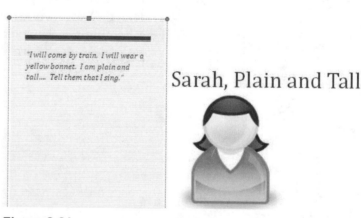

Figure 3.21
Typing in the text box

20. Once the text box is activated in the document, a Text Box Tools Format ribbon will appear. This will allow you to manipulate the text box and the information in it (see Figure 3.22). This ribbon will appear only when the text box is clicked on and "activated."

Figure 3.22
Text Box Tools Format Ribbon

21. Highlight the text you just typed in the text box. Once highlighted, click the right mouse button, and a floating formatting panel will appear. Select the type size of 22, and the text will enlarge to that size. This floating panel is available when you right-click within the Word workspace and no other panel or screen has been activated (see Figure 3.23).

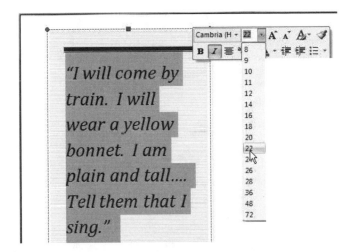

Figure 3.23
Floating formatting panel

22. Place the cursor at the very end of the book report document. Press Enter to place a blank line. You are now going to add a bulleted list of other books that Patricia MacLachlan has written. On the first line, type *Other books that I have read by this author*. Then select the bullet icon from the home ribbon. Use the down arrow by clicking on it with the mouse pointer and select the type of bullet to use in this list (see Figure 3.24).

23. Other books on the list include *Skylark, Caleb's Story*, and *Cassie Binegar*. Press Enter after each title, and this will place another bullet point. Once those titles are typed in, the list should be in bulleted form (see Figure 3.25).

24. Place your cursor at the beginning of the document to start the spell-checking process. To spell-check, click on the Review tab and select *Spelling and Grammar* (see Figure 3.26).

25. The spell-check will highlight any words that may be of question, including proper names. The spell-check and grammar check will not necessarily check words that are substituted, such as *farther* for *father*. The spell-check will provide a screen for you to select changes to spelling or you may choose to ignore the recommendations (see Figure 3.27).

26. After the spell check is complete, it is always a good idea to save your documents about every 5 minutes. To save the book report, click on the Office

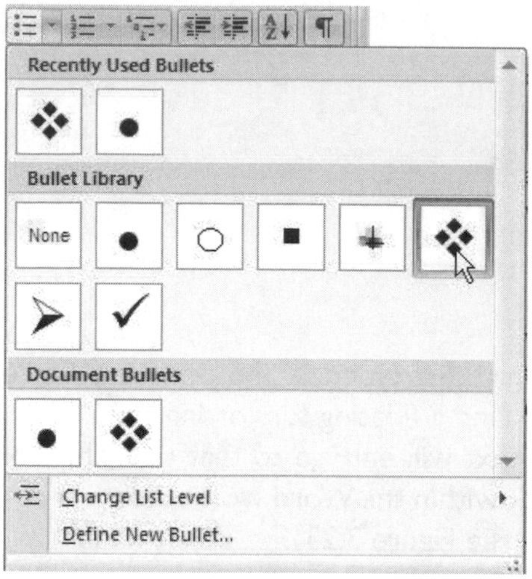

Figure 3.24
Bullet Library

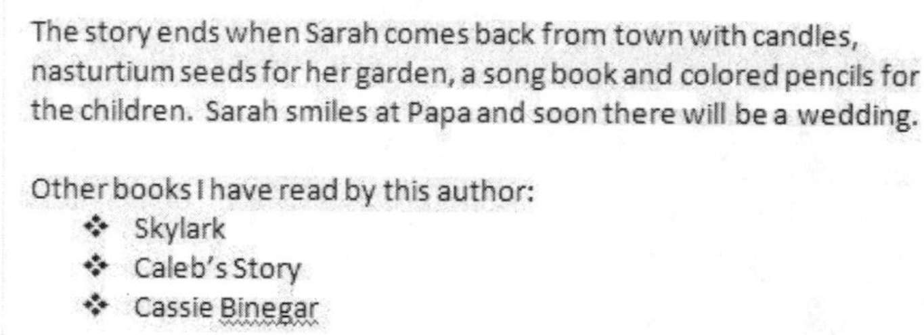

The story ends when Sarah comes back from town with candles, nasturtium seeds for her garden, a song book and colored pencils for the children. Sarah smiles at Papa and soon there will be a wedding.

Other books I have read by this author:
❖ Skylark
❖ Caleb's Story
❖ Cassie Binegar

Figure 3.25
Bulleted list

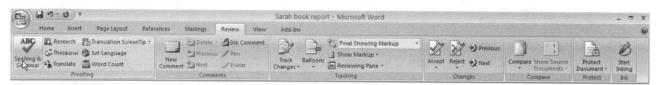

Figure 3.26
Review Ribbon

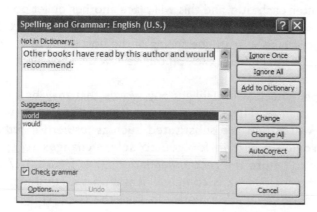

Figure 3.27
Spelling and
Grammar check

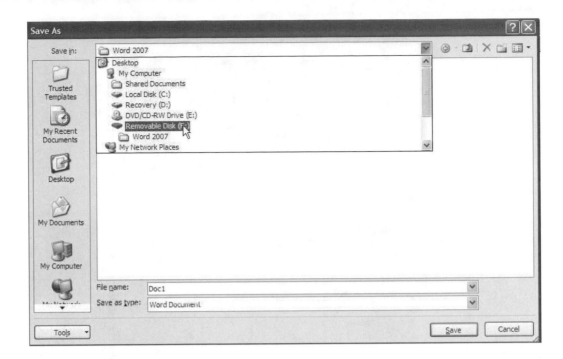

Figure 3.28
Name and save

button and click *Save*. The first time you save a document, you will need to designate where you want to save it (i.e., removable disk F) and name the document and click *Save* when completed (see Figure 3.28).

To preview the document prior to printing, click on the Office button and on the drop-down menu select *Print*. Move the cursor over the word *Print*, and a menu appears. You can select *Print Preview* (which is better than wasting paper) prior to printing, or you can select *Print to default printer* or *Print* and select the printer and designate the number of copies (see Figure 3.29).

27. Click on the Office button and select *Close*, or you can go on to the next project.

Another Project

Periodically, students are asked to provide a diagram of an idea or provide visual images of a process or organization. An example of a project similar to this is to diagram the life cycle of a frog.

1. Open a new document in Word by clicking on the Office button. Because you kept the Word program open from the previous document, you can select *New* from the menu, and a screen will pop up with selections as to what to create. In this case, you want a new blank document, so click on *Create* (see Figure 3.30).
2. Press Enter once and then type in *Life Cycle of a Frog* at the top of the page, highlight the text, and select *Title* from the Styles listing (see Figure 3.31).
3. Press Enter twice to give some space from the title. Select the Insert tab on the Ribbon and then select *SmartArt* on that ribbon. On the menu, select *Cycle* from the choices given (see Figure 3.32).
4. Select *Block Cycle* from the list of possibilities (the third chart on the top row). Once selected, by clicking on the chart type, the chart will appear on

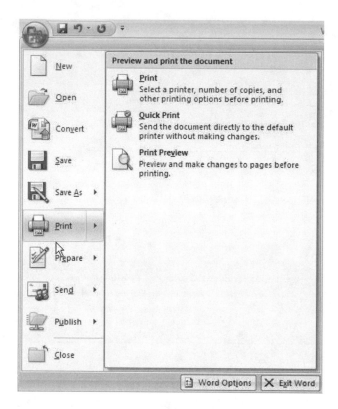

Figure 3.29
Print preview
and printing

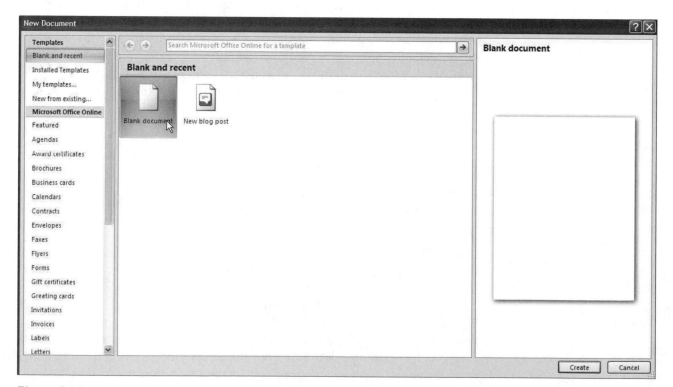

Figure 3.30
Creating a new document

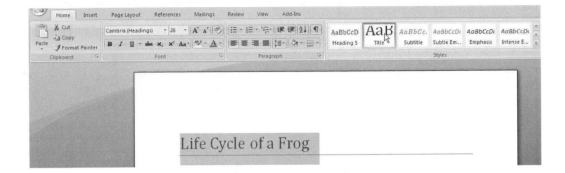

Figure 3.31
Title with style
formatting

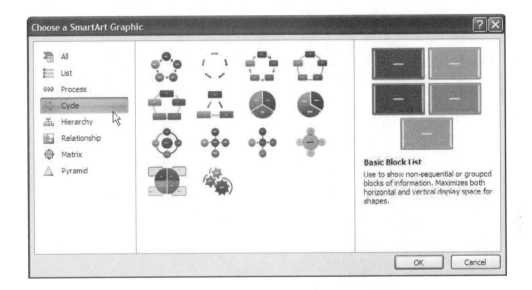

Figure 3.32
SmartArt Graphic

the document with screens where you may type in the text that appears in the box on the chart (see Figure 3.33).

5. When you begin working with SmartArt, a Design Tool ribbon will appear to allow you to make modifications of your artwork (see Figure 3.34).

6. In the space for text on the cycle type, you can type in the terms *Spawn, Egg, Tadpole, Tadpole with legs, Froglet,* and *Frog.* The cycle does not originally have enough blocks, but by pressing Enter after each entry of text, blocks will be added. The finished chart is as follows (see Figure 3.35). The example of the completed document is on the CD.

7. You can change the colors on the cycle by selecting *Change Colors* on the Design view of the SmartArt ribbon. The changes are represented live in the document to give a preview of what the change would look like prior to actually selecting the change. *Change Colors* also allows you to change to an outline box effect in the cycle diagram (see Figure 3.36).

8. If you click the cursor outside the frame around the SmartArt graphic, the frame will disappear, allowing for the addition of text to the document (see Figure 3.37).

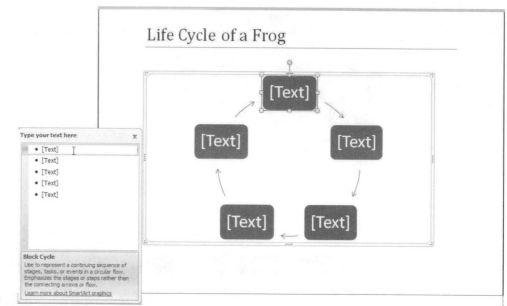

Figure 3.33
Inserting text in the cycle

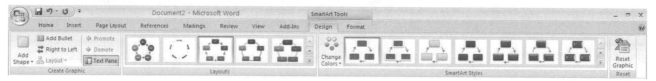

Figure 3.34
Design Ribbon for SmartArt Tools

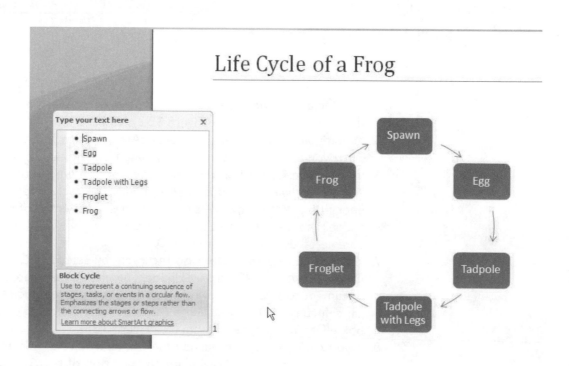

Figure 3.35
Completed cycle

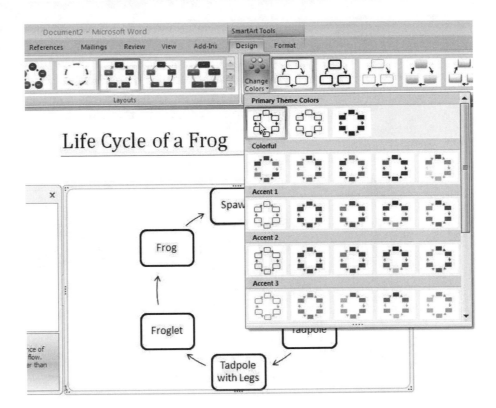

Figure 3.36
Change Colors

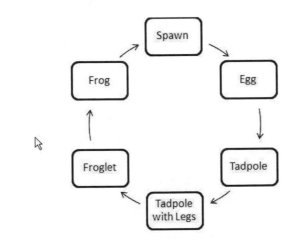

Figure 3.37
Cycle with word processing

By between 12 to 16 weeks, depending on the frog, water and food supply the frog has completed a full growth cycle.

9. The document can be printed or saved by clicking on the Office button and selecting the appropriate action (see Figure 3.38). By selecting *Save As*, you have several options and choices of formats for saving the document. The most common is *Word Document*, which is the default file format.

10. To preview the document prior to printing, you can select *Print Preview* on the menu that appears when you click on the Office button (see Figure 3.39).

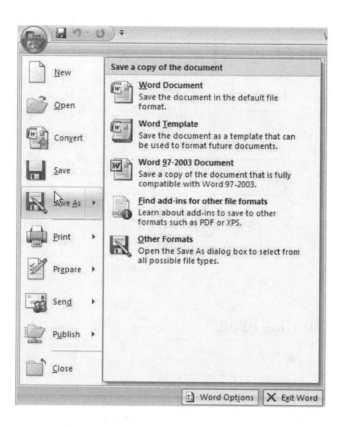

Figure 3.38
Save As

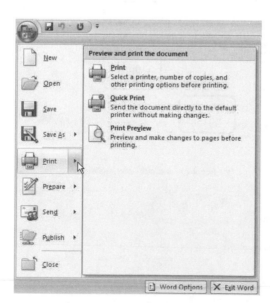

Figure 3.39
Print Preview

11. Along with *Print Preview*, you can also select *Print* and *Quick Print*, depending on your needs. *Quick Print* prints the entire document using the default printer. By clicking on *Print*, you can select what printer you wish to send the document to, select the number of copies, or select the number of pages you wish to print if you do not want to print the entire document. By selecting *Print*, you have several options for printing to select from (see Figure 3.40).

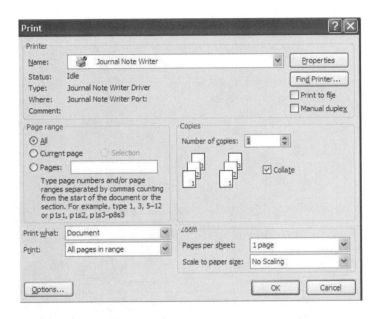

Figure 3.40
Printing

So far we have opened Word 2007 and created a new document that contained centered text and bold text, selected a style, and used SmartArt. We also spell-checked, saved the document, and previewed printing options.

Suppose your students wanted to make a science page that presents information about one of the characters in *Charlotte's Web*. For an example of the completed page, see the "Charlotte's Web" page on the CD.

Creating a Science Page to Be Saved as a Web Page

1. Click on the Office button and select *New* from the menu that appears. Because you want to create a printed document, open this project as a new Word document rather than a blank Web page. Select *Blank document* and click on *Create* (see Figure 3.41).
2. Once the Word workspace appears, press Enter twice and move the cursor down the page. Select the Insert tab and select the WordArt icon, and a WordArt gallery appears (see Figure 3.42).
3. Select the WordArt that you want to use by clicking on the image. Once the type style is selected, type in the words *All About Spiders* and select 48-point typeface for the lettering and click *OK* (see Figure 3.43).

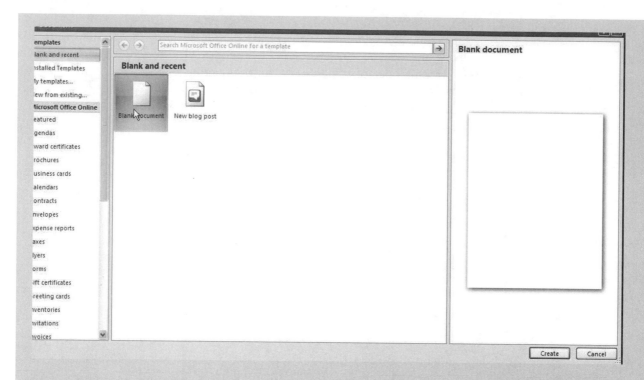

Figure 3.41
New blank document

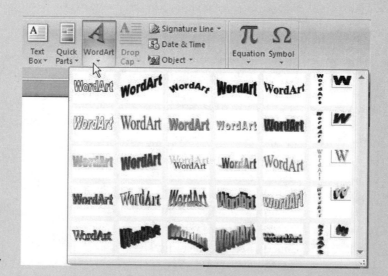

Figure 3.42
WordArt gallery

4. Press Enter twice to add space after the WordArt. The next part of the page will present information about spiders. Set the typeface at 12-point Arial by clicking on the down arrow next to the type style and type size on the Ribbon (as you did in the book report earlier in this chapter). After typing in a short paragraph, press Enter twice.

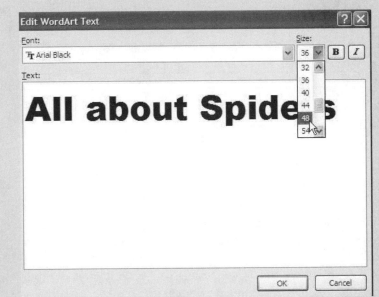

Figure 3.43
Editing WordArt
text

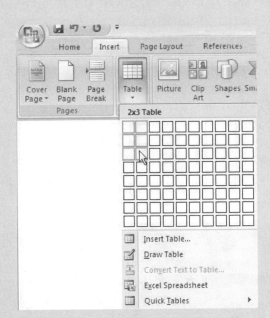

Figure 3.44
Insert Table

5. From the Ribbon, select the Insert tab by clicking it and select *Table* from the Insert ribbon (see Figure 3.44).
6. Select a 2 × 2 cell table by dragging the mouse over 2 × 2 cells and then clicking. You can also insert a table into a document by clicking on *Insert Table* from the drop-down menu and indicating what size table you would like to create wherever your cursor was located when you clicked *Insert Table*.

Spiders	Insects
Eight legs	Six legs
Two-part body	Three-part body
Simple eyes	Complex eyes
No antenna	Antenna

Figure 3.45
Table information

7. The cursor will appear in the first cell of the table. To move from cell to cell in the table, press the Tab key on the keyboard. To add rows, simply press the Tab key while in the rightmost cell of the bottom row. Make the labels *Spiders* and *Insects* bold. Insert the information shown on Figure 3.45 into the table you have created (see Figure 3.45).

8. Click anywhere outside the table to type outside the table. Move your mouse pointer to the beginning of the text at the top of the page. Click the mouse button once. Select the Insert tab from the Ribbon at the top of the screen and select *Clip Art* from the Insert ribbon. From the Clip Art selection, type in the word *spiders* and select a spider from the clip art (see Figure 3.46). You will notice that the illustration indicated that the computer used to bring up the clip art was connected to the World Wide Web and could access clip art from there.

9. Use the picture style of Drop Shadow Rectangle by clicking on the icon on the Picture Tools Format ribbon that appears when you insert clip art. Also, click on the Text Wrapping icon on the ribbon and click on *Tight* (see Figure 3.47). This will bring the text around the picture being inserted into the document.

10. Move down the page, place the mouse pointer below the table, and click one time. This allows you to type on the page in this area. You are going to create a hyperlink to connect to the World Wide Web. Hyperlinks can also link a word or phrase in your document to another document on your computer. For the

Figure 3.46
Clip Art selections

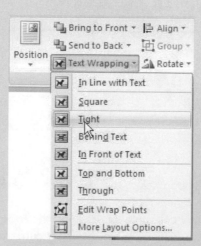

Figure 3.47
Text Wrapping

Figure 3.48
Insert a hyperlink

purposes of this illustration, you will be linking to the following website: http://www.uidaho.edu/so-id/entomology/Spiders.htm. Websites change addresses frequently. If this Web page is not available, go to your favorite search engine and find an appropriate spider website. This address must be typed in exactly as printed here to work.

11. To make a hyperlink, select the Insert tab from the Ribbon and then select *Hyperlink* from the Insert ribbon (see Figure 3.48).

12. Type in the text *A Good World Wide Web Page on Spiders.* Click *Here* in the box that indicates text to be displayed. Type in the Web address in the address section, make sure to type in the *http://* prior to the Web address, and then click *OK* (see Figure 3.49).

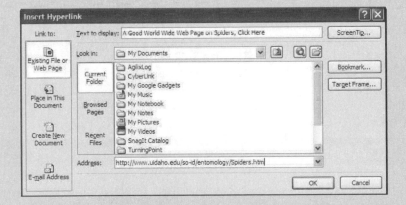

Figure 3.49
Insert Hyperlink
dialog box

13. Select the Page Layout tab on the Ribbon and then select *Page Color* from the Page Background section of the ribbon. There is a pull-down menu of colors to select from as well as *Fill Effects* (see Figure 3.50).

14. From the *Page Color* drop-down list, select *Fill Effects*, then select the Texture tab and select *Stationary* as a background (see Figure 3.51).

15. You can print the page if you are connected to a printer by selecting *Print* from the Office Button menu.

16. To save this document, click on the Office button and select *Save As* and select other formats. You will want to save this document as a single Web page. The completed document is on the CD titled "Spider web page" (see Figure 3.52).

Figure 3.50
Page Color

17. To see how the page looks when posted to the World Wide Web, select the Office button and select *Close* from the menu. When you open the *Spider web page* from My Computer on your operating system, the *Spider web page* will open using whatever browser is installed on your computer, such as Microsoft Internet Explorer.

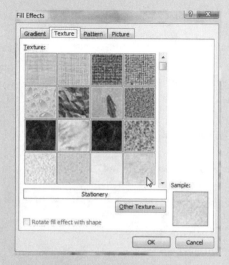

Figure 3.51
Fill Effects—Texture

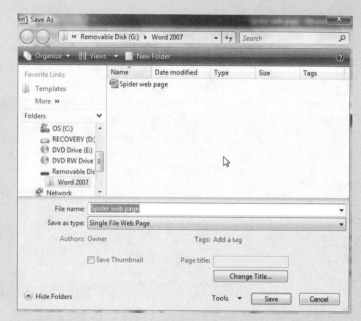

Figure 3.52
Save as a Web page

LET ME TRY, AGAIN

Students are often asked to write letters to senators, other government officials, authors, or other significant individuals in their lives. Word does have several templates that allow students to create letters on stylized letterhead rather than plain paper. These templates offer a variety of documents that the "shell" already created. Templates are also available from Microsoft Online.

1. Open a new document in Word and select *Installed Templates*.
2. Select the *Equity Letter* template from the list, making sure the radio button is highlighted for Document, and click on *Create*. A letter form will appear for the student to fill in the "blanks" created by the template (see Figure 3.53).
3. The template will also provide instructions for modifying the "look" of the letter. Type a letter to your senator indicating that you would like to investigate the opportunities that might be available to visit his or her office during a class trip to Washington, DC.
4. The beginning template will look similar to that shown in Figure 3.54.
5. The finished document for this example is on the accompanying CD titled "Senator Letter."

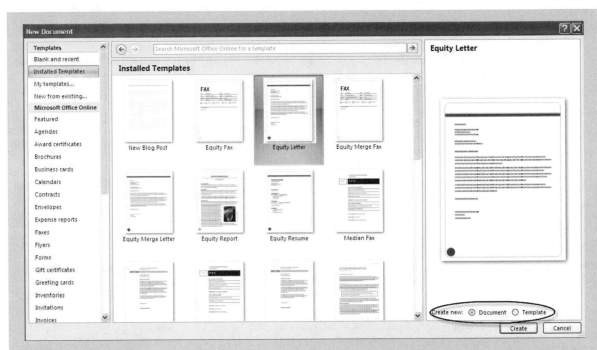

Figure 3.53
Creating a new document from a template

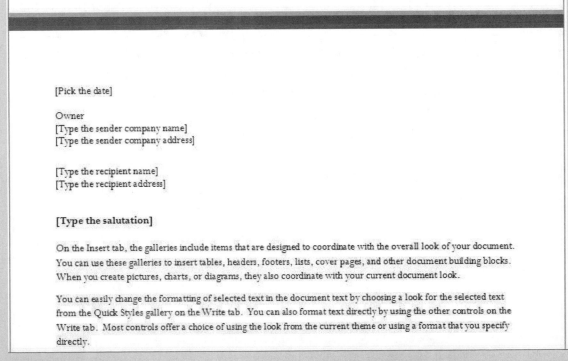

Figure 3.54
Letter template

A CHALLENGE USING WORD 2007

For those who would like a challenge beyond the Let Me Try activities presented in this chapter, try the following exercises.

1. Create an advertisement for a survival kit that you are marketing based on the book *My Side of the Mountain*.
2. Create a newsletter that your students may send home to their parents regarding activities that have taken place or are going to take place in the school next month.
3. Create a résumé for a character of a story they have recently have read.

TYING IT ALL TOGETHER

In this chapter, you created a book report, a Web page with hyperlinks, a chart, and a letter from a template, all of which can be produced by students. You saved documents in Word and Web formats. All these activities will help you and your students begin creating print and electronic documents. These and other activities will allow students to fulfill some of the ISTE standards for creating work using computer technology.

REFERENCES

Bloom, B. (Ed.). (1956). *Taxonomy of educational objectives.* New York: David McKay.

George, J. C. (1991). *My side of the mountain.* New York: Puffin Books.

MacLachlan, P. (1985). *Sarah, plain and tall.* New York: HarperCollins.

Peck, R. (2000). *A year down yonder.* New York: Puffin Books.

White, E. B. (1952). *Charlotte's web.* New York: Scholastic.

4 PowerPoint 2007

Chapter Outline

Learning Objectives

At the completion of this chapter you will be able to:

- Start PowerPoint and create a new presentation
- Navigate the PowerPoint workspace
- Add slides to a presentation in a variety of layouts
- Add clip art to a slide
- Add slide transitions
- Save a presentation
- Save a presentation as a HyperText Markup Language (HTML) document
- Print a presentation
- Copy a presentation to a CD

Chapter Overview

This chapter provides an introduction to PowerPoint 2007. It focuses on helping you learn PowerPoint fundamentals and apply them in developing a presentation. The *Show Me* section presents instructions on how to use many of PowerPoint 2007's tools for creating a slide show. *Let Me Try* exercises, embedded throughout the chapter, give specific step-by-step instructions for quickly accomplishing tasks. They also give you opportunities to practice the information presented. You will find additional Let Me Try exercises in the

PowerPoint folder inside "Let Me Try Exercises" on the CD. Studying the chapter contents and working through the Let Me Try exercises will enable you and your students to develop high-quality presentations suitable for class lectures, student reports and presentations, school board meetings, and other educationally oriented activities.

How Teachers and Students Integrate the Office Products

Microsoft PowerPoint can be used in innovative ways to support various educational activities that benefit students and teachers. In this section, we examine ways in which PowerPoint can be used to support instruction in relation to types of learning outcomes and the National Educational Technology Standards for Students. Looking first at types of learning, the following items identify ways PowerPoint can be used by students:

- *Knowledge*—(a) Students can create their own electronic flash cards games within PowerPoint. The electronic flash cards can take the form of pictures, text, audio, video or any combination of media. (b) Students can be given several historic time periods (e.g., 1861–1865, 1939–1945) and using PowerPoint collect quotes and images that characterize those periods. (c) Students can use PowerPoint to create a shape coloring book. With PowerPoint, they draw shapes and figures and label them and then print the slides for coloring.
- *Comprehension*—(a) Students can create visual stories with images, text, and other media that summarize or describe historical events. (b) Using a digital camera and PowerPoint, they could be asked to visually (without words) describe the habitat in which they live or the habitats of certain animals. (c) For a physics activity, students, using a digital camera and PowerPoint, can be asked to assemble a slide show of images that visually (without words) describes types of motion (forward, backward, upward, and downward).
- *Application*—(a) Students can be asked to use PowerPoint to draw the solar system, labeling each planet and the sun as well as drawing the planets in the appropriate relative positions and sizes. (b) Students can use PowerPoint to visually demonstrate concepts such as justice, legal, happiness, politics, and peace.
- *Analysis*—(a) Students can use PowerPoint to draw shapes and figures and then classify them as rectangles, circles, ellipse, and so on. (b) Similar to photo galleries on news Web sites, students can use PowerPoint and a digital camera to compile a series of photographs that explains important events occurring during the week or month. (c) Inferences—Often what people see is not what is actually taking place. Select students can be given a digital camera with the task of taking action photographs of class members at work or on break. The photographer then infers what is taking place in the photograph or what the subject is thinking. He or she then compiles the photographs and inferences in PowerPoint. After the teacher reviews the PowerPoint slide show, the photographer presents it to the class and explains his or her inferences. Those in the photographs are then given the chance to describe what was really taking place or what they were thinking.
- *Synthesis*—Students can be asked to compile an inventory or images that represent concepts such as peace, justice, family, hope, and health. They could then ask their grandparents and parents to identify a visual inventory of objects that represents those same concepts. The students then need to integrate and/or compare the two inventories and draw conclusions about how the inventories are the same and/or different.
- *Evaluation*—Students could use PowerPoint to make a convincing case for why we should or should not be involved in space travel or similar areas.

NETS for Students[*]

Applications of PowerPoint to educational activities could address the following standards:

- *Creativity and innovation*—Students demonstrate creative and innovative thinking, construct knowledge, and develop innovative visual materials using technology.
- *Communication and collaboration*—Students use mediated materials to communicate and engage with one another and to support each others' learning.
- *Research and information fluency*—Students apply digital tools to gather, evaluate, and use information.
- *Critical thinking, problem-solving, and decision making*—Students use critical thinking skills to plan and conduct research, manage projects, solve problems, and make informed decisions using appropriate digital tools and resources.

What Is New in PowerPoint 2007

Like the other Office products, PowerPoint 2007 has a new interface characterized by the Ribbon, which includes a number of tabs. The Ribbon replaces many of the menus and toolbars of Office 2003, and the associated commands or functions have been grouped under tabs to help you get your work done more quickly. The organization of tabs is based on the type of activity you might perform when creating a presentation, such as animation and slide show. Some tabs display only when you need them. For instance, when you click an image, the Picture Tools tab displays. For additional information about PowerPoint 2007 features, see the *What's New* section of Microsoft Office PowerPoint Help.

About PowerPoint

PowerPoint 2007 is a computer application used to create presentation materials. With PowerPoint, you can create electronic slide shows to display on a computer, printed handouts, overhead transparencies, 2-inch-by-2-inch slides, and Web documents. PowerPoint is commonly used to create and display electronic slide show presentations.

There are many ways to use PowerPoint 2007. Teachers can write and present lecture notes and give students printed handouts of the PowerPoint presentation for review and note taking. Teachers and students can create presentations that include multimedia elements, such as animation, statistical charts and graphs, photographs, video, and audio, to enrich or give emphasis to instructional content. In addition, these presentations can be put on the Web. Media of special school activities may be incorporated into a self-running slide show and displayed at school events. Students can be given research projects that require them to collect and analyze data and to present their findings in a multimedia slide show format. Such a task may cause students to think visually and to collect information of various media formats (in addition to text) and employ them to more fully convey complex concepts. For instance, a student who has researched the rotation of planets in our solar system is likely to have greater impact on his or her audience using animation or video of planet orbits than if he or she attempted to explain the information with text or the spoken word. These are only a few applications of PowerPoint. As you become familiar with PowerPoint, you are likely to find innovative ways to incorporate it into your classroom activities.

[*]Reprinted with permission from *National Educational Technology Standards for Students, Second Edition,* © 2007, ISTE® (International Society for Technology in Education), www.iste.org. All rights reserved.

Working with PowerPoint

Suppose you assign students the task of creating a school weather station. Divide the class into several weather research teams. Students record the daily high and low temperatures, measure precipitation, and calculate wind speed and direction. You correspond with other geographically dispersed schools and arrange for your students to share and compare weather data with them. Students track weather trends throughout the year and each month report their collection methods and analysis to the class. Your classroom is equipped with a computer and projector, so you encourage students to use PowerPoint to present their findings. PowerPoint can help them create visual slide shows with images, colors, text, and animation effects.

This chapter focuses on creating a presentation that students use to present their findings to the class. Although the content used here is specific to creating a student report, the steps and procedures are generic and applicable to a variety of presentation types. Feel free to substitute your content and to modify the materials created in this chapter.

The complete PowerPoint presentation (Our Weather Station) can be found on the accompanying CD in the PowerPoint folder, which is within the Examples folder.

Before developing a presentation, an orientation to the PowerPoint workspace is needed. When opening PowerPoint 2007, you enter the Normal view. It is a workspace comprised of several tabs and panes. Figure 4.1 depicts the different areas of the workspace. The top portion of the screen is referred to as the Ribbon, which contains tabs for functions and tools to assist in creating a presentation. You can minimize the Ribbon by clicking the *Customize Quick Access Toolbar* and selecting *Minimize the Ribbon*.

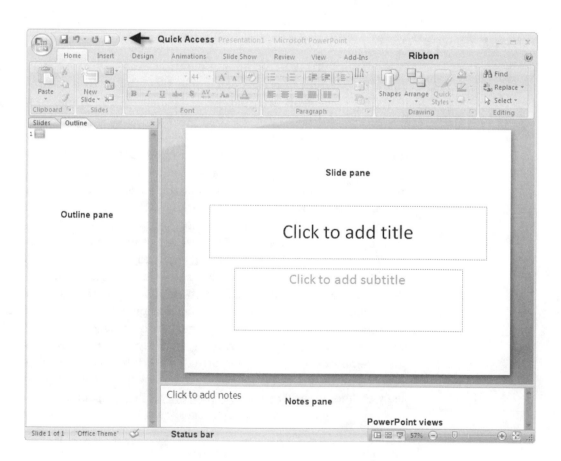

Figure 4.1
PowerPoint
workspace

The middle portion shows three panes—Outline, Slide, and Notes—that divide the PowerPoint workspace. This is the area where most of the slide development work is done. When text, graphics, drawn objects, and so on are added, they appear here and can be arranged and modified to create a professional looking slide. The size and positioning of the panes vary from view to view. You can adjust the size of each pane by positioning the mouse over the pane border (the cursor changes to double arrows), clicking the left mouse button, and then dragging the pane border to the desired size.

The Outline and Slides tabs display a text outline or miniature slides of your presentation, depending on the tab selected. With the Outline tab selected, you can enter the text for your presentation and organize it in list, paragraph, or slide format. With the Slides tab selected, you see thumbnail images of your slides. When you click on text in the Outline tab or the thumbnails in the Slides tab, the corresponding slide appears in the Slide pane.

In the Notes pane, you type notes about your presentation that remind you of a particular point to be made. You can add clip art and pictures to your notes pages. Click *Notes Page* in the Presentation Views group on the view tab to open the notes page. You can then insert objects by clicking the Insert tab and selecting any of the illustration options. The objects and pictures only appear in the notes page view or when printing your slides with notes. When viewing your presentation in the slide show, notes do not display. Exit the notes page by clicking on the View tab and then click *Normal* in the Presentation Views group.

If your computer is equipped with two monitors (e.g., laptop and projector), you can use the Presenter View, which allows you display the slide show to an audience while you control the slide as well as read notes for each slide. Turn the Presenter view on by clicking on the Slide Show tab and check the *Use Presenter View* option. When you view your slide show, slides appear on one screen (i.e., projector), and the Presenter view appears on the screen the audience does not see.

Located at the bottom of the screen, the status bar gives information about the number of slides in your presentation, the current slide number, and the design theme used by the current slide. In addition, the status bar contains the PowerPoint view buttons. PowerPoint provides three views of your presentation: Normal (with Outline and Slides tabs), Slide Sorter, and Slide Show. You can switch between views by clicking the buttons on the View toolbar located in the lower right of the PowerPoint screen. The Normal view has three panes: Outline, Slide, and Notes. There you can work on all the components of your presentation. The Slide Show displays your presentation without menus and toolbars. When presenting to an audience, the Slide Show is used. You can preview your presentation in the Slide Show at any time by clicking the Slide Show button. The Slide Sorter view displays miniatures of each slide in the presentation. In this view, you can reorder the slide sequence, delete slides, and add transitions. Finally, the Zoom slider allows you to zoom in and out on the slide work area. Right-click on the status bar to change the information and options that it displays.

Show Me

1. Open PowerPoint. Click *Start* on the Windows taskbar. On the Start menu, click *All Programs,* move the mouse pointer over *Microsoft Office,* and click *Microsoft PowerPoint 2007*. The PowerPoint workspace appears. You are in PowerPoint's Normal view (see Figure 4.1), and your presentation has one blank slide.

Creating a Title Slide and Inserting Text (Slide 1)

2. Slide layout. PowerPoint offers numerous layouts, such as Title Slide, Title Only, Title and Content, and Blank, among others. Click *Layout* in the Slide group of the Home tab to view slide layouts (see Figure 4.2). Single-click a layout, and

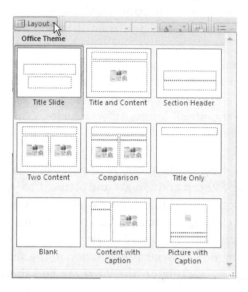

Figure 4.2
Slide layout

the current slide will change to that layout. You can also scroll through layouts by clicking the up and down scroll arrows on the right side of the list.

3. The first slide in a presentation is typically a title slide, which is the layout Power-Point assigns when you create the presentation. If your layout is not a Title slide, click *Layout* on the Home tab and select the Title Slide layout. You may also right-click on the slide and select *Layout* from the menu. Figure 4.3 illustrates a Title slide layout.

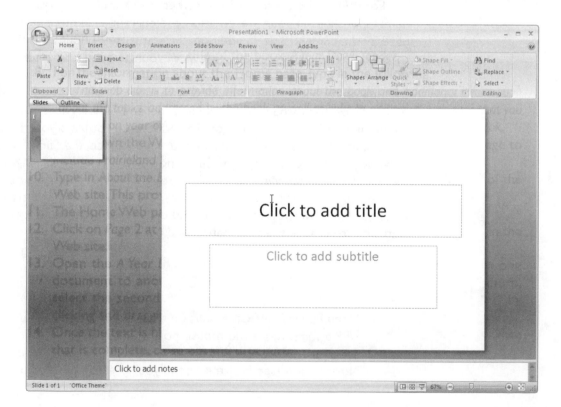

Figure 4.3
Title Slide layout

Inserting Text into a Title Slide

1. You are now in the Normal view of PowerPoint's workspace. You can give the slide a title. On a title slide, there are two text boxes, one for a title and the other for a subtitle (see Figure 4.3).
2. Click inside the text box labeled *Click to add title* and type the title of the presentation, *Our Weather Station: Precipitation Amounts*. Notice that prior to clicking in the *Click to add title* box, the border is a thin dashed line. Clicking inside the box causes the border to change to a thicker dashed line, indicating that it is selected and you can begin typing. Deselect the textbox by clicking anywhere outside of it.
3. Click inside the *Click to add subtitle* box and type *By the Research Weather Team:* and the students' names to signify that this presentation will be a report about precipitation by the school's weather team.

Adding a Design Theme

Design themes consist of predefined colors, layout formats, and font styles that give a presentation a specific look. When applying a design theme, each existing slide receives the same treatment, as do all new slides. PowerPoint provides a number of themes that you can apply to a presentation. It is a good idea to add a theme when starting the presentation. Otherwise, if you add themes after creating numerous slides, you may need to realign objects and reformat text, depending on the themes selected. Select a design theme early to ensure the proper positioning and formatting of slide objects.

1. For the weather team's presentation example, select a theme titled *Flow*. Feel free to select a different theme for your slide show. Click on the Design tab, and thumbnail images of the themes appear. Move the mouse cursor over a theme, and the theme attributes display on your slide. As the cursor moves over a theme, its title displays. Click the *More* option in the Themes group to display a listing of all themes (see Figure 4.4). Click on a theme to apply it to your slide.
2. To remove the design, select *Office Theme* in the Themes group of the Design tab.
3. The slide should now look similar to Figure 4.5.

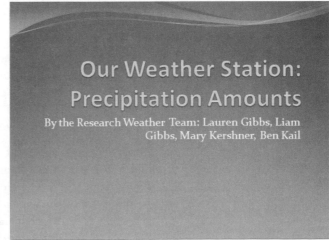

Figure 4.4
More arrow

Figure 4.5
Slide 1

LET ME TRY

At this point, you have created a new presentation that has one title slide. In addition, you added text and a design template to the slide. Let's practice what we have covered so far.

Suppose your principal asked you to deliver a presentation to the school board. The topic is your plan for establishing new graduation requirements. She gives you 2 days notice and states emphatically, "Dazzle them!" Additionally, she indicates that "it won't hurt to be high-tech, so feel free to use the computer/video projector in the meeting room." As your excitement, and perhaps apprehension, of presenting to the school board rises you begin to consider all the tasks before you, one of which is creating high-quality, easy-to-understand visuals that illustrate and support the points of your talk. Knowing that the room is equipped with a computer/video projector, you decide to develop your visuals using a portable computer (which you will connect to the projector during the presentation) and PowerPoint 2007. PowerPoint will enable you to create a visual slide show with images, colored charts and graphs, text, and animation effects, among other things. The steps for getting started are presented next. *To view a completed version of the school board presentation, open SchoolBoard_ Complete.pptx on the CD in the PowerPoint folder in Examples.*

1. Open PowerPoint. A blank presentation opens with one title slide. If you do not see a blank title slide, then select *Layout* from the Slides group of the Home tab and click *Title Slide.* This action creates one blank presentation that contains one blank title slide.
2. Insert text in the title slide. To enter a title, click inside the *Click to add title* box and type the title of the presentation, *Level Five.* Click anywhere outside the text object to deselect it.
3. Add a subtitle by clicking inside the *Click to add subtitle* box and type *Board Work Session by Lauren Marie Gibbs.*
4. Select a theme from the Themes group on the Design tab. Apply a theme of your choice by clicking its icon.

Inserting Slides and Adding Content

Title Only Slide (Slide 2)

A second slide can now be added to the weather station presentation. For this slide, you will choose a Title Only layout, which provides a text area for the slide title. The Title Only layout refers to the slide's title and not the title slide of the presentation.

After entering a title, you will create a second text box in which to type the purpose of the presentation. When you are finished, the slide will look similar to Figure 4.6.

1. There are several ways to add a new slide. Click the New Slide button in the Slides group on the Home tab or use the key combination of Ctrl+M.
2. PowerPoint adds a new slide to the presentation and by default assigns it a Title and Content layout. You want the layout to be Title Only, so click *Layout* in the Slides group on the Home tab and click the *Title Only* layout option (see Figure 4.7).
3. Add a title to slide 2 by clicking inside the *Click to add title* box and typing the following: *Reporting the Weather.* Another way to add a title is by making the Outline tab (on the left side of screen) active. Select the small slide icon that

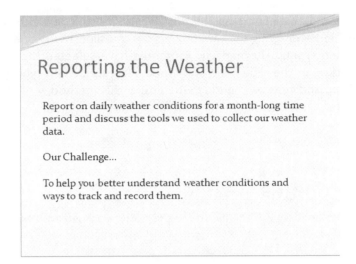

Figure 4.6
Title Only slide

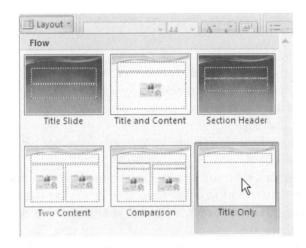

Figure 4.7
Title Only layout

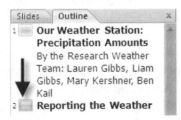

Figure 4.8
Slide title in Outline tab

Figure 4.9
Text Box

Figure 4.10
Cursor after selecting
Text Box

corresponds to slide 2 and type the title (see Figure 4.8). The title appears in the slide pane when typing.

4. This slide presents the purpose of the presentation. Currently, it has one text box that contains the slide title. You will now create a second text box for the text describing the presentation's purpose. Create a text box by clicking the Insert tab and then select the Text Box tool in the Text group (see Figure 4.9). When you click on the Text box tool, the mouse cursor changes to the vertical line (see Figure 4.10).

5. Place (click) the cursor in the slide pane where you want the text box to begin. While holding the left mouse button down, drag the cursor to the right side of

the slide pane. Release the mouse, and a blank text box appears (see Figure 4.11). By dragging the text box across the slide, the text wraps to the next line when typing. Alternatively, you could have selected the text tool and simply clicked in the slide pane and typed. However, when typing, the text does not wrap and runs off the slide when using this method.

Figure 4.11
Empty text box

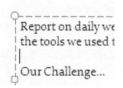

Figure 4.12
Text box border—
dashed line

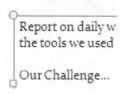

Figure 4.13
Text box border—
solid line

6. Now, type the purpose of the presentation:
   Report on daily weather conditions for a monthlong time period and discuss the tools we used to collect our weather data.
   Our Challenge . . . ?
   To help you better understand weather conditions and ways to track and record them.
7. Change the font style and size by clicking the text box border, then selecting a desired font style and size from the font group on the Home tab. When you click a text box to select it, a border appears with a dashed line (see Figure 4.12), indicating that you can insert or modify text. Clicking the text box border a second time changes it to a solid line (see Figure 4.13). The solid line indicates that the contents of the text box are selected. Any changes (e.g., font size or style) that you make alter the entire contents of the box.
8. If you chose the Flow theme, PowerPoint assigned the slides a font type of Constantia. If you want to change the font type, click the text object to select it and then click the border of the object so it changes from a dashed to a solid line. Make the Home tab active and in Font group click the small downward arrow in the font box to display a list of available fonts (see Figure 4.14). Select a font by clicking on the font name.
9. To change the font size, click the small downward arrow in the font size box, which is located on the right side of the font type box (see Figure 4.14). Select a size of 18 or 24 by clicking on the number. Currently, the Times New Roman font is set to 24.
10. The slide should look like Figure 4.6.

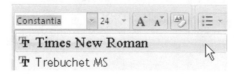

Figure 4.14
Font type

Navigating Between Slides

We now have two slides and can navigate from one to the other using one of the following methods:

1. Using either the Outline or the Slide tab, click on the slide icon that represents the slide to which you want to navigate. The slide appears in the slide pane.
2. In the slide pane, click the scroll bar arrows. The up arrow takes you to the previous slide, and the down arrow takes you to the next slide.
3. Use the arrow keys on your keyboard. The down arrow moves you forward through the slide show. The up arrow moves you back through the slide show.

LET ME TRY

Continuing with the school board presentation example, let's practice what we've covered so far. You created a slide with a Title Only layout, created a text box, and modified and set text attributes. Here are the steps you followed:

1. Add a new slide. Click *New Slide* in the Slides group of the Home tab or press Ctrl+M.
2. Select *Title Only* under the Layout option in the Slides group of the Home tab.
3. Click in the *Click to add title* box and enter the following: *Our Work Here Today . . .*
4. Create a text box to place the text describing the presentation's purpose. Select the Text Box tool in the Text group of the Insert tab. The mouse cursor changes to a vertical line when you click on the Text Box tool and then move the cursor to the slide pane.
5. With the cursor appearing as a vertical line, click in the slide pane where the text box begins and, while holding the left mouse button down, drag it to the right side of the slide pane. Release the mouse button, and a blank text box appears.
6. Type the purpose of the presentation in the text box:
   Establish new graduation requirements and standards that ensure high levels of student achievement versus traditional time and attendance requirements.
   Our Challenge . . .
   Invent a new system that prepares ALL graduates for society.
7. With the text box selected and the border as a solid line, click the small downward arrow in the font box on the Formatting toolbar. Select *Arial* font by clicking on the font name.
8. With the text box selected and the border as a solid line, click the small downward arrow in the Font Size box on the Formatting toolbar. Select a text size of 24.

Title and Content Slide (Slide 3)

Now let's add the third slide to the presentation. For this slide, choose a Title and Content layout, which provides text areas for the slide title and a text list. When you enter text into a list, PowerPoint separates it with bullets, checkmarks, hyphens, and so on. Lists are an easy and useful way to format text on a slide. When you are finished, the slide will look similar to Figure 4.15.

1. Add a new slide by selecting *New Slide* from the Slides group of the Home tab. By default, PowerPoint assigns a Title and Content layout, which is the layout

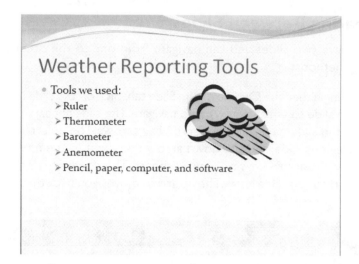

Figure 4.15
Title and Content slide

you want to use in this example. If your layout is not Title and Content, choose it by clicking *Layout* on the Slides groups of the Home tab.

2. Click in the *Click to add title* box and type the following title: *Weather Reporting Tools.*

3. Click inside the *Click to add text* box and type *The tools we used:*

4. Press Enter, and a bullet character (ellipse) appears on the next line. In Figure 4.15, notice that the first line uses the bullet character and that the remaining lines indent with an arrow character. After typing the first line in the bullet list and pressing Enter, the next text line (Ruler) does not indent. To indent it, position the cursor at the beginning of the line and press the Tab key. Type *Ruler* and press Enter, and subsequent lines indent.

5. Type the remaining items:
   - *Thermometer*
   - *Barometer*
   - *Anemometer*
   - *Pencil, paper, computer, and software*

6. By indenting these lines, the bullets become ellipses different in color from the first bullet item. To change the ellipses to arrows, select the five indented bullet items by positioning the cursor before the word *Ruler* and, while holding down the left mouse button, drag downward to after the word *software,* and release the mouse. The text should appear highlighted (highlighting text in this manner is referred to as *selecting*). With the text selected, click the right mouse button in the highlighted area and select *Bullets* and then choose arrow bullets from the submenu (see Figure 4.16). If you do not see this option, then choose

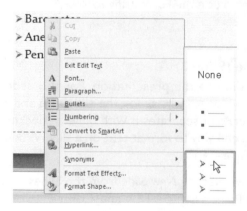

Figure 4.16
Bullets and numbering

Bullets and Numbering. The Bullets and Numbering dialog box appears, which presents various bullet types. Select the arrow bullet type by clicking the Bulleted tab and clicking the appropriate option.

7. To deselect the text, click anywhere outside the text box.

Adding Clip Art

1. You will insert a clip art image that represents or supports your topic about weather. Images are available from PowerPoint's clip art library. To insert clip art onto a slide, make the Insert tab active and click the Clip Art button in the Illustrations group (see Figure 4.17). The task pane displays the Clip Art options

Figure 4.17
Clip art

(see Figure 4.18). To search for clip art, type a key word in the *Search for:* box and click *Go* or press Enter. Using the *Search in:* and *Results should be:* options, you can specify the location that you want to search and the file types that you are seeking (e.g., sounds, movies, photographs, and clip art).

2. In the *Search for:* box, type *weather* and click *Go.* Small images (thumbnails) representing weather clip art will be displayed in the task pane (see Figure 4.18). If you do not want any of the images, you may also click the *Clip Art on Office Online* link at the bottom of the task pane. This option links to Microsoft's Clip Art and Media Web site containing numerous images that you can download.

3. For this presentation, select the rain clouds image located at the top left of the task pane. Insert it onto the slide by clicking on it. You can also insert the image

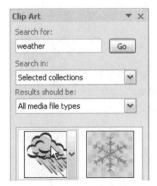

Figure 4.18
Inserting clip art

by selecting *Insert* from the drop-down menu that becomes available by positioning the mouse cursor over the image icon and clicking the downward arrow that appears on the right side of the thumbnail.

Tools

Figure 4.19
Inserting sizing
handles

Moving Clip Art and Resizing Text Objects

1. Now that you have inserted the clip art, its size and placement need adjustment. There are eight small sizing handles around the image (see Figure 4.19) that you can use to resize it. The handles also indicate that you selected the object. If you do not see the sizing handles around your clip art image, click on the image to select it, and the handles appear.
2. To make the image larger, move the mouse cursor over one of the sizing handles, and the cursor changes to an arrow. Click the upper-left sizing handle of the image and, while holding the left mouse button down, drag the sizing handle to the upper left. The image resizes. Pressing the Ctrl key while dragging resizes the image proportionally. If you need to reposition the image, click the left mouse button in the center of the image and, while holding the left mouse button down, drag the image to the desired location. You may also notice a green dot attached to the sizing handle. Dragging this dot to the left or right rotates the image.

LET ME TRY

Let's get back to the school board presentation example and practice what we covered. You created a slide with a Title and Content layout, modified the bullets in the list, and added a clip art image to the slide. Here are the steps you followed:

1. Add a new slide by selecting *New slide* from the Slides group on the Home tab.
2. Select a Title and Content layout from the Layout option in the Slides group.
3. Click in the *Click to add title* box and type the title *Time-Based System*.
4. Click inside the *Click to add text* box and type *Credits based on:* and press Enter.
5. Indent subbullets. With the cursor positioned at the beginning of the line, press the Tab key. Type the following bullet items and press Enter after each line:
   - *Time spent in class*
   - *Grade of D or better*
   - *Lack of consistency or uniform expectations for performance to earn diploma*
   Each item will indent under the *Credits based on:* text.
6. Select the three indented bullet items. Click the right mouse button in the selected area and select *Bullets* and then click the checkmarks cell.
7. Click anywhere outside the text box to deselect the text.
8. Select the Insert tab and then click *Clip Art*.
9. Enter a search term or key word (e.g., *education*) in the *Search for:* box of the task pane to search for an image.
10. When PowerPoint retrieves the images that relate to your search term, click one of them to insert it onto the slide.
11. Position and resize the image on the slide.

Adding a Title, Text, and Picture to a Slide (Slide 4)

A fourth slide can now be added to the presentation. This slide has a Two Content layout. When you are finished, the slide will look similar to Figure 4.20.

1. Add a new slide by selecting *New Slide* from the Slides group on the Home tab.
2. Select a Two Content layout from the layout options. After clicking the layout, the slide view looks like Figure 4.21.

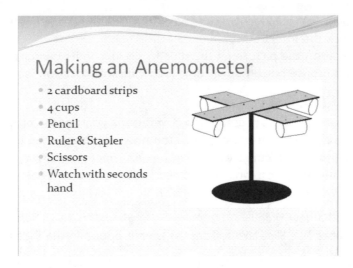

Figure 4.20
Two Content

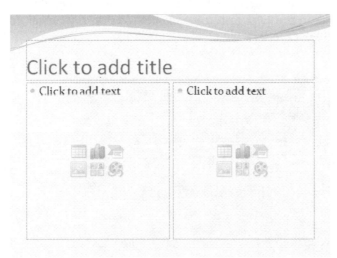

Figure 4.21
Two Content layout

3. Click inside the *Click to add title* box and type the following title: *Making an Anemometer.*
4. Click inside the *Click to add text* box on the left side of the screen and type the following text list:
   - *2 cardboard strips*
   - *Ruler & Stapler*
   - *4 cups*
   - *Scissors*
   - *Pencil*
   - *Watch with second hand*
5. Add a picture to the slide. Suppose the project involves making an anemometer, which measures wind speed and direction. Let's also suppose that when making the anemometer, you created a picture of it in a drawing program and saved it on the computer.
6. Notice that the slide has a placeholder for content (see Figure 4.21). The six icons in the placeholder area represent different types of content that can be added to a slide, such as tables, graphs, clip art, pictures, diagrams, and media (audio and video).
7. Click the Insert Picture icon, and the Insert Picture dialog box appears. *On the CD, locate the drawing of the anemometer,* anemometer.tif. *It is in the WeatherData*

folder within PowerPoint and Examples. Click the image one time to select it, then click the Insert button.

8. Position the picture on the slide by clicking in its center and, while holding the left mouse button down, drag it to a desired location (see Figure 4.20).

Title Slide (Slide 5)

The first portion of the presentation covered the goals of the project, weather reporting tools, and making an anemometer. You now will change the presentation topic and discuss weather data collected in October. You need to convey to your audience that you are changing topics, and a way to accomplish this is to insert a title slide. The complete slide will look similar to Figure 4.22.

1. Add a new slide.
2. Select *Title Slide* layout from the Layout option in the Slides group on the Home tab.
3. Click in the *Click to add title* box and type *Our Weather in October.*
4. Click in the *Click to add subtitle* box and type *Weather data: Recorded October 1 through October 31.*

Figure 4.22
Title slide for
new topic

Modifying Text

You can now adjust the font type, style, size, and positioning of the text.

1. To modify the title, click the title text box to select it. The first time you click the box, a dashed line border appears with sizing handles. Click the border again to change its appearance from a dashed to a solid line. Notice that as you pass the mouse pointer over the border, it changes to a four-pointed cross. When the border is selected, changes (e.g., font size or style) can be made to the contents of the text box.
2. On the Home tab and in the Font group, click the small downward arrow in the font box to display a list of fonts (see Figure 4.23). Select a font by clicking on the font name. For this slide, set the font set to Impact. If you want to choose a different font, scroll through the font list and click a font name.
3. Click the small downward arrow in the font size box to display a list of font sizes. Select a size by clicking on the number. Choose a font size of 60 (see Figure 4.24).

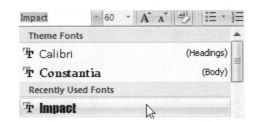

Figure 4.23
Font selection

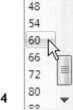

Figure 4.24
Font size

4. In the Font group, set the font style to bold and the text to shadow by clicking the Bold (B) and Shadow (S) icons (see Figure 4.25). In the Paragraph group (Home tab), click the Center icon to center the text (see Figure 4.26). The Center icon centers the contents inside the text box. It does not center the text box relative to the screen.

5. With the title selected, click the Format tab, and in the WordArt Styles group click the down arrow for *Text Effects* and select *Shadow* and then *Perspective Diagonal Upper Left* (see Figure 4.27).

Figure 4.25
Font attributes

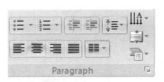

Figure 4.26
Font attributes

Figure 4.27
Font styles

Figure 4.28
Alignment

Figure 4.29
Alignment

6. Click the subtitle text box and set the font style to shadow (S).

7. The subtitle is directly under the title. You can move the subtitle to the lower portion of the slide by selecting it (clicking on it), clicking on its border, and then dragging the box. If the text box is not selected or the border is a dashed line, the text box will not move. A more accurate way to align the text box in the lower portion of the slide is to use *Align or Distribute*. However, before you use *Align or Distribute*, let's align the text in the middle of its own text box. Notice in Figure 4.28 that the text is aligned at the top of the text box. PowerPoint provides options for aligning text in the top, middle, or bottom of the text box. To align the text in the middle of the box, such as in Figure 4.29, go to the Home tab and in the Paragraph group click *Align Text* and select *Middle* (see Figure 4.30).

8. Next you'll align the entire text box at the bottom of the screen. The steps are as follows:

■ Select the subtitle and ensure that a solid line border displays around it.

■ Select the Home tab and click the Arrange button in the Drawing group. Pass the mouse pointer over *Align* and from the drop-down menu click *Align to Slide*. A check appears next to the Align to Slide menu item. The menu disappears.

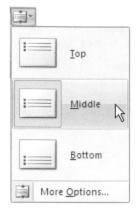

Figure 4.30
Alignment options

- Click *Arrange* in the Drawing group. Pass the mouse pointer over *Align* and from the drop-down menu click *Align Bottom*. The text box appears toward the bottom of the slide.
- Alternatively, you can align the text using the *Align* button in the Arrange group on the Format tab.
- Click the subtitle text box to select it. Click the Format tab and in the WordArt Styles group click the down arrow for *Text Effects* and select *Shadow* and then *Perspective Diagonal Upper Left.*

Adding a Title, Text, and Content Slide (Slide 6)

For this slide, choose the Two Content layout. The final slide will look similar to Figure 4.31.

1. Add a new slide by selecting *New Slide* from the Slides group on the Home tab.
2. Choose the Two Content layout from the Slides group.
3. Click in the *Click to add title* box and type the following title: *October Assignments.*

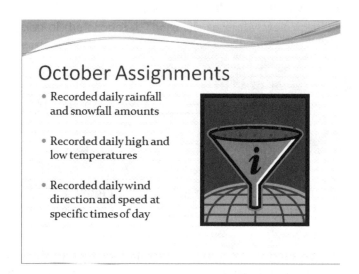

Figure 4.31
Complete slide

4. Enter the following three items in the bullet list on the left side of the two content areas:
   - *Recorded daily rainfall and snowfall amounts*
   - *Recorded daily high and low temperatures*
   - *Recorded daily wind direction and speed at specific times of day*
5. Set the line spacing. The list items are close together, and readers may have difficulty discerning one item from another. Select the list text box and click on its border so it becomes a solid line. Click the Line Spacing button in the Paragraph group on the Home tab and select *Line Spacing Options*. The Paragraph box appears (see Figure 4.32).
6. Type *30* in the *After* box located in the Spacing area, which adds space between list items.
7. Click the Clip Art icon in the content area on the right side of the slide to add a clip art image. Adjust its size and position as needed.

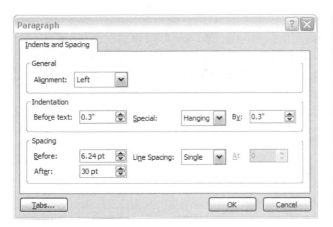

Figure 4.32
Line spacing

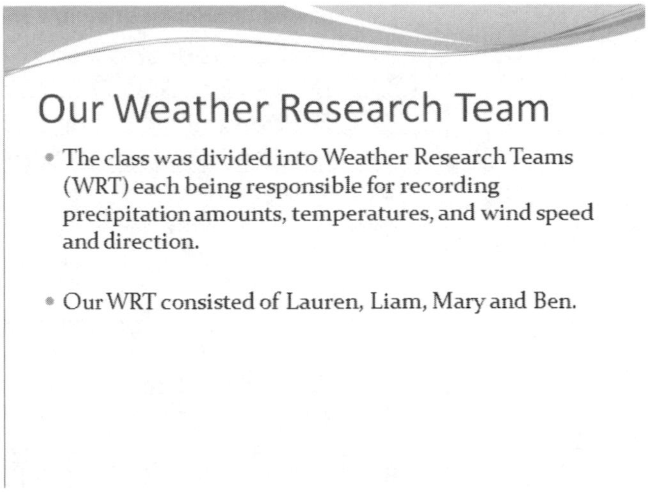

Our Weather Research Team

- The class was divided into Weather Research Teams (WRT) each being responsible for recording precipitation amounts, temperatures, and wind speed and direction.

- Our WRT consisted of Lauren, Liam, Mary and Ben.

Figure 4.33
Title and content

Adding a Title and Content Slide (Slide 7)

For this slide, choose a Title and Content layout. The final slide will look similar to Figure 4.33.

1. Add a new slide by selecting *New Slide* from the Slides group on the Home tab.
2. Choose Title and Content layout from the task pane.
3. Click in the *Click to add title* box to enter the following title: *Our Weather Research Team.*
4. Type the following bullet list items:
   - *The class was divided into Weather Research Teams (WRT), each being responsible for recording precipitation amounts, temperatures, and wind speed and direction.*
   - *Our WRT consisted of Lauren, Liam, Ben.*
5. Select the text box and in the Line Spacing options and set the *Spacing After* to 30, which adds space between list items.

LET ME TRY

Returning to our school board presentation example, let's create three slides based on what we covered so far.

Two Content Slides

1. Add a new slide by selecting *New Slide*.
2. Click the *Two Content* layout.
3. Click inside the *Click to add title* box and type the following title: *Performance-based System.*
4. Click inside the *Click to add text* box and type the following text list:
   - *Students demonstrate proficiency in all graduation requirements.*
   - *Seat time and passing grade no longer earns a degree.*

5. Add a picture or clip art to the slide. Click the Clip Art icon in the content area on the right side of the slide to add a clip art image.
6. Position the picture or clip art on the slide by clicking in its center and, while holding the left mouse button down, drag it to a desired location.

Title Slide

At this point in the school board presentation, the topic focus changes, and you will indicate this shift in focus using a title slide.

1. Add a new slide.
2. Click the *Title Slide* layout.
3. Click in the *Click to add title* box and type *Why Change?*
4. Click in the *Click to add subtitle* box and type *Some important reasons.*
5. Click the title text box to select it. Click the border again so that a solid line appears. With the border as a solid line, choose a font.
6. Set the font size to 66.
7. Set the font style to bold, the text to shadowed, and the text alignment to centered by clicking the Bold (B), Shadow (S), and Center icons.
8. Click the subtitle text box and set the font size to 36 and the style to shadow (S) and bold (B).

Title and Content Slide

The next slide will state reasons for why change is needed. This slide will have a Title and Content layout. Because there is an existing slide with a Title and Content layout, you will use the Slide Sorter to copy and paste it.

1. Click the *Slide Sorter View* button located in the lower-right portion of the PowerPoint workspace to enter the Slide Sorter.
2. Click the Title and Content slide (e.g., slide 3) to select it.
3. With the slide selected, choose *Copy* from the Edit menu. Click the last slide in the presentation (slide 5) and select *Paste* from the Edit menu. There are now six slides.
4. Change the text on the sixth slide. Double-click it to exit the Slide Sorter and return to the Normal view.
5. Click on the Title box to select it. A dashed line border appears around the box. Click on the border again, and it changes to a solid line. Press the Delete key, and the text changes to *Click to add title.* Type the new title: *America Is Unprepared.*
6. Click the bullet list text box to select it. A dashed line border appears around the box. Click on the border again, and it changes to a solid line. Press the Delete key, and the text changes to *Click to add text.* Type a new list by entering the following items:
   - *"Literacy and the ability to think are the underpinnings of a free society." Thomas Jefferson.*
   - *Provide students with a proper background in history, economics, government, language, literature, science, technology, philosophy, and the arts.*
7. Add clip art.

Adding a Title Only Slide with an Object (Slide 8)

For this slide, choose a *Title Only* layout. We will insert an Excel worksheet onto the slide to represent the data recorded for the first 15 days in October. The final slide will look similar to the screen shown in Figure 4.34.

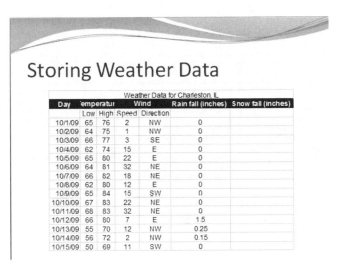

Storing Weather Data

Day	Temperature		Wind		Rain fall (inches)	Snow fall (inches)
	Low	High	Speed	Direction		
10/1/09	65	76	2	NW	0	
10/2/09	64	75	1	NW	0	
10/3/09	66	77	3	SE	0	
10/4/09	62	74	15	E	0	
10/5/09	65	80	22	E	0	
10/6/09	64	81	32	NE	0	
10/7/09	66	82	18	NE	0	
10/8/09	62	80	12	E	0	
10/9/09	65	84	15	SW	0	
10/10/09	67	83	22	NE	0	
10/11/09	68	83	32	NE	0	
10/12/09	66	80	7	E	1.5	
10/13/09	55	70	12	NW	0.25	
10/14/09	56	72	2	NW	0.15	
10/15/09	50	69	11	SW	0	

Weather Data for Charleston, IL.

Figure 4.34
Completed slide with worksheet

1. Add a new slide.
2. Choose *Title Only*.
3. Click in the *Click to add title* box and type the following title: *Storing Weather Data*.
4. Place an Excel worksheet on the slide. Click anywhere on the slide to deselect the title. Click the Insert tab and select *Object* in the Text group (see Figure 4.35). The Insert Object dialogue box appears (see Figure 4.36).
5. Click the *Create from file* option. Click *Browse*, and the Browse dialog box appears.
6. Locate the worksheet named *OctoberWeatherData.xlsx* in the WeatherData folder (in PowerPoint and Examples) on the CD. Click the *OctoberWeather Data.xlsx* file one time to select it and then click *OK*, and you will return to the Insert dialog box.

Figure 4.35
Insert object

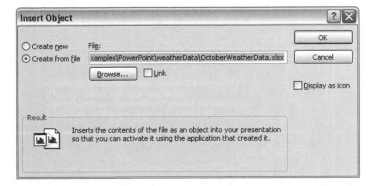

Figure 4.36
Insert Object box

7. Click *OK*, and the worksheet should appear on the slide. Adjust the size of the worksheet by clicking and dragging the corner to expand or contract it.

Adding a Chart Slide (Slide 9)

Add the ninth slide to the presentation, which will include a chart. Suppose a weather research team located in Charleston, Illinois, and another team in Philadelphia, Pennsylvania, want to compare precipitation amounts for the month of October over a 3-year period. One way to present the data is shown in Figure 4.37.

1. Add a new slide by selecting *New Slide* from the Insert menu.
2. Choose a Title and Content layout.
3. Click in the *Click to add title* box and enter the following title: *Precipitation Amount.*

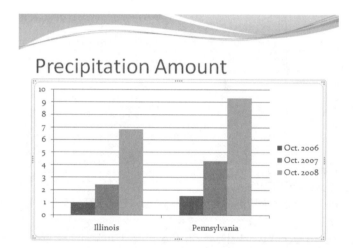

Figure 4.37
Column chart emphasizing state

Figure 4.38
Insert Chart icon

4. Click the Insert Chart icon (see Figure 4.38), and the Insert Chart box appears (see Figure 4.39). On the left side of the Insert Chart box, select *Column* and, under the column subtype area, choose *Clustered Column* and click *OK*. An Excel worksheet opens with sample data.
5. Enter the data as shown in Figure 4.40. Notice in Figure 4.40 that there are Category 3 and Category 4 items with data that do not display in the chart. You

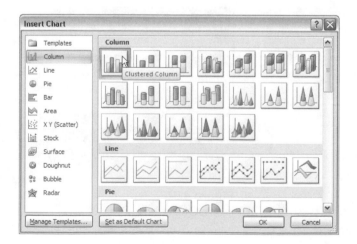

Figure 4.39
Chart type options

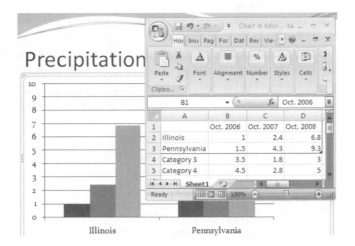

Figure 4.40
Data entry End

can either delete these data items or simply drag the Range rectangle so that it encompasses only the data to be shown in the chart. In this example, the Range rectangle encompasses data in cells A1 down through cell D3. To close the data sheet, click the Close button (X) on the upper-right corner of the data sheet.

6. Close the Excel worksheet and view the chart (see Figure 4.41). If you need to edit the data, click the chart, and the *Chart Tools* tab becomes active. Under the Chart Tools tab, click the *Design* tab and in the Data group click *Edit data*.

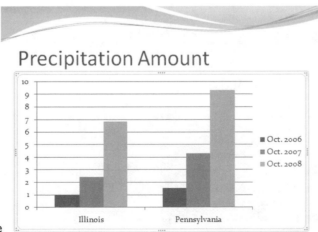

Figure 4.41
Chart emphasizing time

Ordering Data
Before continuing, review quickly how to order data in the data sheet. The ordering of data in Excel determines how data are plotted. For instance, in the previous example, there are two categories labeled *Illinois* and *Pennsylvania*. Enter the Illinois data in cells A2 through D2 and then the Pennsylvania data in cells A3 through D3. PowerPoint plots the Illinois data first on the left side of the chart with data points in subsequent columns and rows appearing next and so on. Notice in Figure 4.40 that row 1 is the

data series column. Data entered there appear in the chart legend. The legend in Figure 4.41 appears on the right side of the chart.

Various aspects of data can be emphasized or grouped depending on their ordering. For example, data can be ordered to show how precipitation varied for each state over time, as shown in Figure 4.41. Alternatively, placing the states in the data series column and time periods in Categories 1, 2, and 3 (see Figure 4.42) emphasizes

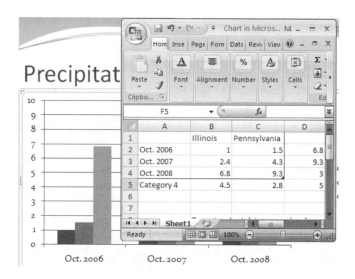

Figure 4.42
Editing data

precipitation over time. The ordering of data illustrated in Figure 4.42 produces the chart shown in Figure 4.43. In this example, the chart emphasizes time period and plots the state categories as the data series.

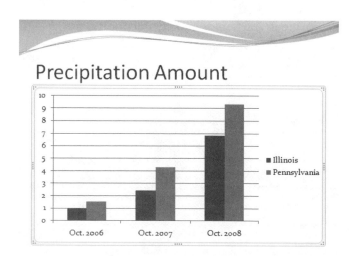

Figure 4.43
Complete slide

Inserting a Chart

In this example, you will create the chart shown in Figure 4.43 using the Insert Chart command.

1. Add a new slide.
2. Choose a Blank layout.

3. Make the Insert tab active and click the Chart button. The Insert Chart box appears. Click *Column* and then *Clustered Column*. Click *OK*. An Excel worksheet displays.

4. Enter the data as shown in Figure 4.42 and move the Range rectangle so that it encompasses cells A1 down through C4. Close the worksheet.

Changing the Chart Layout

1. Click the chart to select it, and the Chart Tools tab becomes active. Click the Design tab and in the Chart Layouts group select *Layout 2*. Clicking the *More* arrow in the Chart Layouts group will display the available chart layouts. Move the mouse cursor over each item, and the layout name appears. When you se-lect the layout, the chart appearance changes, and a Chart title box appears at the top of the chart. Type *October Precipitation: Illinois and Pennsylvania* in the Title box.

2. Enlarge the chart by clicking and dragging one of the sizing handles (three small dots) around its borders.

3. Click the chart to select it, and the Chart Tools tab becomes active. Click the Design tab and in the Chart Styles group choose *Style 39* or another style of your choice.

4. With the chart selected, position the cursor over its border, right-click, and select *Format Chart Area . . .* The Format Chart Area box displays. On the left portion of the box, click *Border Color*, and the Border Color options display. Select *No line* and then click *Close*.

5. The completed chart should look like Figure 4.44.

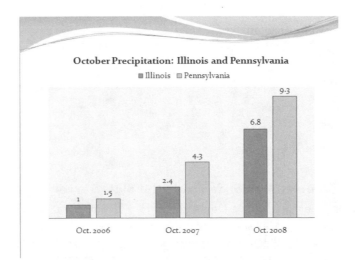

Figure 4.44
Complete chart

Changing the Chart Type

1. To change the chart type, click on the chart, and the Chart Tools tab becomes active. Click the Design tab and in the Type group click *Change Chart Type*. The Change Chart Type box appears from which you can choose another type.

2. You can edit the chart by double-clicking in the chart area and then selecting the commands on the Chart Tools Design tab or right-clicking in the chart area and selecting *Edit data* or *Change chart type*.

Returning to the school board presentation example, let's practice what we've covered so far. You created a slide with a chart, entered data into a worksheet, and modified the chart layout. Here are the steps you followed:

1. Add a new slide.
2. Choose Title and Content layout from the task pane.
3. Click in the *Click to add title* box and enter the following title: *Skills Needed: Critical Thinking and Problem Solving.*
4. Click the Insert Chart icon (see Figure 4.38), and the Insert Chart box appears.
5. On the left side of the Insert Chart box, select *Bar*; then under *Chart sub-type*, select the Cluster Bar format by clicking the appropriate icon.
6. Click *OK* to set the chart options. An Excel worksheet opens with sample data.
7. In the data sheet, type *(%) of Jobs Requiring Skills* in the Category 1 cell of column A and *(%) of Today's Workforce with Skills* in the Category 2 cell of column A. Adjust the column widths as needed.
8. Enter three time periods for the data series: *1900* in the data series column B, row 1; *1950* in the data series column C, row 1; and *2000* in the data series column D, row 1.
9. Enter the values of 10, 30, and 60 in cells B2, C2, and D2, respectively.
10. Enter the values of 4, 14, and 20 in cells B3, C3, and D3, respectively.
11. Set the Range rectangle so that it encompasses cell A1 down through cell D3 (see Figure 4.45).
12. Close the worksheet by clicking *Close* on the upper-right corner.

	A	B	C	D
1		1900	1950	2000
2	*(%) of Jobs Requiring Skill*	10	30	60
3	*(%) of Today's Workforce w*	4	14	20

Figure 4.45
Data range

Adding a Title and Text Slide Using the Slide Sorter (Slide 10)

Now add another slide with a Title and Content layout. For this slide, use the Slide Sorter to make a copy of an existing slide, paste it, and alter its text to create the 10th slide. Copying and pasting slides in the Slide Sorter is one of the many approaches you can use to work efficiently. When you are finished, the slide will look similar to Figure 4.46.

1. Click the *Slide Sorter View* button located in the lower-right portion of the PowerPoint workspace to enter the Slide Sorter (see Figure 4.47). The Slide Sorter presents images of each slide in the slide show (see Figure 4.48). In this view, slides can be easily copied, pasted, reordered, and deleted. To reorder a slide, click on it and drag it to a new location in the slide show sequence. To delete a slide, click on it and press Delete. You can also accomplish many of the previously mentioned tasks in the Slide pane of the Normal view.
2. To copy and paste a slide, click one of the Title and Content layout slides (e.g., slide 7) to select it. A border appears around it. With the slide selected, click

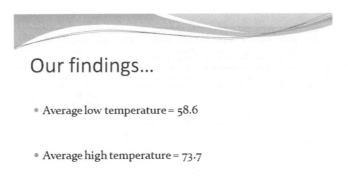

Figure 4.46
Complete slide

Figure 4.47
Slide Sorter

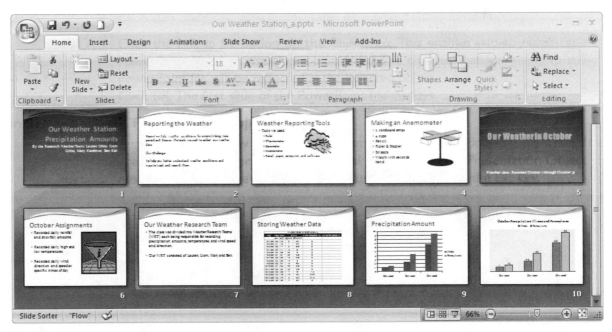

Figure 4.48
Slide Sorter view

Copy on the Clipboard group of the Home tab or press Ctrl+C. Click the last slide in the presentation (slide 10) and click *Paste* in the Clipboard group or press Ctrl+V. The 11th slide appears. Note that the pasted slide appears after the slide (i.e., slide 10) you selected.

3. There are now 11 slides, two of which are duplicates, slides 7 and 11. Change the text on the 11th slide. Double-click it to exit the Slide Sorter and return to the Normal view.

4. Slide 11's title box has text in it that can be replaced with *Our findings . . .* To replace the text, click on the Title box to select it. A dashed line border appears around the box. Click on the border again, and it changes to a solid line. Press Delete, and the text changes to *Click to add title*. Type the new title: *Our findings . . .*

5. To enter bullet items, click the bullet list text box to select it. As in the previous step, press Delete, and the text changes to *Click to add text*. Type a new list by entering the following items:
   - *Average low temperature = 58.6*
   - *Average high temperature = 73.7*
   - *Total precipitation = 5.9*
6. Select the bullet list textbox. Choose *Line Spacing* from the Paragraph group on the Home tab and select *3.0*.

Adding a Title, Text, and Content Slide (Slide 12)

To complete the presentation, add one more slide. Again, use the Slide Sorter to copy and paste a slide.

1. Click the Slide Sorter View button to enter the Slide Sorter.
2. Click a Two Content slide (e.g., slide 4) to select it. A border appears around it. With the slide selected, choose *Copy*. Click the last slide in the presentation (slide 11) and select *Paste*. The 12th slide appears.
3. To change the text on the slide, double-click slide 12 to exit the Slide Sorter and return to the Normal view. The slide you create will look like the screen shown in Figure 4.49.

Figure 4.49
Complete slide

4. Replace the text in the title text box with *Weather Reporting Team*.
5. Enter the bullet items. Click the bullet list text box to select it. A dashed line border appears around the box. Click on the border again, and it changes to a solid line pattern. Press Delete, and the text changes to *Click to add text*. Type the new list. Enter the following items:
   - *From Lauren, Liam, Mary and Ben, this has been our monthly weather report. . . .*
   - *Until next time—Thanks!!!*
6. Select the text list and then click *Line Spacing* in the Paragraph group of the Home tab. Select the *Line Spacing* options and type *30* in the *After* box.
7. Delete the existing clip art image. Click it to select it and then press Delete. Add clip art representative of the topic and position it in a desired location.

LET ME TRY

Let's continue creating the school board presentation by adding two slides with a Title and Content layout and one slide with a Two Content layout.

Title and Content Slides

1. Because we already have a slide (slide 6) with a Title and Content layout, use the Slide Sorter to copy it and paste it. Because we need two slides with this layout, paste the copied slide twice. Paste the slides after the last slide (slide 7). The presentation now has nine slides.

2. In the Slide Sorter, double-click slide 8 to return to the Normal view. Click on slide 8's Title box to select it. Delete the existing text and type *The Five New Performance Standards Are:*

3. Click the bullet list text box to select it. Delete the existing text and enter the following items:
   - *Quantitative and scientific reasoning*
   - *Communication (including a culminating project)*
   - *Citizenship (including a service learning component)*
   - *Culture*
   - *School-to-career (including an education and future plans and a field experience)*

4. Add clip art.

5. Repeat these steps for slide 9. Enter the following title: *What Will Be Done to Ensure All Students Meet These Standards?*

6. Enter the following list items:
   - *Students who perform poorly on the 4th, 7th, and 10th grade WASL exams will be identified for additional support.*
   - *Support programs will exist in K-12.*
   - *Students will be given multiple chances to show they can meet the standards.*

Two Content Slide

To complete the presentation, add one more slide with a Two Content layout. Again, use the Slide Sorter to copy and paste a slide.

7. Click the Slide Sorter View button to enter the Slide Sorter.

8. Click a Two Content slide (e.g., slide 4) to select it. Copy the slide and paste it after the last slide.

9. Replace the text in title text box with *Gradual Phases*.

10. Enter the following bullet items:
    - *2005 Communication Requirements*
    - *2006 Quantitative and Scientific Reasoning Requirements + Requirements for 2005*
    - *2007 Citizenship and Culture Requirements + Requirements for 2006*
    - *2008 School-to-Career and Life Skills Requirements + Requirements for 2007*
    - *Certificate of Mastery required for Graduation*

Previewing the PowerPoint Presentation in the Slide Show

You can now view the presentation in the Slide Show. Click the *Slide Show* button located in the lower left portion of the PowerPoint workspace to enter the Slide Show. Advance the slides by clicking the left mouse button. To exit the Slide Show, press the

Escape (Esc) key or click the right mouse button on the slide and select *End Show* from the menu. Remember that at any point when you are developing the presentation, you can view it in the Slide Show.

Saving the Presentation

It is a good idea to save your work frequently. Keep in mind that even though you see your presentation on-screen, it may not be saved. The more often you save your work, the less chance there is of losing a presentation or a portion of it. Any portion of your presentation that you do not save disappears when the computer is turned off.

There are two Save options, *Save* and *Save As,* located under the Office button.

Save

When you create a new presentation and select *Save,* the Save As dialog box appears (see Figure 4.50), prompting you to determine a location in which to save the file, give the file a name, and specify a file format. When saving a new presentation, you will likely do the following:

- Click in the *Save in* box to specify the location to save the presentation.
- Type a name in the *File name* field.
- Assign a file format by clicking in the *Save as type* box.

If you do not provide a name, PowerPoint gives the presentation the name of *Presentation1.pptx.* By default, PowerPoint appends the .pptx extension to the file name and saves the file in a presentation (*.pptx) format. Several other file format options are available, such as .html, .mht, and PowerPoint 97.

Once you have designated a location, name, and format for your presentation, PowerPoint saves all future changes accordingly. If you created a new presentation,

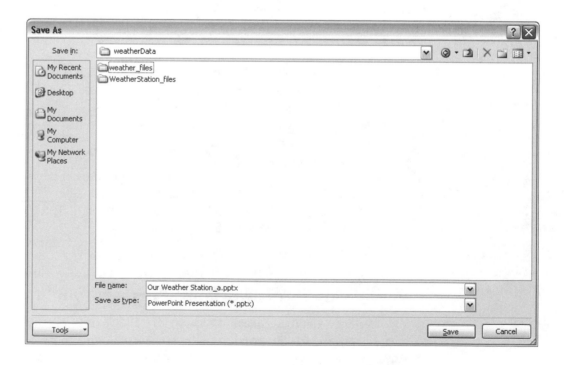

Figure 4.50
Save As box

added five slides, and saved it in the Office folder with the name *WeatherData.pptx,* a file named *WeatherData.pptx* would appear in the Office folder on your computer's hard drive. If you reopened the presentation, added two additional slides, and clicked *Save,* the two new slides would be automatically saved with the original five, and the Save As dialog box would not appear. The presentation would have seven slides.

1. Because the presentation in this chapter has not yet been saved, click the Office button and select *Save.*
2. Click in the *Save in* box on the Save As dialog box to locate the Office folder or another folder of your choice.
3. Type a name for the presentation in the *File name* box. Use *WeatherStation* for the name. Remember, PowerPoint appends the .pptx extension to the file name, resulting in *WeatherStation.pptx.* The file is saved to your computer.
4. In addition to saving the file, save the file as a PowerPoint show format. Click the Office button, select *Save as,* and then select the *PowerPoint Show* option. The Save As box appears. Specify the location to save the show and click *Save. View the WeatherStation.ppsx on the CD (WeatherData folder) to see an example of the PowerPoint show.*

Save As

The Save As option allows you to save an existing presentation in a different location, under a different file name, or in a different file format.

Adding Slide Transitions

You can add slide transitions, such as wipes, dissolves, and fades, between slides. The effects display when viewing the presentation in the Slide Show.

1. Make the Animations tab active.
2. Select a transition from the Transition to This Slide group (see Figure 4.51). To add a transition to all slides, click *Apply to All* after selecting the transition. If you want to add a transition to only a single slide, then select the slide and then choose a transition. You can also adjust the speed of the transition using the options on the Transition to This Slide group.

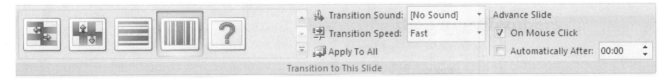

Figure 4.51
Slide transition

3. For this example, click a transition (e.g., blinds horizontal, blinds vertical wipe, dissolve, and so on) and then click *Apply to All Slides.*
4. Set the speed of the transition and a sound.
5. Under *Advance slide,* check *On mouse click* so the slide advances and the transition takes place when the mouse button is clicked.
6. You can also select *Automatically after* to advance slides after a designated number of seconds. Checking this option and specifying a number of

seconds sets the transition to occur and the slide to advance automatically after the specified time. This option is useful for creating self-running slide shows. *See the Schoolboard_SelRun.pptx and Schoolboard_SelfRun.pps files on the CD for examples.* Checking both *On mouse click* and *Automatically after* (and specifying a time) sets the transition to occur automatically after the preset number of seconds. To advance the slide before the designated time, click the mouse.

7. Set the transition to apply to all the slides by clicking *Apply to All Slides*. To preview the transitions, click the Preview button on the Animations tab.

Saving as a Web Page

Suppose the weather research team wants to share the presentation with parents, teachers, and other students. One way to disseminate the presentation to a large audience is to make it available on the Web. In PowerPoint, you can save a presentation as a Web page (.htm or .html) or as a single file Web page (.mht or .mhtml), both of which can be viewed in a Web browser. *See WeatherStation.htm and WeatherStation.mht on the CD in the WeatherData folder for examples.*

As a Web Page

The Web Page (.htm or .html) option converts the presentation to HTML and stores all associated files on your computer or on removal disks. PowerPoint appends the .htm extension to the file name. For example, when saving *WeatherStation.ppt* as a Web page, PowerPoint assigns it the name *WeatherStation.htm.* In addition, PowerPoint creates a folder named *WeatherStation_files* that contains the HTML and graphic files associated with the presentation. You will need both the *WeatherStation.htm* and the *WeatherStation_files* folder or the presentation will not display properly on the Web. Thus, when uploading the presentation to the Web, you must upload the .htm file and the folder.

As a Single File Web Page

The Single File Web Page (.mht or .mhtml) option creates a single file with the .mht extension. For example, when saving *WeatherStation.ppt* as a Single File Web Page, PowerPoint assigns it the name *WeatherStation.mht,* and it creates one file containing the presentation. The Single File Web Page format is convenient because the presentation is contained in a single file, unlike the Web Page format that creates several files and a folder. However, the Single File Web Page format typically produces a larger file size than the Web Page format.

It is important to note that even though you save a presentation as a Web page or a single file Web page and can view it, the Web-formatted presentation files need to be placed on a computer server for them to be available worldwide. A server is a computer (with server software) set up to perform many different functions. One of its primary uses is to serve applications and files. With respect to the Web, a server permits people from around the world to view Web documents using a browser (e.g., Internet Explorer, Netscape, Mozilla FireFox, and so on). Thus, after saving your presentation as HTML, you need the following to make it available on the Web:

- Access to a Web server that stores and serves your HTML files and graphics. Internet service providers provide this service.
- File transfer software that transfers the HTML files and graphics from your computer to a server.

Saving the Presentation as a Web Page

1. Click the Office button, select *Save as,* and then select *Other Formats.*
2. The Save As dialog box appears (see Figure 4.52). Locate the folder in which you want to save the files by clicking in the *Save in* box. In this example, you will save it in a folder titled *WeatherData* located in the Office folder on your computer's C: drive. If you do not have a folder with this name and want to create one, click the Create New Folder button on the top right (third option from right) of the Save As dialog box. When the *New Folder* box appears, enter a folder name and click *OK.*

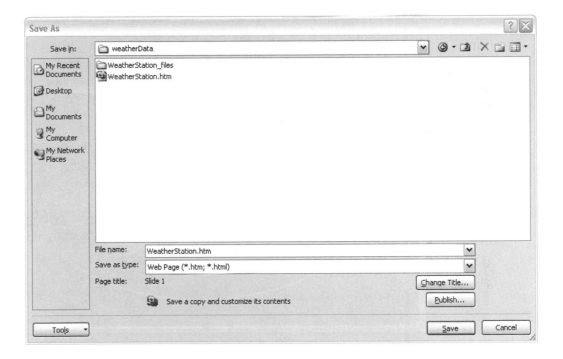

Figure 4.52
Save As box

3. Click the Change Title button and type *Weather Station* in the Page title box.
4. Click the Publish button, which provides several options for saving the presentation, including the following:
   - *Publish what?* Specify the range of slides to be saved and whether to display speaker notes. For this presentation, select *Complete presentation* to save all slides.
   - *Browser support:* HTML files display differently depending on the browser and version. Specify the browser version that is most compatible with users' systems. Click *All browsers listed above.* This option creates a larger file but gives users greater flexibility in terms of the browser they use to view the presentation.
   - *Publish a copy as:* Change the page title by clicking the Change button—you set this in a previous step. Use the *File name* box to specify a location to save the Web-formatted file and assign it a name. The Browse button allows you to specify a location other than the one presented. For this presentation, there is no need to change anything.
5. Click the Publish button, and PowerPoint converts the presentation to a Web format. Note that when you click the Publish button on the *Save As* box,

PowerPoint saves the presentation as a Web page (.htm) and not as a Single File Web Page (*.mht).

If you do not want to modify any of the Publish options, click *Save* on the *Save As* box and PowerPoint converts the entire presentation to a Single File Web Page (*.mht). If you want to save the presentation in a Web Page format, choose *Web Page (*.htm; *.html)* from the *Save as type* section on the Save As box.

When saving a presentation as a Web page, it is preferable to remove blank spaces in the file name. The computer server may not recognize file names containing blank spaces. For example, when converting a presentation named *Weather Station.pptx .pptx* to a Web page, the file should be saved as *WeatherStation.htm*.

Opening the Presentation in a Web Browser

1. Open a Web browser (e.g., Internet Explorer) to view the presentation. In this example, use Internet Explorer. Press Crtl+O to display the Open dialog box. If you know the location or path of your presentation, type it into the location box. If not, click *Browse,* and the Microsoft Internet Explorer dialog box appears.
2. Locate the file on your computer. The file in this example is titled *WeatherStation.htm* and is located on the computer's C: drive within Office in a folder called WeatherData. After locating the file, click *Open.* Return to the Open dialogue box and click *OK.*
3. The presentation opens in the browser (see Figure 4.53). The left portion of the browser window contains the title of each slide. Clicking on a title

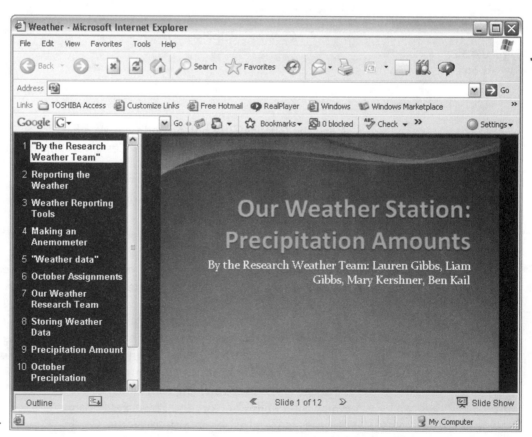

Figure 4.53
Slide show in browser

displays the corresponding slide in the right portion of the browser window. Clicking the Slide Show button at the bottom right of the window displays the presentation in full screen. Keep in mind that the presentation is not on the Web even though you can view it in a Web browser. At this point, you need to transfer the HTML-formatted files to a server to make them available worldwide.

Spell Checking the PowerPoint Presentation

Check the presentation for spelling errors by selecting *Spelling* in the Proofing group on the Review tab. When PowerPoint does not recognize a word, it displays it in the Spelling box (see Figure 4.54). In most cases, PowerPoint offers suggestions for correcting misspelled words. By clicking *Ignore,* the spell check disregards the suggestion. By clicking *Ignore All,* it disregards all future instances of the word in the spell-check session. You can make the suggested change by clicking *Change. Change All* changes all future instances of the word in the spell-check session.

Figure 4.54
Spell checking

If the word in the *Not in Dictionary* box is spelled correctly and PowerPoint does not recognize it, you can add it to PowerPoint's dictionary by clicking *Add.* Clicking *Suggest* causes PowerPoint to search the currently selected dictionary for possible suggestions of the correct word. Clicking *AutoCorrect* adds the spelling mistake to a list of errors and automatically corrects it on subsequent occurrences. The Ignore button changes to *Resume* when you exit the spell-check session. Clicking *Resume* resumes the session. Clicking *Close* closes the Spelling dialog box.

Printing the PowerPoint Presentation

PowerPoint provides several options for printing, such as slides, handouts, notes, or an outline. For this example, print handouts of the presentation. This is particularly useful if you want students or audience members to take notes while they listen to the presentation.

1. To print, click the Office button and select *Print,* and the *Print* dialog box appears (see Figure 4.55).
   - **Printer Name box:** Selects the printer that will print the handouts.
   - **Print range:** Specifies a range of slides to print. For your presentation, select *All.*

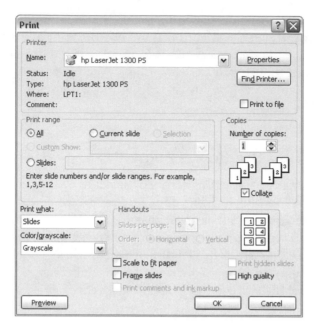

Figure 4.55
Print box

- **Copies:** Specifies the number of copies you want to print. If there will be 20 students in class, print 20 copies. Click the upward arrow under *Number of copies* until the number 20 appears. With each mouse click, depending on whether the upward or downward arrow is clicked, the number increases or decreases by increments of 1.
- **Print what:** Specifies whether to print slides, handouts, notes, or the outline. For this presentation, select *Handouts* by clicking the downward arrow. Click *Handouts* from the drop-down list. When the *Handouts* option is selected, the Handouts area becomes active and you can specify how many slides to print on each page of the handout. Select six slides per page.

2. Check the *Color* and *Frame Slides* options and click *OK*.

Packaging a Presentation on CD

Make an autorun CD of your presentation and share it with colleagues and students. Those who view it do not need to install a viewer or PowerPoint. PowerPoint 2007's viewer runs on Microsoft Windows 98 or later.

1. Open the presentation that you want to copy to a CD.
2. Click the Office button and select *Package for CD* from the File menu. The *Package for CD* box will be displayed (see Figure 4.56).
3. Type a name for the CD in the *Name the CD* box (e.g., *Weather Research*).
4. The Add Files button allows you to add additional files to the CD. To the left of the Add Files button is the name of the file that will be copied. In Figure 4.56, the file name is *Our Weather Station.ppt*.
5. Click the Copy to CD button, and recording begins. When recording is complete, several files will appear on the CD, and the CD title will correspond to the title you typed in the *Name the CD* box. The *ppviewer.exe* runs the presentation. When you insert the CD into a computer, the presentation opens automatically in the Slide Show mode. To open the presentation manually, double-click *pptviewer.exe*. You will be prompted to select a PowerPoint (.pptx) file. Select a file and click *Open*. The presentation opens in the Slide Show.

LET ME TRY

This Let Me Try activity builds on the other exercises in the chapter. In addition, it provides you with the steps needed to include photographs, video, and animation in your slide show. This Let Me Try is based on a genealogy assignment. It is abbreviated, and you will develop only the first two slides of the genealogy assignment, which has a total of seven slides. *You can work through an enhanced version of the Let Me Try by accessing My family Tree.docx in the Family Tree folder in Let Me Try on the accompanying CD.* You can view a complete version of the slide show by opening *Family Tree.pptx* or *Family Tree.ppsx* in the Family Tree folder. A copy of the Family Tree folder is also in PowerPoint inside the Examples folder on the CD.

Let's suppose that you give your students a genealogy exercise. Students must trace their family heritage back at least two generations and create a visual presentation about their family. This activity creates the presentation, and in doing so, it integrates audio, video, and photographs into the slide show.

Slide 1: The Opening Slide

When complete, slide 1 will look like Figure 4.56.

Figure 4.56
Complete slide

1. Open a new PowerPoint presentation.
2. Select *Blank slide* for the slide layout. The first slide of this presentation has a slightly different appearance than all other slides.
3. You'll begin by placing a photograph in the background. Click the Design tab and then click *Background Styles* in the Background group. Select *Format Background* (see Figure 4.57) on the *Background Styles* box. Click *Fill* on the left side of the *Format Background* box and then click the *Picture or texture fill* option (see Figure 4.58).
4. Click the *File . . .* button and browse to the *background.png* file located in the FamilyTree_images folder. This folder can be found in the Examples folder under PowerPoint and FamilyTree. Click the Insert button on the Insert Picture box, and you return to the *Format Background* box, where you should set all the off-sets to 0 (see Figure 4.58) Click *Close* on the *Background* box (do not click *Apply to All*). A photograph should appear on the slide.

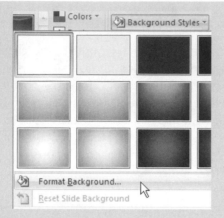

Figure 4.57
Format background

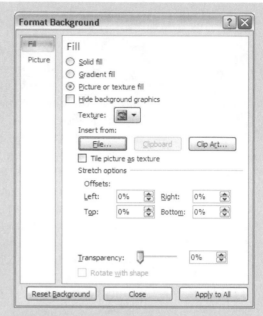

Figure 4.58
Format Background box

5. Insert an image title. Click the Insert tab and then click the Picture button. Locate *title.png* in the FamilyTree_Images folder and insert it. Position the image at the top left of the screen.

6. You have not named this slide yet. Click the Outline tab in the Outline pane. You will use the slide title to place your name. Type *By Calia Walters*. Set the font type to Verdana and the size to 32 and make the text bold.

7. Click on the text box to select it. Click the Home tab and then expand the Font Color list in the Font group and select *More Colors* (see Figure 4.59). Click the Custom tab and set the colors to the following values: Red—111, Green—105, and Blue—61 (see Figure 4.60). Click *OK*.

Figure 4.59
Set color

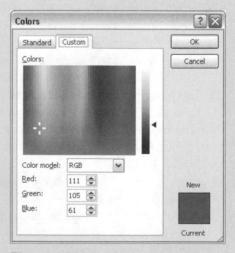

Figure 4.60
Color box

8. Place a glow effect on the text. With the text box still selected, click the Format tab (under the Drawing Tools tab). In the Work Styles group, click *Text Effects* and *Glow* and then choose one of the Glow Variations (see Figure 4.61).

9. Now you will add two objects. Click the Home tab and then click the Shapes button in the Drawing group. Select the rectangle tool (see Figure 4.62). With the rectangle tool selected, create a rectangle about 1.5 inches by 1.5 inches.

10. Right-click the rectangle and select *Format Shape* from the drop-down menu, and the *Format Shape* box appears. Click *Fill* on the left side of the box and then select *Picture or texture fill*.

11. Click the File . . . button . . . Locate the *background.png* image again and insert it. Check *Rotate with shape*.

12. Set the Transparency to 60% (see Figure 4.63)

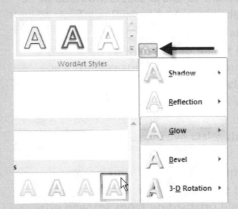

Figure 4.61
WordArt styles

Figure 4.62
Shapes

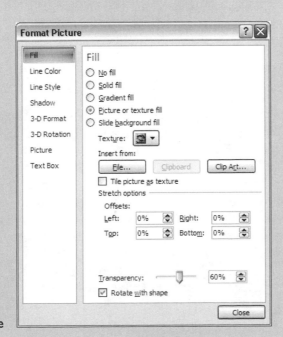

Figure 4.63
Format picture

13. Click *Line Color* on the left side of the *Format* box. Next, click *Solid Line* and then click the Color button. The color pallet appears. Choose *Tan, Background 2, Darker 10%* (see Figure 4.64).

Figure 4.64
Line color

14. Click *Line Style* on the left side of the *Format* box and set the line width to 1. Click *Close*
15. The rectangle should be selected, and a green dot should appear at the top. Move the cursor over the green dot and rotate the rectangle to the left.
16. Repeat this procedure two more times. First, create a rectangle and insert the *letter.jpg* file. Set its transparency to 60%. Next, create another rectangle and insert the *girl.png* file. Set its transparency to 84%. After you have inserted the *girl.png* file, rotate it slightly to the left.
17. Finally, click the Home tab and then click the Shapes button. Select *Curved Right Arrow* from *Block Arrows* in *Autoshapes* on the drawing toolbar (see Figure 4.65).

Figure 4.65
Block arrows

Drag the arrow on the screen. With the arrow selected, click the Format tab under the Drawing Tools tab. In the Arrange group, click *Rotate* and select *Rotate Left 90*. In the Size group, set the Shape Height to 8.5 and the Shape Width to 5.5. Click the curved right arrow to select it. Activate the Format tab (under Drawing Tools) and click *Align* in the Arrange group. Ensure that a check appears next to *Align to Slide* and then choose center alignment and then bottom alignment.

18. Refer to Figure 4.65 to see how to position the arrow. In Figure 4.65, the curve arrow extends across the slide.
19. Right-click on the curved right arrow and then select the *Format Shape* option.
20. Click *Fill* and select *Solid fill*. Click the Color button and choose *More Colors*. In the *Colors* box, click the Custom tab. Select *RGB* for color mode and enter the following values: Red—111, Green—105, and Blue—61. Click *OK*.

21. Set the Transparency to 76%.
22. Click *Line Color* on the left side of the *Format Shape* box and then select *No Line*.

Slide 2: Images and Video

23. Create a new slide. Select a blank slide for the Slide layout.
24. Click the Design tab and in the Themes group locate the Paper theme. When you locate it, right-click on it and select *Apply to Selected Slides*.
25. In the Themes group, click *Colors* and then select *Create New Theme Colors* (see Figure 4.66).

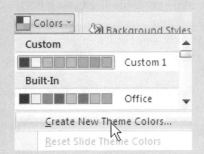

Figure 4.66
Themes

26. Under Theme Colors, click the button to the right of Text/Background—Dark 2 and select *More Colors* . . . Click the Custom tab on the *Colors* box. Select *RGB* for color mode and enter the following values: Red—111, Green—105, and Blue—61. Click *OK* and then click OK.
27. Insert an image title. Click the Insert tab and select *Picture (From File)*. Locate *title.png* in the FamilyTree_Images folder and insert it. Position the image at the top left of the screen. Alternatively, you can go to slide 1 and copy it and then paste it on slide 2.
28. Because this slide show is about a student's family tree, you'll insert a drawing of a tree. Click *Picture (From File)* on the Insert tab. Locate *tree.png* in the FamilyTree_Images folder and insert it. The image extends beyond the dimensions of the screen. Position the cursor over the bottom right or left sizing handle and while pressing the Ctrl key down, drag the sizing handle up, and it resizes proportionally. Position the drawing in the middle of the screen.
29. With the drawing selected, click the Format tab under Picture Tools and choose *Send to Back* in the Arrange group.
30. Next you will insert seven images to place on the family tree. Select *Picture (From File)* on the Insert tab. Locate the following image files in the FamilyTree_ Images folder and insert them. Place the images around the tree.
    - *grandParentD.png*
    - *grndParentM.png*
    - *ggparentD1.png*
    - *ggparentD2.png*
    - *ggparentM2.png*
    - *Mom.png*
    - *Parents.png*
31. Resize each image by selecting it and pressing the Ctrl key while dragging the sizing handle.

Video

32. Next you'll insert a video. Click *Movie (From File)* in the Media Clips group on the Insert tab. Locate the *Family.avi* file in the FamilyTree_Images folder. When inserting the movie, a prompt appears. Click *Automatically*. Position the video on the right side of the tree. To see where to position the video, open *FamilyTree.pptx* or *FamilyTree.ppsx* on the CD.

33. You have not named this slide yet. Click the Outline tab in the Outline pane. You will use the slide title to place your name. Type *My Family*. Set the font type to Verdana, the size to 48, and make the text bold. Click on the text box to select it. Select *More Colors* from the Font Color button on the drawing toolbar. Click the Custom tab and set the colors to following values: Red—111, Green—105, and Blue—61. Click *OK*.

34. Rotate the text. With the text box selected, a green dot appears at the top of the text box. Position the cursor over the box and then drag, and the text will rotate.

35. The first two slides of the My Family Tree activity are complete.

LET ME TRY AGAIN

In this final Let Me Try, we will use many of the concepts presented in the chapter to create a game of Jeopardy for multiplication tables. In chapter 9, "Integrating Office 2007," you will expand on this activity by placing your questions into an Excel worksheet and then link the worksheet to PowerPoint. Thus, when you want to change questions, you change them in Excel. Only the questions change in PowerPoint, and all the formatting remains the same, which can be a big time-saver.

One of the ways the game created here can be used is during class with the PowerPoint slides projected onto a screen. Ask students or student teams to select a topic and point value. The student might say, for example, *I select the 3 Times Table for 5 points*. After the student or team makes the selection, you click the point presented on the slide, which then displays the question. The student is given a time to respond, after which you click the slide and the correct answer displays.

1. Open a new PowerPoint presentation.
2. Select a Title Only layout.
3. Click the Design tab and in the Themes group choose the Foundry theme.
4. Type *Jeopardy* in the *Click to add title* box.
5. Click the title text box border so that the border appears as a solid line. With the text box selected, set the font size (Font group on Home tab) to 72.
6. Under the Drawing Tools tab, click the Format tab. In the Word Styles group, apply the *Gradient fill—Accent 4, Reflection* style.
7. Create a table for the categories and points. Make the Insert tab active and click the Tables button, and the Insert Table palette appears. Drag your mouse over the small rectangles to create a 4-by-6 table, 4 columns by 6 rows (see Figure 4.67).
8. After you selected the rectangles, click on the last rectangle to place the table on the slide.

Figure 4.67
Table

9. Click on the table and then, under the Table Tools tab, click *Design*. In the Table Styles group, apply the *Medium style 2, Accent 1* style to the table.
10. With the table selected, click the Home tab and in the Drawing group click the Arrange button and select *Align*. Ensure that the *Align to Slide* item is checked and then choose *Align Center* and *Align Middle*.
11. In the first row, type *3 Times Table* in cell 1, *4 Times Table* in cell 2, *5 Times Table* in cell 3, and *6 Times Table* in cell 4.
12. With the table selected, click the Home tab and then click the Center Align text button in the Paragraph group. Row 1 of the table should look like that shown in Figure 4.68.

3 Times Table	4 Times Table	5 Times Table	6 Times Table

Figure 4.68
Table row

13. In this example, you will create only the items for the 3 Times Table. Beginning in row 2, type the amount of points allotted for each question. Replicate the format shown in Figure 4.69.

3 Times Table	4 Times Table	5 Times Table	6 Times Table
1 Point	1 Point	1 Point	1 Point
2 Points	2 Points	2 Points	2 Points
3 Points	3 Points	3 Points	3 Points
4 Points	4 Points	4 Points	4 Points
5 Points	5 Points	5 Points	5 Points

Figure 4.69
Table

14. Add a new slide with a Title only layout. Copy the *Jeopardy* text from slide 1 to slide 2. Alternatively, you may copy slide 1 and paste it as slide 2.

15. On slide 1 under the 3 Times Table, there are five alternatives for points 1 through 5 (see Figure 4.69). When playing the game, you may ask the class to pick a point value. When you click a point value, PowerPoint links to the associated question slide. After the question, the answer appears. This approach to the game requires at least two screens for each point value.

16. On slide 2, type the question *3 Times 4* and place it in the center of the screen. Click the Insert tab and then click the Text Box button in the Text group. Click in the slide area and, while holding the mouse down, drag to extend the text box. Type *3 Times 4* in the text box.

17. With the text box selected, click the Home tab and set the font to Arial Black and the size to 72. Choose a font color. Click the Format tab under Drawing Tools (the text box must be selected) and in the Arrange group set the alignment of the text box to the middle of the slide (see Figure 4.70).

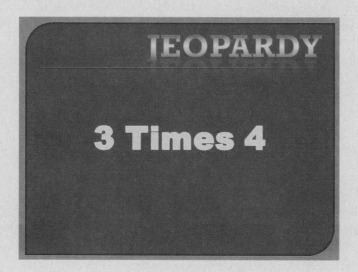

Figure 4.70
Background

18. Copy slide 2 and paste it so there is a total of three slides. On slide 3, replace the *3 Times 4* text with *What is 12?* Triple-click inside the text box to select the text and then type *What is 12?*

19. Go back to slide 2, which should read *3 Times 4*. Click the Home tab and click *Shapes* in the Drawing group. When the Shapes palette displays, choose *Right Arrow* under the Block Arrows category. When you select the right arrow, the cursor changes to a crosshair. Click in the lower right portion of the screen and drag so that an arrow is drawn about one-half inch by one-half inch.

20. After drawing the arrow, type *Answer*. You may have to readjust the size of the arrow so the text fits.

21. With the arrow selected (ensure that the selection border is a solid line around the arrow), click the Insert tab and then select *Action* in the Links group.

22. In the *Action Settings* box, click the Mouse Click tab and select *Hyperlink* and choose *Slide. . . .* The *Hyperlink to Slide* box displays. Select the third item, which should correspond to the third slide, the answer (see Figure 4.71). Click *OK*.

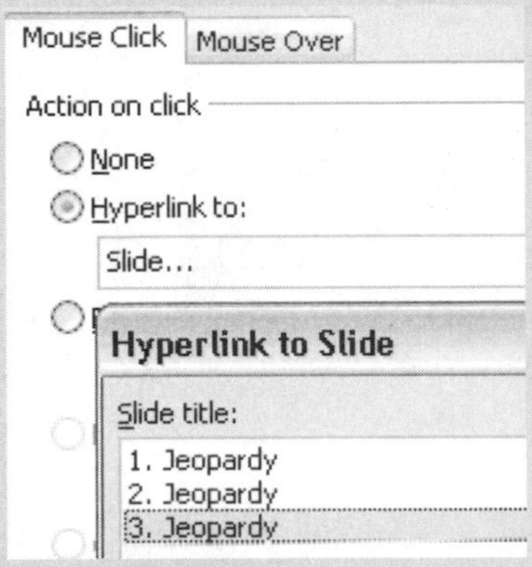

Figure 4.71
Hyperlink

23. Click the *Mouse Over* tab. The item under *Action on mouse over* should be *None*. Check the item *Highlight when mouse over*.

24. Click *OK* to close the *Action Settings* box. This action links the answer arrow to slide 3. In this example, you will copy and paste several slides. Each time you make a copy of the slide with the answer arrow, you need to change the slide to which It links. To do so, select the arrow, make the Insert tab active, and click *Action* in the Links group. On the Mouse Click tab, under Hyperlink to: select *Slide* and then browse to the appropriate slide.

25. Click the View tab. In the Presentation Views group, click *Slide Master*, and the slide master displays.

26. Click the Insert tab while still in the slide master. Click *Shapes* in the Illustrations group and select *Up Arrow* in the Block Arrows category. The cursor changes to a crosshair. Click and drag to draw an arrow about one-half inch by one-half inch. Release the mouse and type *Back*.

27. With the arrow selected (ensure that a solid-line border appears when selecting), click *Action* on the Insert tab. Click the Mouse Click tab and select *Slide . . .* from the *Hyperlink to*: list. When the Hyperlink to Slide box appears, choose the first item (slide 1) and click *OK*.

28. Check *Highlight click*.

29. On the Mouse Over tab, check *Highlight when mouse over*. Click *OK*.

30. Click the View tab and in the Presentation Views group click *Normal*. When you preview your slides, the back arrow should be present. When clicked, you go back to the first slide.

31. Go to the Slide Sorter view. Select slides 2 and, 3. Click on slide 2 and, while holding the Ctrl key down, click on slide 3. Press Ctrl+C to copy. Click on slide 3 and press Ctrl+V to paste the slides. You should now have a total of five slides.

32. Double-click slide 4 to exit the Slide Sorter view. Replace the *3 Times 4* text with *3 Times 8*. Remember to change the slide to which the answer arrow links. Right-click on the arrow and select *Edit Hyperlink*. On the Mouse Click tab under *Hyperlink to*, set the link to go to slide 5.

33. Go to slide 5 and replace the *What is 12?* with *What is 24?*

34. Go to slide 1. Select the text 1 point. With the text selected, right-click and select *Hyperlink*. The *Insert Hyperlink* box appears (see Figure 4.72). Click the *Place in This Document* option on the left and under Slide Titles click *Slide 2*. Click OK.

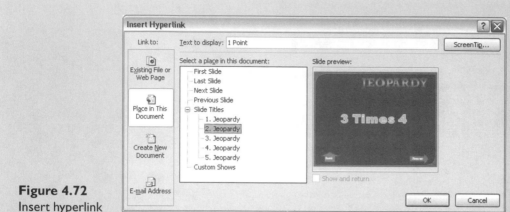

Figure 4.72
Insert hyperlink

35. Repeat this step for the *2 Points* item. The *2 Points* link should go to slide 4.
36. So far you have five slides. You can add many more slides repeating the previous steps. If you would like to view the example we just made, see the *Jeopardy_Game.pptx* file in the PowerPoint folder inside Examples.

A CHALLENGE USING POWERPOINT 2007

For those who would like a challenge beyond the Let Me Try activities presented in this chapter, try the following exercises:

1. Have students create a genealogy presentation that includes various font types and styles, design templates, and clip art that complement the older-style photographs that students scan and include in the presentation. The presentations should depict at least one generation beginning with the most recent generation.
2. Have students present a book report on *Charlotte's Web*. The presentation should include photographs or clip art of all the animals depicted in the book.
3. For a science project, have students make an anemometer. While making this device, students should document the process with a camera and notes. Compile the notes and photographs in a PowerPoint presentation and present it to the class. The presentation may also include video of the anemometer rotating.
4. Create a class or school presentation portfolio. Have students collect photographs, write stories and poems, and create drawings representative of their positive feelings and attitudes about the class or school. Incorporate the photographs, stories, drawings, and so forth into a self-running presentation displayed in public areas (e.g., school lounge). The presentation may also include audio and video segments of school activities, students, and teachers.
5. Create an art exhibit presentation. Scan students' drawings and artwork into a PowerPoint presentation. Save the presentation as a Web page and distribute it on the Web for parents, teachers, and classmates to view.
6. Assign a design theme and give a background color to only one slide in the presentation.

7. Assign a design theme to a presentation and assign a different template to one slide.
8. Create a five-slide presentation that includes linked action buttons.
9. Create a slide that imports a chart created in Excel.

TYING IT ALL TOGETHER

This chapter presents many fundamentals to help you get started with PowerPoint. We created a presentation consisting of 12 slides with varying layouts. The slides contained text, clip art, and a chart. We saved the presentation in presentation (.pptx) and Web (.htm; .mht) formats and printed handouts. In addition, we copied the presentation to a CD.

CHAPTER OUTLINE

LEARNING OBJECTIVES

At the completion of this chapter you will be able to:

- Start Excel and create a new workbook suitable for use in a variety of student learning activities
- Navigate the Excel workspace
- Add, modify, and manipulate data in a worksheet
- Chart worksheet data
- Add worksheets to a workbook

- Add formulas and functions in a worksheet
- Save a workbook
- Save workbooks as Web documents
- Print a workbook

CHAPTER OVERVIEW

This chapter provides an introduction to Excel 2007. It focuses on Excel fundamentals and how to apply them to a variety of learning activities. The chapter's Show Me sections present instructions on how to use many of Excel's tools to create workbooks and edit and manipulate data in worksheets. The chapter presents two Show Me activities. The first uses the example of a school weather station that tracks weather conditions. As you work though the data collection and analysis examples, you will become familiar with many essential features and functions. The second Show Me is more focused. Using data about the American presidency, it explores PivotTables and PivotCharts, which are powerful data analysis tools that can help you and your students examine data in in-depth and in diverse ways. Several Let Me Try student-oriented exercises give specific examples and step-by-step instructions for using Excel to accomplish a variety of learn-ing tasks. Studying the chapter contents and working through the Let Me Try exercises will enable you to create workbooks suitable for many classroom learning activities.

How Teachers and Students Can Use Excel

Microsoft Excel can be used in innovative ways to support various educational activities that benefit students and teachers. In this section, we examine ways in which Excel can be used to support educational activities in relation to types of learning outcomes and the National Educational Technology Standards for Students. Looking first at types of learning, the ways in which Excel can be used by students include the following:

- *Knowledge*—(a) Students can create their own Excel worksheets of historical facts, vocabulary words, multiplication tables, or science facts. As they read and study, they can enter these facts into the worksheet. (b) Data in the worksheets could then be linked across applications to create electronic flash cards games within PowerPoint, or they could be used to create print flash cards in Word. (c) Students can create worksheets that list all the states in the United States, the date when the state became part of the union, and the population of those states.
- *Comprehension*—(a) Students can create book or laboratory reports that include data tables from Excel that help them interpret results and explain a topic or experiment. (b) Using a worksheet based on state information, stu-dents could summarize state data and contrast one state with another.
- *Application*—(a) Students can collect precipitation data about specific regions and, examining these data, classify regions as low-, moderate-, or heavy-precipitation areas. They could then assess if there are relationships between the data and regional characteristics, such as population, employment, and recreational activities.
- *Analysis*—(a) Students could use Excel to project costs for a summer vacation traveling from their home town to Yellowstone National Park. (b) Based on the travel data collected, students could make inferences about the fastest route, the least expensive route, and arrival time.
- *Synthesis*—(a) Students could integrate participation data, temperature data, and population density for specific regions of the United States to formulate projections about the most livable areas in the country.

■ *Evaluation*—(a) Students could make recommendations about the best cars or bicycles to purchase based on data (cost, safety features, and so on) entered into a worksheet.

NETS for Students*

Applications of Excel to educational activities could address the following:

■ *Creativity and innovation*—Students demonstrate creative and innovative thinking, construct knowledge, and develop innovative materials and processes using technology.
■ *Communication and collaboration*—Students use mediated materials to communicate and work collaboratively and to support the learning of others.
■ *Research and information fluency*—Students apply digital tools to gather, evaluate, and use information.
■ *Critical thinking, problem solving, and decision-making*—Students use critical thinking skills to plan and conduct research, manage projects, solve problems, and make informed decisions using appropriate digital tools and resources.

What Is New in Excel

Like the other Office products, one of the main features new to Excel is the interface, characterized by the Ribbon. As you become accustomed to the new interface, you may find that, in many cases, the steps to accomplish certain tasks are reduced, allowing you to work more efficiently. The Ribbon replaces many of the menus and toolbars of Office 2003, and the associated commands or functions have been grouped under tabs intended to help you get your work done more quickly. The organization of tabs is based on the type of activity you might perform when working with data and worksheets.

About Excel

Excel is a tool that you and your students can use to record, organize, and analyze information. With Excel, you can perform mathematical calculations, sort data, and produce charts and graphs to visually represent information, among other things.

As you become familiar with Excel, you will come to realize the use of this application for many student learning and classroom management activities. Teachers can create Excel workbooks that contain information about student learning progress, or they can create electronic grade books for entering and calculating student performance scores. In addition, they can create worksheets to record and maintain information about classroom equipment and supply costs.

Students can use Excel as an electronic data recorder to help them collect, record, and analyze information and data sets. They can manage projects with it. When given an assignment that requires a team effort, students can log project details and progress to ensure that the team is on task and on schedule. Suppose your students set up a school weather station to record local weather data throughout the school year. They can use Excel worksheets to make daily entries of temperatures, wind speeds, precipitation, and barometric pressures for specific time periods. At the end of each month, students graph their data to visually depict the weather patterns that occurred during the month and present their findings to the class. Their worksheets include statistical charts and graphs and photographs or videos of weather conditions to help enrich the presentations.

Using Excel, students can save their weather data in a Web format and place it on the Web to share with other students locally and around the world. These are only a few applications of Excel. As you become familiar with it, you are likely to find innovative ways to incorporate it into your classroom management and student learning activities.

Working with Excel

The primary purpose of this chapter is to introduce fundamental components and features of Excel so that you may use them in productive ways. To accomplish this objective, we present several examples throughout the chapter. Although the examples are specific, the steps and procedures they present for developing workbooks and worksheets are generic and applicable to a variety of classroom management tasks and learning activities. As you work through the chapter's content, substitute our examples with your own. *In addition, you can locate files that correspond to the chapter activities on the CD in the Excel folder under* Examples. *Additional Let Me Try activities can be found on the CD in the Let Me Try Exercises folder.*

A Word About the Excel Workspace

Before we create a workbook and corresponding worksheets, it is important to examine the Excel workspace, including the screen layout, functions, and tools. When you open Excel, it presents a new blank document, referred to as a *workbook*. Figure 5.1 depicts a new workbook. The Ribbon, located in the top portion of the workbook, contains functions and tools to assist you with entering, modifying, and analyzing data. For additional workspace, you can minimize the Ribbon by clicking the *Customize Quick Access Toolbar* option, the selection arrow to the right of the Quick Access Toolbar. With a few exceptions, the tabs on the Ribbon are the same as those in other Office applications. You may notice, for example, that except for the Formulas and Data tabs, Excel's Ribbon is almost identical to that of Word. The Formulas tab contains four main groups labeled Function Library, Defined Names, Formula Auditing, and Calculation. With the tools in these groups, you can write formulas and include Excel functions in worksheets that can assist you with performing calculations and data analysis. The Data tab has five major groups: Get External Data, Connections, Sort & Filter, Data Tools, and Outline. These groups offer functions for acquiring, organizing, and examining data. For example, you may have data in a text file that you want import into a worksheet. The Get External Data group provides an option to import the file.

As shown in Figure 5.1, the Home tab contains seven groups, two of which (Number and Cells) are most unique to Excel. The Number group provides options for number formatting: Currency Style, Percent Style, Comma Style, Increase Decimal, and Decrease Decimal. Number format allows you to set how Excel displays the cell values in a worksheet. The Currency Style option sets the cell format to a dollar value. Percent Style sets the cell value to a percentage. The Comma Style option sets the cell value to a number with a decimal point. Finally, Increase and Decrease Decimal specify the number of decimal points in a cell value.

The Cells group contains options to insert and delete rows and columns and to set the cell formatting options. The Alignment group is similar to Word's Paragraph group.

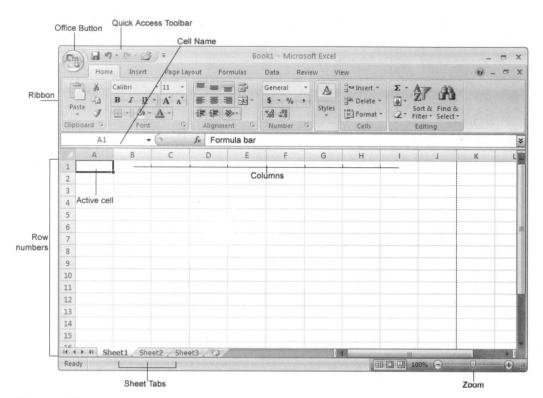

Figure 5.1
The Excel workspace

However, it contains the Wrap Text and Merge and Center options. Wrap Text, when clicked, wraps the text in the cell. The Merge and Center option combines multiple cells into a single cell and aligns the cell's contents to Center.

Below the Ribbon is the worksheet area where you will perform most of your data entry, modification, and analysis. This is also referred to as the Normal view. There are several alternative ways you can view a worksheet, such as Page Layout (worksheets are laid out side to side) and Page Break (allows you to see page breaks in a document). These options are found under the View tab.

A new workbook is made up of three blank worksheets or sheets. When the workbook opens, Sheet 1 appears foremost on the screen with Sheets 2 and 3 layered behind it. The Sheet tabs can be used to navigate sheets. Each worksheet contains column and row headings, cells, gridlines, worksheet tabs, and scroll bars. Excel labels columns with letters (e.g., A, B, and C) and rows with numbers. Columns extend vertically down the worksheet, and rows extend horizontally. Excel designates cell names by the intersection of the column and row. For example, cell A1 is located in the first row (row 1) in column A. When you click inside a cell, its name or cell reference appears in the cell name box. Grid lines separate cells, columns, and rows.

Worksheet tabs and scroll bars are located at the bottom right of the worksheet. The tabs provide easy movement between worksheets. Clicking on a tab moves the selected worksheet to the foreground.

As data sets become large, columns and rows extend beyond the viewing areas of the computer monitor. To see them, scroll using the scroll bars and arrows located to the right of the worksheet. Click or hold the mouse button down on the scroll arrows, and the screen moves in the corresponding direction. You may also drag the scroll bar in the desired direction while holding the mouse button down. The zoom control can be used to zoom in and out of worksheets so that data can be viewed more easily.

Moving About in a Worksheet

There are several ways to move across cells, columns, and rows. When you open a new workbook, cell A1 is active and ready for input. Begin to type, and the information appears in the cell as well as in the formula bar. After typing the information, pressing Enter moves the active cell down one row. Pressing the keyboard arrow keys moves the active cell in the direction corresponding to the arrow key. For instance, if the active cell is A1 and you press the down arrow key, the active cell moves down from A1 to A2.

Pressing the arrow keys does not move the active cell when you are editing a cell's contents. If cell B2 contains a misspelled word, double-click in the cell, and the cursor will appear in the cell as a flashing line (insertion point). The arrow keys allow you to move the cursor within the cell so that you may edit the word. To move the active cell when in the Edit mode, you must press Enter or the Tab key.

Pressing the Tab key moves the active cell one column to the right. Pressing the Tab key while holding the Shift key moves the active cell one column to the left. Clicking the cursor in any cell on the worksheet makes that cell active. Clicking and typing in a cell that contains information replaces the cell's contents. Double-clicking in a cell that contains information enables you to edit the cell's contents.

Show Me

Creating a Workbook and Worksheets

1. To create a workbook and corresponding worksheets, you need to open Excel. Click the Start button on the Windows taskbar. On the Start menu, click *All Programs*, and the Programs list appears. Click *Microsoft Office* to expand the Microsoft Office list. Click *Microsoft Office Excel 2007*, and Excel opens. *Note:* Depending on how you installed Excel, it may be in a different location on the Start menu. In most cases, it can be found under All Programs or within the Microsoft Office folder.
2. An Excel workbook opens, containing three blank worksheets (see Figure 5.2). Cell A1 is the active cell. If you begin to type, the information appears in cell A1.

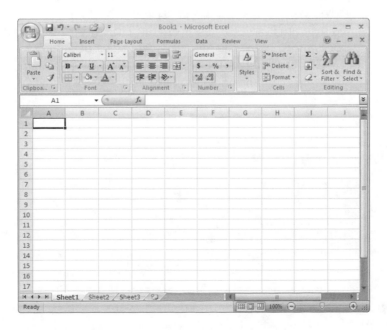

Figure 5.2
Blank worksheet

Entering Data in a Worksheet

Suppose you and your students form a school weather station. Using Excel, you record the daily low and high temperatures and precipitation. You are interested in collecting these data to observe weather patterns. Each month you ask students to analyze the data and present their findings (monthly high and low temperatures and precipitation) to the class. *To view an example of the final workbook, open the weather.xlsx file on the CD inside the Excel folder under Examples.*

1. For this example, you will create a simple monthly weather reporting sheet. Check that cell A1 is the active cell, indicated by a black frame around its border. Enter *Weather Data for Charleston IL: October 2008* into A1 and then press Enter. As you type, the text appears in the formula bar. *Weather Data for Charleston IL: October 2008* appears in cell A1, and cell A2 becomes the active cell after you press Enter. Note that although *Weather Data for Charleston IL: October 2008* may appear to extend beyond cell A1 to cells B1, C1, and D1, it is contained only in cell A1 (see Figure 5.3).

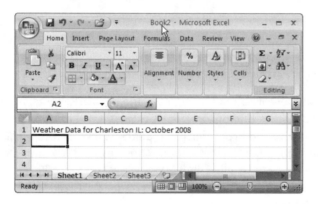

Figure 5.3
Data title

2. Create titles to describe the weather data collected by students. With cell A2 active, type *Day* and then press the Tab key (cell B2 becomes active). Type *Temperature* in cell B2 and press the Tab key two times, leaving cell C2 empty. Continue to enter the following data titles beginning in cell D2 and ending in cell G2: *Rain Fall (inches), Avg. Low, Avg. High,* and *Total Precipitation.* When complete, your screen should look like Figure 5.4.

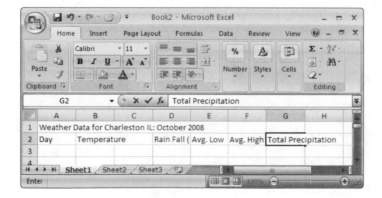

Figure 5.4
Weather data titles

Merge and Center

Before continuing, format the data titles. Formatting helps with entering the data correctly. Adjust the columns and cells so that all the data titles are readable. The main title for this data set is *Weather Data for Charleston IL: October 2008,* which should extend across columns A through G. To extend this title, use the Merge command.

1. Select cells A1 through G1. Click in cell A1 and, while holding the mouse button down, drag across to cell G1 (see Figure 5.5).

Figure 5.5
Multiple cell selection

2. Click the Merge and Center button (see Figure 5.6). The seven cells merge into one, and the text becomes centered.

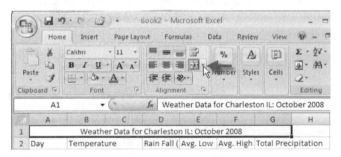

Figure 5.6
Merge and Center sheet title

You can merge cells B2 and C2 so that the *Temperature* title appears as a header for the daily low and high temperatures (see Figure 5.7). Select cells B2 and C2. Click in cell B2 and, while holding the mouse button down, drag across to cell C2. Click the Merge and Center button. The two cells merge into one, and the text becomes centered.

Figure 5.7
Merge and Center subtitle

3. Create titles to indicate the low and high temperatures for each day of the month. Make cell B3 active by clicking in it. Type *Low,* then press the Tab key. In cell C3, type *High.* This completes the titles, but before you can enter the data, you need to do more formatting.

Modifying Worksheets: Adjusting Columns and Rows

You probably noticed that the formatting of the worksheet contents appears incomplete. The cell contents cannot be seen, or they extend beyond the cell borders and into other cells. In this section, you will adjust the column widths and format the data titles. There are several ways to adjust the column width. For your purposes, Excel's *AutoFit Column Width* is a good option.

1. Adjust the width of a specific column by clicking on the column header or within a cell (see Figure 5.8). In Figure 5.8, *Rain Fall* (*inches*) does not fit in the cell D2 and needs adjusting. Click in cell D2.

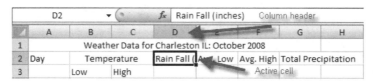

Figure 5.8
Adjust column width

2. On the Home tab and in the Cells group, click the selection arrow under Format and select *AutoFit Column Width* (see Figure 5.9). The column width adjusts to fit the cell content.

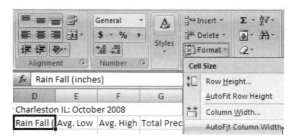

Figure 5.9
AutoFit column width

3. Alternatively, you could format all the column titles simultaneously by clicking cell A2 and, while holding the mouse button down, dragging across to the G2 header. The columns are highlighted, or selected, as you drag across them (see Figure 5.10). With the column titles selected, click the selection arrow under Format in the Cells group and select *AutoFit Column Width*. The columns adjust

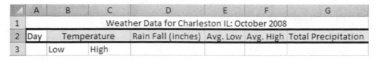

Figure 5.10
Column selection

to the data. If the columns are still selected, deselect them by clicking anywhere on the worksheet.

In the Format options there are several additional items useful for formatting cells: Column Width, Hide & Unhide, and *Default Width.* Each of the items is described briefly as follows:

Column Width: Displays a box in which you can enter a dimension for the column width.

Hide (columns, rows, or sheets): Hides a column, row, or selected set of columns or rows from view. This option may be useful when you want to view only specific segments of your data set.

Unhide (columns, rows, or sheets): Reveals columns or rows that have been hidden using the Hide option. To reveal a hidden column or row, select the columns to the left and right of the hidden column and choose *Unhide.* For example, if you hide column B from view, you need to select columns A and C, then choose *Unhide* to reveal column B. To reveal rows, select the rows above and below the hidden row and choose *Unhide.*

Default Width: Allows you to define a standard width for all columns in a worksheet. However, the standard width will not apply to columns that have been adjusted previously. To set a standard width, click the Format option in the Cells group and select the *Default Width* submenu item. The *Standard Width* box appears in which you can specify a width value and then click *OK.* All previously unadjusted columns are set to the designated width.

Adjusting Row Height

To make the data title more pronounced, increase the height of the second row to set it apart from the main title and weather data.

4. Click in any cell of row 2. On the Home tab, click the selection arrow under Format in the Cells group and select *Row Height.* The *Row Height* box appears (see Figure 5.11). Enter a row height of 24 and click *OK.* The row height increases across all columns (see Figure 5.12).

Figure 5.11
Set row height

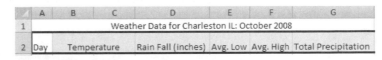

Figure 5.12
Increasing row height

Notice that the titles are aligned at the bottom of row 2. To align the text in the center of row 2, click the row number to select row 2. Click the selection arrow under Format in the Cells group and select *Format Cells,* and the *Format Cells* box appears (see Figure 5.13). You can also right-click in row 2 and select Format Cells from the shortcut menu. Click the Alignment tab. Under Vertical, select *Center,* then click *OK.* The text appears in the center of row 2 (see Figure 5.14). You can now continue to enter data. For this example, enter the day of the month, temperatures (low and high), and rainfall in inches for each day, even though your students will likely record this information daily. The average temperature and total precipitation will be handled later.

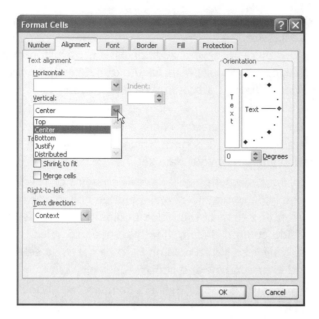

Figure 5.13
Format Cells box

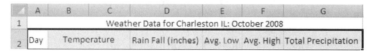

Figure 5.14
Center aligned

5. Column A will contain dates corresponding to each day of the month. Format the column for this data type. Select column A by clicking on the column header. Click the selection arrow under Format in the Cells group and select *Format Cells*, and the *Format Cells* box appears (see Figure 5.15). Click the Number tab, select *Date* from the Category area, choose a date type or the way you want the date to appear, and then click *OK*.

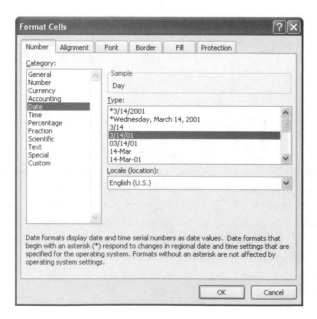

Figure 5.15
Format Cells box

6. Click in cell A4 and type the first date, *10/01/08*. You may notice an #### error after typing the date, which indicates that the column width is too narrow. If this occurs, select column A by clicking on the column header, then click the selection arrow under Format in the Cells group and select *AutoFit Column Width*. Your screen should look like Figure 5.16.

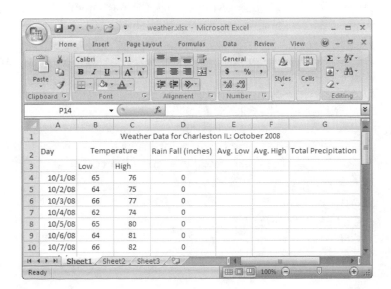

	A	B	C	D	E	F	G
			fx	10/1/2008			
1				Weather Data for Charleston IL: October 2008			
2	Day	Temperature		Rain Fall (inches)	Avg. Low	Avg. High	Total Precipitation
3		Low	High				
4	10/1/08						

Figure 5.16
Enter data

7. Press the Tab key to accept the data, then cell B4 becomes active. Type the low temperature for the day and press the Tab key to make cell C4 active. Type the high temperature for the day. Press the Tab key again to make cell D4 active and type the amount of rainfall (in inches) for that day. Press Enter to move down to the next row. *Note:* Format cells containing temperatures and precipitation amount as *General*. Select the range of cells or columns to be formatted. From the Format options (Cells group on the Home tab), select *Format Cells*. On the *Format Cells* box, click the Number tab and under Category select *General*.

Enter a date, low and high temperatures, and rainfall amounts for each day of the month. Remember to press the Tab key to move to a cell in the adjacent column on the right. If you prefer, you can auto fill the date column by dragging the selection down. After entering the first date, click in the cell to make it active (see Figure 5.17). At the bottom right of the Active cell is a small square. Position the cursor over it and, while holding the mouse button down, drag down, and the dates will auto fill. Drag down to cell A34, and the data that appears in the cell should be *10/31/08*. When you are finished, the worksheet should look similar to Figure 5.18.

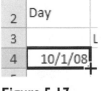

Figure 5.17
Auto Fill cells

Figure 5.18
Completed
worksheet

	A	B	C	D	E	F	G
1				Weather Data for Charleston IL: October 2008			
2	Day	Temperature		Rain Fall (inches)	Avg. Low	Avg. High	Total Precipitation
3		Low	High				
4	10/1/08	65	76	0			
5	10/2/08	64	75	0			
6	10/3/08	66	77	0			
7	10/4/08	62	74	0			
8	10/5/08	65	80	0			
9	10/6/08	64	81	0			
10	10/7/08	66	82	0			

LET ME TRY: ENTERING PRESIDENTIAL DATA

So far, you have opened Excel and created a new workbook that contains three worksheets. You entered data in one of the worksheets (Sheet 1) and navigated around it using the Enter, Tab, and arrow keys. Finally, you modified worksheet columns and rows. In this section, you will incorporate what you have learned by using a new workbook example pertaining to the presidents of the United States.

Ask students to research and collect information about all the presidents of the United States. Specifically, they should find out the following information about each president:

- Month and year of birth
- State of birth
- Year elected
- Year term ended as president
- Occupation other than president
- Year of death

Once students collect this information, they can enter it into an Excel workbook for analysis. From the information, students can, among other things, calculate the age of the president when elected, his age at death, the states in which the majority of elected presidents were born, and the most common occupation of presidents other than the presidency. To view an example of a final workbook, open *presidents.xlsx* on the CD.

Creating a Presidential Information Workbook

1. Open Excel 2007.
2. When you open Excel, cell A1 is the active cell. Type *Presidential Information* in cell A1.
3. After typing *Presidential Information,* click anywhere outside cell A1 to deselect it and to exit the cell's text-editing mode. Now, select cells A1 through H1 and then click the Merge and Center button to center the title.
4. If cell A1 is not active, click it. From the Format options (Home tab, Cells group), select *Row Height.* Type *24* in the *Row Height* box and click *OK.*
5. With cell A1 active, click *Format* (Home tab, Cells group) and select *Format Cells,* and the *Format Cells* box displays. Click the Alignment tab. Set the Horizontal and Vertical text alignment to *Center* and then click *OK.*
6. Click in cell A2 to make it active. Type the word *Name* for the column title. Press the Tab key to accept the data and move the active cell to B2 and type *Birth Month.*
7. Type the following six titles: *Birth, Death, Year Elected, Term Ended, Occupation,* and *State of Birth* in cells C2, D2, E2, F2, G2, and H2, respectively.
8. Click cell A3 to make it active and type *George Washington.* Press the Tab key to move to cell B3 and type *February* for his birth month. Enter the following information for George Washington in each of the corresponding cells:

   - Cell C3, *Birth:*   1732
   - Cell D3, *Death:*   1799
   - Cell E3, *Year Elected:* 1789
   - Cell F3, *Term Ended:*   1797

- Cell G3, *Occupation:*   *Planter, Soldier*
- Cell H3, *State of Birth:*   *Virginia* (Grolier, 1994)

9. After entering Washington's state of birth, Virginia, in cell H3, click in cell A4 to make it active. Alternatively, you can press Enter, which should make cell H4 active, and then press the left arrow key seven times until you reach cell A4.

10. Begin entering information about the next president, John Adams, and continue for as many presidents as you'd like.

11. Select *Save* from the Office button. Assign the workbook a name and designate a location to save it. Click the Save button. Saving workbooks is discussed in more detail in the "Saving and Naming a Workbook" section of this chapter.

Modifying Worksheets: Formatting Text

In this section, we return to our weather data and adjust the text of the worksheet by modifying the font type, size, style, and color of cell contents.

1. Click in cell A1. Set the font type to Arial. Click the Home tab. In the Font group, click the *Font* box (see Figure 5.19) and select *Arial.* Notice that as you move the mouse over the font types, the changes appear in your text.

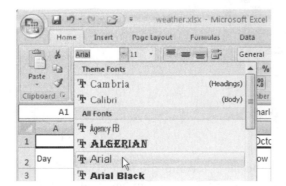

Figure 5.19
Font type

2. Set the font size 14 by clicking the *Font Size* box (see Figure 5.20) in the Font group (Home tab) and selecting *14.* The result of the font type and size changes can be seen in Figure 5.21.

3. Adjust the font style of the titles. Select cells A2 through G2 by clicking in cell A2 and, while holding the mouse button down, dragging to cell G2.

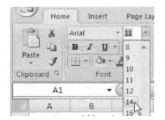

Figure 5.20
Font sizes

Figure 5.21
Adjusted font type
and size

Figure 5.22
Set font styles

4. Click the Bold button in the Font group (Home tab). The Bold button appears as a B on the formatting toolbar (see Figure 5.22).

5. After setting the style to Bold, you may notice that portions of the titles in columns D through G do not display. To adjust this, select cells D2 through G2 and then on the Home tab click the selection arrow under Format (Cells group) and select *AutoFit Column Width*.

6. You can now assign a Fill Color of black to row 2 and set the font color to white. On the left side of the worksheet, click the row heading number 2, which represents the second row. Clicking 2 selects the entire row. Alternatively, you can select cells A2 through G2 by dragging across them.

7. On the Home tab in the Font group, click the down arrow located on the right side of the Fill Color tool. A palette of color choices displays (see Figure 5.23). Click on the black square and the row fill color changes to black.

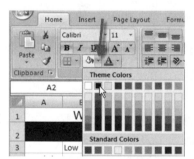

Figure 5.23
Set fill color

8. Because both the fill color and the font color of row 2 are set to black, you cannot see the text titles (*Day, Temperature, Rain Fall (inches), Avg. Low, Avg. High, Total Precipitation*). With row 2 selected, click the down arrow located on the right side of the font color tool. The color choices palette will display (see Figure 5.24). Click on the white square, and the font color changes to white. Row 2 should now have a black background with white text (see Figure 5.25).

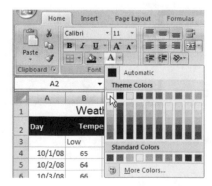

Figure 5.24
Set font color

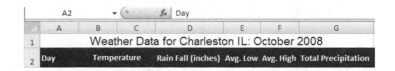

Figure 5.25
Row text and background color

Alternatively, you can set the style of row 2. Select row 2, on the Home tab click *Cell Styles* in the Styles group, and the cell styles box appears. Move your cursor over the styles to see their effects. Select *Accent 1*, and the font and background colors of the row change (see Figure 5.26).

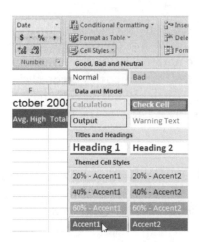

Figure 5.26
Cell styles

Figure 5.27
Format Painter icon

If you prefer, you can apply the same attributes (font type, color, and so on) to the *Low* and *High* titles under *Temperature*. One way to set these attributes is to select cells B3 and C3 and repeat the steps previously presented. Alternatively, using the Format Painter icon in the Clipboard group (see Figure 5.27), you can apply the attributes of one cell or a group of cells to another cell or range of cells.

For example, select cells E2 and F2 and then click the Format Painter icon. Click cell B3, and the attributes of cells E2 and F2 are applied to B3 and C3. Notice that Excel applies the attributes to the same number of cells that you selected prior to clicking the Format Painter icon.

Modifying Worksheets: Editing Data

In this section, you will alter the data entered into the school weather station workbook. Specifically, you will edit the contents of a cell, replace the contents of a cell, and delete data.

Edit Data

1. Suppose one of the titles is misspelled in the school weather station worksheet. Assume that the last column title is spelled *Total Percipitation* instead of *Total Precipitation*. Double-click cell G2, which contains the misspelled title. After double-clicking in the cell, the cursor appears inside the cell as a flashing line, referred

to as the *insertion point*. You are now able to edit the text (e.g., select, add, delete, and so on).

2. Select the second and third letters of *Percipitation* (see Figure 5.28) and, with the letters selected, type *re*. Press Enter or the Tab key to accept the changes and move the active cell. You can also edit *Percipitation* on the formula bar.

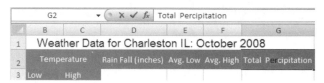

Figure 5.28
Edit cell data

Replace Data

Suppose you inadvertently assigned a wrong low temperature amount for a particular day in the worksheet. You may have entered 23 for the low temperature on October 2 when, in fact, it should have been 64. To correct this error, click on the cell containing the value that needs to be changed. Click cell B5. Type the new temperature of 64. The old value of 23 is replaced with 64. Press Enter or the Tab key to accept the change and move the active cell.

Delete Data

Suppose you mistakenly entered data in the *Avg. Low* and *Avg. High* columns for October 2 and now need to remove it. Click on the cell(s) containing the data you want to delete. Select cells E4 and F4 and press Delete. The contents of the cell are removed.

Saving and Naming a Workbook

Before continuing, you need to save your workbook. It is important to save your Excel documents frequently because any unsaved portion of a workbook disappears when you turn the computer off. In this section, we describe naming and saving a workbook. There are two save options available by clicking the Office button: *Save* and *Save As*. Under *Save As*, there are numerous options for saving the workbook, including options for the Web and for earlier Office versions.

Save

When you create a new workbook and then select Save, the *Save As* dialog box (see Figure 5.29) appears, requesting that you assign the file a location in which to be saved, give the file a name, and specify a file format. When saving a new workbook, you will most likely do the following:

- Click in the *Save in* box to specify the location to save the workbook.
- Type a name in the *File name* field.
- Assign a file format by clicking in the *Save as type* box.

If you do not provide a name, Excel gives the workbook the name of *Book1.xlsx*. By default, Excel appends the *.xlsx* extension to the file name and saves the file in a Microsoft Excel workbook (* .xlsx) format. A number of formats are available for saving documents, including *Web Page, Microsoft Excel 97–2003, XML,* and *text* (.txt).

Once you have designated a location, name, and format for your workbook, Excel saves all future changes accordingly. For example, if you created a new workbook,

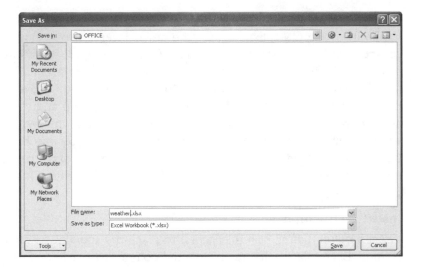

Figure 5.29
Save As box

added 10 rows and five columns of data, and then saved it in the Office folder with the name *weather.xlsx*, a file named *weather.xlsx* appears in the Office folder on your computer's hard drive. If you reopened the workbook, added five additional rows of data, and clicked *Save*, the five new rows are automatically saved with the original 10, and the *Save As* dialog box does not appear. The workbook now has a total of 15 rows and five columns.

1. Because you have not yet saved the workbook, click the Office button and select *Save*. You can also click the *Save* icon on the Quick Access Toolbar.
2. Click in the *Save in* box on the *Save As* dialog box to locate the Office folder (or select another folder of your choice).
3. Type a name for the workbook in the *File name* box. Use *weather* for the name. Remember, Excel appends the .xlsx extension to the file name, resulting in *weather.xlsx*. The document should be saved as a *Microsoft Office Excel Workbook*.xlsx file, so be sure that this format type appears in the *Save as type* box. Click *Save*.

Save As

The Save As option allows you to save an existing Excel workbook in a different location, under a different file name, or in a different file format.

Save as Web Page

To save a workbook for the Web, select *Save As* from the Office button and then in the *Save as type* box choose either Web Page (.htm; .html) or as a Single File Web Page (.mht; .mhtml), both of which can be viewed in a Web browser.

Modifying Worksheets: Inserting Rows and Columns

So far you have created a worksheet to record daily weather data and formatted its appearance. In the following sections, you will expand on this example by adding data to the worksheet and performing calculations.

Suppose that after creating the weather station worksheet, you found that you overlooked a date (October 4) and a column for snowfall. To add the *October 4* data and a *snowfall* column, first insert a row below rows 6 and 7 and then insert a column after *Rain Fall (inches)*. These actions provide the space to place the previously unrecorded data.

Inserting a Row

When inserting rows, Excel places the newly inserted row above the cursor position or active cell. For example, if the active cell is row 23, the contents of row 23 are pushed down into row 24, and the inserted row becomes row 23.

To insert the *October 4* data, position the cursor within row 7. On the Home tab, click the selection arrow under Insert in the Cells group and select *Insert Sheet Rows,* and a new empty row appears. Enter the following data in row 7: *10/4/08, 62, 74, 0.* If you auto filled your date column in earlier steps, then you may have more than 31 days because you added the extra row. You may delete the extra row by clicking the row number to select it and then click the selection arrow under Delete in the Cells group and choose *Delete sheet rows.*

Inserting a Column

Insert a column after *Rain Fall (inches)* to place the snowfall amounts. When inserting a column, Excel places the newly inserted column to the left of the cursor position or active cell. For example, if the active cell is in column E, the contents of column E, are pushed to the right into column F and the inserted column becomes column E.

Click anywhere in column E (*Avg. Low*). On the Home tab, click the selection arrow under Insert in the Cells group and select *Insert Sheet Columns,* and a new empty column appears in which you can enter snowfall amounts (see Figure 5.30). Add the title *Snowfall (inches)* to cell E2.

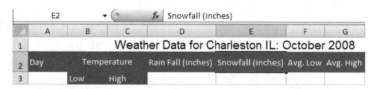

Figure 5.30
Inserting a column

After inserting a column or row, the Format Painter icon appears and presents cell formatting options. Clicking the down arrow next to the Format Painter icon displays a list of formatting choices (see Figure 5.31). You can format the inserted row or column like the row or column adjacent to it, or you can clear the formatting. For our purposes, select the default option: *Format Same as Above* for a row and *Format Same as Left* for a column.

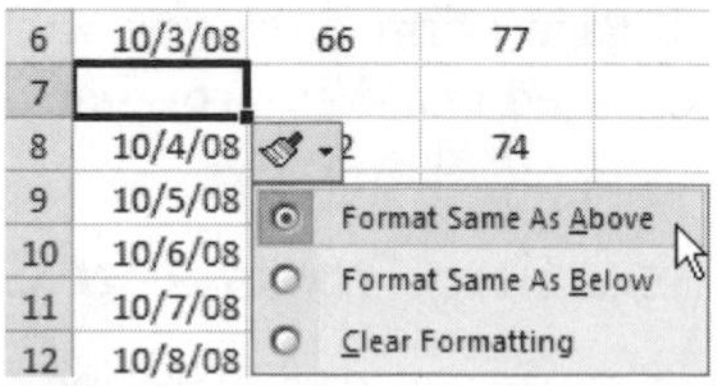

Figure 5.31
Format Painter

Formulas

Excel allows you to write formulas to make calculations. A formula can be a series of numbers, cell references, or names that, when placed in a specific sequence or combination, produce a new value. All formulas start with an equals sign (=). Suppose you want to place the sum of three cells (A1, A2, and A3) of data into a new cell, A4. Double-click in cell A4, which activates the formula bar. On the formula bar, type an equals sign (=) and then type the formula *A1+A2+A3* to add the values in the three cells (see Figure 5.32).

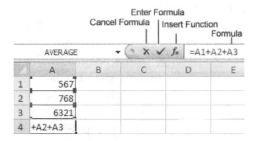

Figure 5.32
Formula bar

This formula adds the contents of cells A1, A2, and A3, and the sum of the cells appears in cell A4. After typing the formula, click the Enter Formula option or press Enter. You can cancel the formula by clicking the Cancel Formula option.

For the weather station example, suppose you want to determine the differences between the low and high temperatures for a particular number of days. To get a cursory look at how many degrees the temperature increased, calculate the differences between the low and high temperatures for the first 5 days in October.

1. Insert a column to calculate the temperature difference. In the weather station workbook (*weather.xls*), click anywhere in column D. Click the selection arrow under Insert in the Cells group and click *Insert Sheet Columns*, and a new empty column appears to calculate the temperature differences (see Figure 5.33). Click in cell D2 and give the column the title of *Degree Change*. Notice that a portion of the title in D2 does not display. To adjust the title, select cell D2, then click the selection arrow under Format in the Cells group and then choose *AutoFit Column Width*.

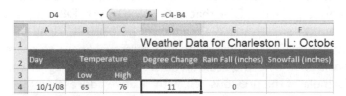

Figure 5.33
Cell formula

2. For this example, you will calculate temperature differences for the first 5 days of October. Begin by subtracting the low temperature in cell B4 from the high temperature in C4 to get the degree difference.

    Click in the cell that corresponds to *October 1*, which is D4. Type an equals sign (=) followed by *C4-B4*. Once you type the equals sign, Excel displays the *Formula Cancel* and Enter options. Double-clicking in cell D4 makes the Formula options appear automatically. The complete formula should look like the following: =*C4-B4*.

3. Click the Enter Formula option or press Enter to accept the formula. If the temperatures in cells C4 and B4 in your workbook were 76 and 65, respectively, 11 should appear in cell D4.

Copy and Paste Formulas

You could calculate the temperature differences for October 2 through October 5 by entering a formula for each day. However, a more expedient approach is to copy the formula in cell D4 and paste it for each of the other days.

4. Click in cell D4 to make it active.
5. Click the Copy button in the Clipboard group on the Home tab or press Ctrl+C. Notice that the cell becomes surrounded with a marquee (blinking dots) border to indicate that the computer copied the cell contents.
6. Click in cell D5 to make it active and, while holding the mouse button down, drag to cell D8, which should correspond to October 5. All cells from D5 to D8 should be selected.
7. Click the Paste button in the Clipboard group (Home tab) or press Ctrl+V. The formula is pasted in each cell, and the calculated values are displayed (see Figure 5.34). Click in each cell of column D and look closely at the formulas. Excel automatically adjusted each cell, reference to the appropriate row. So, for example,

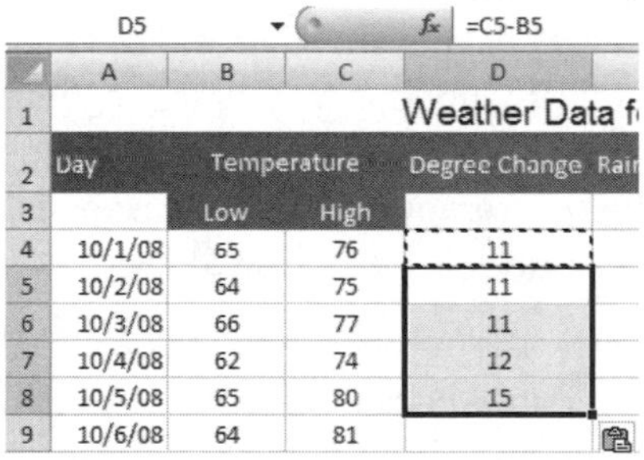

Figure 5.34
Copy and paste formulas

	A	B	C	D
1				Weather Data f
2	Day	Temperature		Degree Change Rai
3		Low	High	
4	10/1/08	65	76	11
5	10/2/08	64	75	11
6	10/3/08	66	77	11
7	10/4/08	62	74	12
8	10/5/08	65	80	15
9	10/6/08	64	81	

D5 ▾ f_x =C5-B5

cell D5 contains the formula =*C5-B5,* cell D6 contains the formula =*C6-B6,* and so on. The automatic referencing of cells is referred to as *relative addressing.*

8. In addition to copying and pasting the formula, you can use the Auto Fill option. Notice in Figure 5.34 that cells D5 through D8 have a black border around them. A small square appears at the bottom right of the border. Pass the mouse over the square and the cursor changes to a cross. With the cursor positioned over the square, and set to a cross, drag down, and Excel copies the formula of the previous cell, with relative addressing.

A review of the data in column D indicates that the greatest temperature change between October 1 and October 5 occurred on October 5, with 15 degrees difference between the low and high temperatures.

Functions

In the previous example, you created a formula (=C4-B4) to calculate the differences between daily low and high temperatures. Excel provides built-in formulas called *functions* that perform calculations. For instance, to find the average temperature change for October 1 through October 31, you could use the AVERAGE function.

For this example, you will place the average temperature difference in cell D35. Copy and paste or use the Auto Fill to complete the degree change column so that column D (Degree Change) has values for each day of the month up until October 31. Click in the cell (D35) at the bottom of column D, after the last degree change figure.

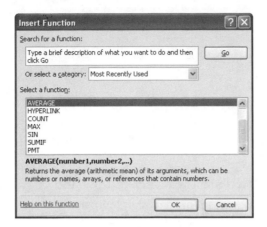

Figure 5.35
Insert function

On the Formula bar, click the Insert Function option, and the *Insert Function* box appears (see Figure 5.35). This box presents a number of functions that you can use. You can also search for function. Click *AVERAGE* under *Select a function* and then click *OK*.

The *Function Arguments* box appears (see Figure 5.36) and requests a defined range of cells for the average. Your cell range is D4 through D34. To define the cell range for

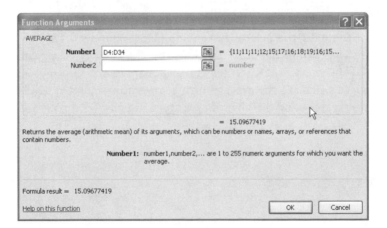

Figure 5.36
Function arguments box

the function arguments, click in the beginning cell (D4) and, while holding the mouse down, drag to cell D34. D4:D34 displays in the *Number 1* field of the *Function Arguments* box, indicating that the average of these cells will be calculated. Click *OK*. These steps average the values in cells D4 through D34 by placing the following function in cell D35:

$$=AVERAGE\ (D4:D34)$$

The result is 15.09. The AVERAGE formula is built into Excel, and thus we refer to it as a function. Alternatively, you could write your own formula to average the column D values, but it would be less efficient to do so. Entering the function $=AVERAGE\ (D4:D34)$ into cell D35 produces the same result as entering the following formula: $=(D4+ D5+ D6+ D7+ D8+ \cdots D34)/31$.

Structure of Functions

In Figure 5.37, notice that the structure of the function begins with an equals sign followed by the function name. The function arguments (I4:I18), or the range of cells on which the SUM function is performed, are enclosed in parentheses.

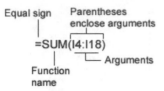

Figure 5.37
Function structure

Using Functions to Calculate the Average Low and High Temperatures

You can now calculate the average low and high temperatures for the month of October.

1. Click in cell G3 to make it active. G3 will record the average low temperature.
2. On the Formula bar, click the Insert Formula option, and the *Insert Function* box appears.
3. Click *AVERAGE* under *Select a function* and then click *OK*. The *Function Arguments* box appears to specify the arguments or range of cells for the AVERAGE function. For the average low temperature, the argument or cell range is B4 through B34 (B4:B34). Select the range of cells by clicking in the beginning cell (i.e., B4) and dragging to the last cell (i.e., B34). A marquee (blinking dots) border appears around the cells to indicate that they are selected. After selecting the cells, the cell range appears in the *Number 1* field of the *Function Arguments* box (see Figure 5.38). Click *OK* on the *Function Arguments* box.
4. The average low temperature appears in cell G3.
5. To calculate the average high temperature, click in cell H3. Repeat the preceding steps for the high temperature in cells C4 through C34.

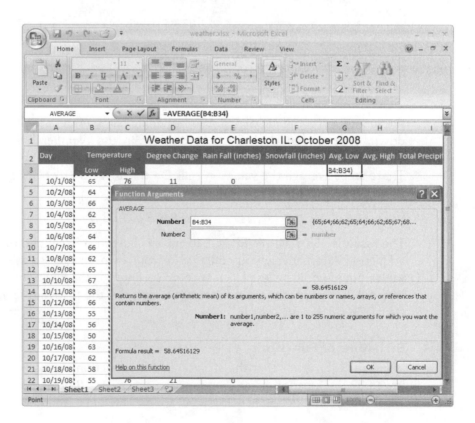

Figure 5.38
Average function

6. The average low and high temperatures for October are 58.64516 and 73.741935, respectively. These cells can be formatted to display only one decimal point. Select cells G3 and H3. On the Home tab, click the selection arrow under Format (Cells group) and choose *Format Cells*. Click the Number tab and under Category select *Number*. In the *Decimal Places* box, type *1* or use the down arrow to decrease the decimal places.

Using Functions to Calculate the Total Precipitation for the Month

You can use the SUM function to calculate the total precipitation for October. Before performing the calculations, suppose that on October 29 the amount of snowfall was 1 inch and that on October 31 it was 0.5 inch. In cell F32, enter the value of 1 and in cell F34 enter the value of 0.5.

1. Click in cell I3 to make it active. I3 will record the total precipitation.
2. On the formula bar, click the Insert Formula option, and the *Insert Function* box appears.
3. Click *SUM* under *Select a function* and then click *OK*. The *Function Arguments* box appears to specify the arguments or range of cells for the SUM function. For the total precipitation, the cell range includes both columns E and F (remember, snowfall amounts are in column F for October 29 and 31).
4. Select the range of cells to perform the SUM function by clicking in the beginning cell (i.e., E4) and dragging to the last cell (i.e., F34). A blinking dotted border appears around the cells to indicate that they are selected. After selecting the cells, the cell range appears in the *Number 1* field of the *Function Arguments* box (see Figure 5.39).
5. Click *OK* on the *Function Arguments* box. The total precipitation for October is 5.9 inches.

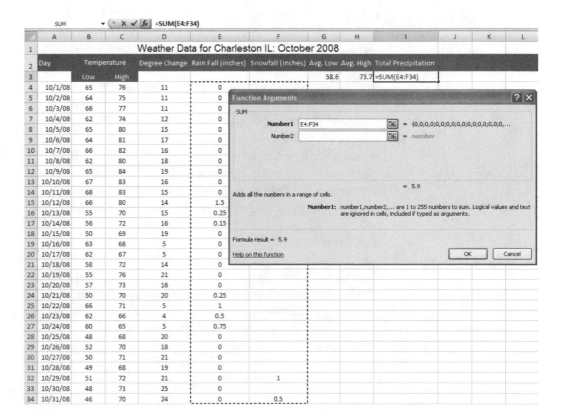

Figure 5.39
Sum function—
selecting multiple
columns

LET ME TRY: MY FAMILY TREE QUIZ

To practice using Excel functions, let's work on another Let Me Try that creates a short quiz. In this activity, you will create a matching question that requires the student to match photographs to a text label. For a completed version of this activity, go to the CD and open the *FamilyTree_Quiz.xlsx* file in the Family Tree folder. *Family Tree* is inside the Excel folder under *Examples*.

1. Open Excel and create a new worksheet.
2. Save the worksheet as *familyTree_Quiz.xlsx*.
3. Select cells A1 down through H4. With the cells selected, choose *Merge and Center*.
4. Type *My Family Tree Quiz* in the merged cells. Set the font to Verdana at a size of 28 points and bold.
5. Set the alignment of the merged cells to *Top*. Set the alignment by clicking the selection arrow under Format in the Cells group on the Home tab. Select *Format Cells* and click the Alignment tab and select *General* under Horizontal and *Top* under Vertical on the *Format Cells* box.
6. Select cells A5 through H8 and choose *Merge and Center*. Type the following:
7. *Match the item in the Relative column with the Photograph in the Photograph column. Type the letter of photograph in the Answer column next to the label the photo matches.*
8. To ensure that the text fits in the merged cell, select *Wrap text* under Text Control in the *Format Cell* box (click the selection arrow under Format in the Cells group on the Home tab and select *Format Cells* and click the Alignment tab). Set the alignment of the text to *Center*.
9. Enter the labels:
    - In cell C11, type *Mother*
    - In cell C12, type *Father*
    - In cell C13, type *Mother's Parents*
    - In cell C14, type *Father's Parents*
10. Set the font of the text in cells C11 through C14 to Verdana and 12 point with no bold. Select *AutoFit Column Width* from Format in the Cells group (Home tab).
11. Type *Feedback* in cell A10. Set the font to Verdana, bold, and 12 point. Select *AutoFit Column Width* from Format in the Cells group (*Home* tab).
12. Type *Answer* in cell B10. Set the font to Verdana, bold, and 12 point. Select *AutoFit Column Width* from Format in the Cells group (Home tab).
13. Select cells E10 through I10 and click *Merge and Center*. Type the following label: *Photographs*. Set the font to Verdana, bold, and 12 point. Select *AutoFit Column Width* from Format in the Cells group (Home tab).
14. Select cells D12 through D14 and click *Merge and Center*. Type the letter A. in the merged cells and set the alignment to Center. Set the font to Verdana, bold, and 12 point. Set this font type and size for all remaining photo letters (B, C, and D).
15. Select cells E11 through F16 and click *Merge and Center*. Place a solid border around the merged cells and fill them with a light gray background color. These options are under Format in the Cells group (Home tab).
16. Select cells G12 through G14 and click *Merge and Center*. Type the letter B. in the merged cells and set the alignment to Center.
17. Select cells H11 through I16 and click *Merge and Center*.
18. Select Cells D19 through D21 and click *Merge and Center*. Type the letter C. in the merged cells and set the alignment to Center.

19. Select cells E18 through F23 and click *Merge and Center*. Place a solid border around the merged cells and fill them with a light gray background color.

20. Select cells G19 through G21 and click *Merge and Center*. Type the letter D. in the merged cells and set the alignment to Center.

21. Select cells H18 through I23 and click *Merge and Center*. Place a solid border around the merged cells and fill them with a light gray background color.

22. Insert the following images located on the CD in the Family Tree folder—Family Tree is inside the Excel folder under Examples:

    ■ *Dad.png*
    ■ *Mom.png*
    ■ *grandparentD.png*
    ■ *grandparentM.png*

23. Insert the images by selecting the Insert tab and clicking the Picture button. Place each image over one of merged cell blocks. See Figure 5.40 for an example.

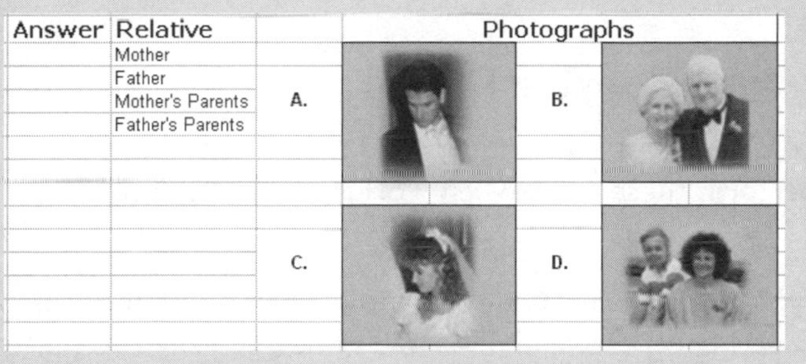

Figure 5.40
Image placement

Answer	Relative		Photographs		
	Mother				
	Father				
	Mother's Parents	A.		B.	
	Father's Parents				
		C.		D.	

Defining the Correct and Incorrect Answers

You need to determine the correct and incorrect answers. For instance, the *Relative* column lists *Mother* in cell C11 (see Figure 5.40). The photograph of the mother is labeled as C. in Figure 5.40. Therefore, to respond correctly to this item, the student must type a C in the *Answer* column in the cell to the left of the label *Mother*. Here is how the answer looks if you follow the layout in Figure 5.40:

C: Mother
A: Father
D: Mother's Parents
B: Father's Parents

24. With this information, type the following in cells K11 through K14:

    ■ In cell K11, type *C*
    ■ In cell K12, type *A*
    ■ In cell K13, type *D*
    ■ In cell K14, type *B*

The Formula

25. Click in cell A11, which should be in the same row as the *Mother* label. Type the following formula:

$$=IF(B11=K11, \text{"Correct"}, \text{"Try again"})$$

26. This formula checks to see if what the student types in cell B11 matches what you defined as the correct answer in cell K11. If it does match, then it displays "Correct." If it does not match, then it displays "Try again."
27. Click in cell A11 and copy the formula and paste it into cells A12, A13, and A14. You should notice that the cell references change to match the row numbers. When you enter the correct letter, the content of the A11–A14 cells should change.
28. To hide the correct answers, select column K and then choose *Hide Columns* from the Hide and Unhide options under Format in the Cells group.

To practice using the IF function, open the NumberPatterns.xlsx or the Jellybeans.xlsx files on the CD in the Excel folder under Examples. *The NumberPatterns.xlsx worksheet uses the IF function along with the AND logical function. The Jelly beans worksheet uses the IF function along with the OR logical function.*

Moving and Copying Data

This section describes how to copy and move data within a worksheet; you will often need to perform these tasks when working with data sets.

Moving Data

Suppose you entered the October snowfall amounts incorrectly. Instead of snowfall events occurring on October 29 and 31, they actually took place on October 26 and 28, so these values need to be moved to the appropriate cells.

1. Select cells F32 and F34. Click cell F32 to make it the active cell and, while holding the mouse button down, drag downward to cell F34.
2. Position the cursor over the selected area's border, and the cursor changes to a four-point arrow. Click on the border and drag the selection to the appropriate cells, F29 and F31. As you drag the selection, its border becomes shaded, and it snaps to the cell's border.
3. Release the mouse button when the values are over cells F29 and F31, and the values move.
4. Another way to move data is to select the data that you want to move and click the Cut button in the Clipboard group (Home tab) or press Ctrl+X. Click in the location where you want to move the data. Click the Paste button or press Ctrl+V.

Copying Data

Data can be copied from one group of cells to another or from one column to another. Suppose you want to make a copy of column A (the days of the month) on the right side of your worksheet to more easily view the precipitation amounts with their corresponding dates.

1. Select cells A4 through A34.
2. Position the cursor over the selected area's border, and the cursor changes to a four-point arrow. Press the Control (Ctrl) key while clicking on the border and drag the selection to the desired column, J. As you drag the selection, its border becomes shaded, and it snaps to the column's border. Note that pressing Ctrl while moving the selection copies it to the destination. If you do not press Ctrl, Excel moves the selection instead of copying it.

3. Release the mouse when the values are over column J, and the selection is copied.

4. Another method of copying data is to select the data that you want to copy and click the Copy button in the Clipboard group (Home tab) or press Ctrl+C. Click in the location where you want to copy the data. Click the Paste button or press Ctrl+V.

LET ME TRY: NUMBER PATTERNS

In the previous sections, you learned how modify the appearance of a worksheet and to use formulas and functions. Let's practice some of these concepts using a number patterns example. This Let Me Try will get you started creating a worksheet that requires students to recognize number patterns. Here you will build the first number sequence to which you can add your own sequences. The workbook will present a series of numbers (e.g., 2, 6, 10, 12, 16, and 20), and students must fill in the missing values. For instance, in the preceding sequence, the missing values are 4, 8, 14, and 18. The workbook will check the entered values and give feedback.

1. Create a New workbook. Click the *Office* button and select *New*, and the *New Workbook* box appears.

2. Click the *Blank Workbook* icon and click *Create*.

3. Select cells A1 through S1 and then click *Merge and Center* in the Alignment group of the Home tab.

4. Type *NUMBER PATTERNS*.

5. With the cursor still in the cell, click *Cell Styles* in the Styles group (Home tab) and choose *Accent 2*.

6. Set the text to size 36, bold, and the font to Broadway or Comic Sans. Set the font color to white. If the color is not already set, set the font color by clicking the font color button in the Font group (Home tab). Align the text to the left.

7. Click the Column A header to select the column and set the fill color to the same color as row 1. Set the fill color by clicking the fill color button in the Font group (Home tab).

8. Click in cell A4 and type the letter *A* to signify the first numbered sequence. Set the text to size 36, bold, and the font to Comic Sans. Choose a font color.

9. Type *2, 6, 8, 12, 18,* and *20* in cells B4, D4, E4, G4, J4, and K4, respectively.

10. Select cells B4 through K4 and set the text to size 24, bold, and the font to Comic Sans. Center align the numbers in their cells.

11. With cells B4 through K4 still selected, click the Borders button in the Font group (Home tab) and set the border to *All borders*.

12. Click in each cell that is empty between B4 and K4. If you hold the Control key down while clicking, you can select multiple cells at one time. Set the fill color of the empty cells to distinguish them from the cells containing numbers. Set the fill color by clicking the Fill color button in the Font group (Home tab).

13. Select cells M4 through O4 and then click *Merge and Center* in the Alignment group (Home tab). Set the text size to 14 and the font to Comic Sans. Set a fill color and a font color.

14. With the cursor still in the cell, enter the following formula in the Formula bar:

   =IF(AND(c4=4,f4=10,H4=14,i4=16),"You got it. Great Job!","Keep trying")

15. Test your formula by entering values in cells C4, F4, H4, and I4. If the values are correct (C4=4, F4=10, H4=14 and I4=16), then feedback (*You got it*) displays. If you don't get the values correct, *Keep trying* displays.

16. Copy and paste this row down though the worksheet to add more number sequences. Modify the formula in the new sequences to correspond to the cells and values you choose.

17. Currently, all values in the row can be changed, even those that need to remain unaltered. To protect the values in cells B4, D4, E4, G4, J4, and K4 so they cannot be changed, hold the Control key and click the cells in which students will enter values. Those cells should be C4, F4, H4, and I4. With the cells selected, right-click and select *Format Cell*. On the *Format Cells* box, click the Protection tab and uncheck *Locked*. Click *OK*. Check to ensure that the other cells (those that should remain unchanged) are locked. Right-click on a cell, select *Format Cells*, and then click the Protection tab. *Locked* should be checked.

18. Click the Review tab on the Ribbon and then click the Protect sheet button on the Changes group. The *Protect Sheet* box appears. Uncheck *Select locked cells* and check *Select Unlocked cells* and click *OK*. You should now be able to open the worksheet and enter values only in the cells that are blank. If you need to edit any of the protected cells, unprotect the worksheet by clicking the Review tab and click *Unprotect sheet* in the Changes group.

19. Click the Office button and select *Save* to save your workbook.

A copy of this starter worksheet (*NumberPatterns_Starter.xlsx*) is located in the Examples folder within the Excel folder. The *NumberPatterns.xlsx* sheet can be found there also. Another related Let Me Try (*Let me try Excel.docx*) activity, *Calculating the age of presidents*, can be found on the CD in the Let Me Try folder. It uses formulas to calculate the ages of presidents.

Charting Excel Data

In this section, you will use the weather data to chart daily temperatures. When you complete this section, you will have produced the line chart shown in Figure 5.41.

1. Select the range of cells from B3 through C34, which are the low and high temperatures for the month of October.

2. Click the Insert tab and then click the selection arrow below Line in the Charts group. Select the *Stacked Line with Markers* chart type (see Figure 5.42). The Charts group offers options for Column, Line, Bar, Area, and Scatter chart types. There is also an Other charts option that includes surface, donut, bubble, and radar categories. Notice within each type that the charts are categorized and that icons of the chart types appear. Clicking on an icon selects that particular chart type. Moving the cursor over the icons displays a pop-up description of the charts.

3. The Line chart displays in the worksheet. Click the chart to select it, and the Chart Tools tab becomes active. Under the Chart Tools tab, click the *More* arrow in the Charts Layout group and select *Layout 1* (see Figure 5.43). In the Chart Styles group, select *Style 2* (see Figure 5.44).

4. Click on the chart title and type *October Low and High Temperature*. Click on the axis title and type *Temperature*.

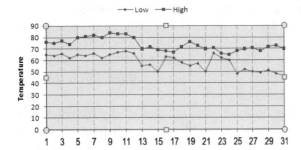

Figure 5.41
Completed chart

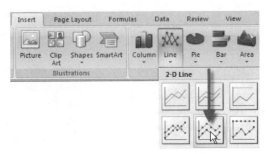

Figure 5.42
Line chart

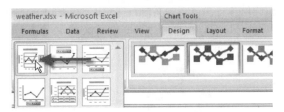

Figure 5.43
Chart layout

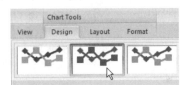

Figure 5.44
Chart styles

5. Click on the Series line for the high temperature to select it (see Figure 5.45). Under the Chart Tools tab, click the Format tab and then click the selection arrow for Shape Outline in the Shape Styles group (see Figure 5.46). Select *Weight* and ¼ *pt* to set the weight of the high temperature series line (see Figure 5.47). Repeat this step for the low temperature series line.

Figure 5.45
Chart series lines

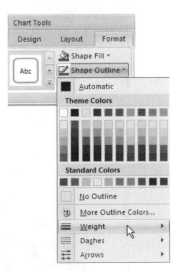

Figure 5.46
Select chart series
lines weight

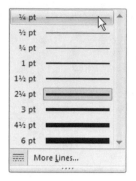

Figure 5.47
Chart series line weights

6. Click the chart if it is not already selected. Right-click on the Horizontal/ Category Axis and select *Format Axis* (see Figure 5.48), and the *Format Axis* box appears. Click on *Axis Options* on the left side of the box. For *Major Unit*, choose *Fixed* and enter *2 Days*. For *Major tick* marks, select *Outside*, and for Position Axis choose *On tick marks* (see Figure 5.49). These options display every other date on the horizontal axis. They place tick marks on the chart and center the horizontal axis values on them.

7. Click the Number option on the left side of the *Format Axis* box. Currently, the dates on the horizontal axis take up too much space, so you'll change them. With *Number* on the left side of the *Format Axis* box selected, choose *Custom* (under Category). In the Type box select *m/d;@*, and this code for the day and month will appear in the *Format Code* box. In the *Format Code* box, change *m/d;@* to *d;@* and click the Add button. Click *Close*. This changes the horizontal axis so that only the day appears (see Figure 5.50).

8. Click the chart to select it, and the Chart Tools tab becomes active. Click the Layout tab under Chart Tools. In the Labels group, choose *Legend* and *Show Legend at Top* (see Figure 5.51).

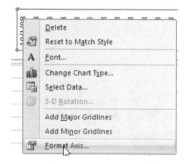

Figure 5.48
Format axis

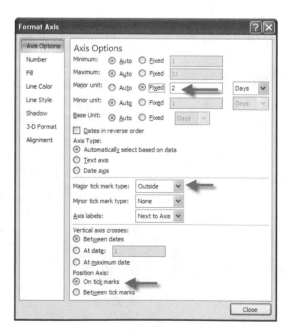

Figure 5.49
Format axis box

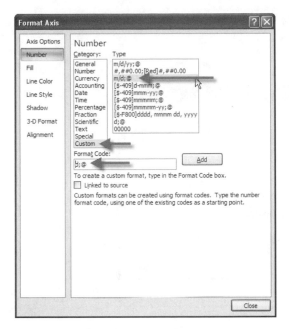

Figure 5.50
For axis—date
format

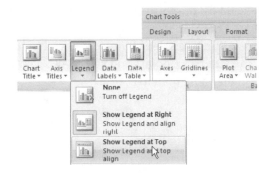

Figure 5.51
Chart legend

Modifying the Chart

Adjust X-Axis Labels: Orientation

Notice that as you click on various sections of the chart, they become selected. For example, clicking on the chart title *October: Low and High Temperature* selects it. A border and four small dots appear around it, indicating that it is selected (see Figure 5.52). Once selected, the title can be moved, edited, or deleted.

Figure 5.52
Chart title

October Low and High Temperature

Adjust X-Axis Labels: Font Type, Style, and Size

1. Right-click the X-axis labels section (the numbers representing the days of month) of the chart located below the columns (see Figure 5.53). A border and four small dots on the X-axis label indicate that it is selected. Choose *Font* from the shortcut menu, and the *Font* box appears. Set the font to Arial, size 10, and check the Equalize Character Height option (see Figure 5.54).

Figure 5.53
Chart X-axis

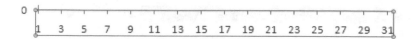

Figure 5.54
Chart X-axis font

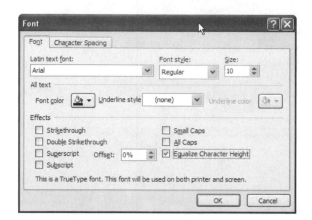

Adjust Data Labels: Font Type, Style, and Size

2. Click the Chart title (*October: Low and High Temperature*). Clicking on the title selects it, as indicated by the four small dots appearing around it (see Figure 5.55).

3. Right-click the chart title and select *Font* from the shortcut menu. Set the font type to Arial and the size to 12 points and select *All Caps* (see Figure 5.56). Click *OK* to accept the changes to the chart title.

Figure 5.55
Chart title selected

October Low and High Temperature

Figure 5.56
Chart title—font

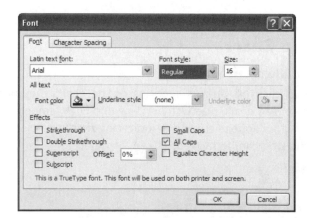

Adjust Chart Gridlines

Gridlines are horizontal and vertical lines running through the chart. They provide a visual referent for the data series lines and the X- and Y-axes. However, the lines in your chart may interfere with the visual clarity of the data points, so they can be adjusted. In this example, you want to see exactly where the data points fall in terms of data and temperature. As a result, you'll turn on both the horizontal and the vertical axes.

1. Click the chart to select it, and the Chart Tools tab becomes active. Click the Layout tab. In the Axes group, click the Gridlines option and select *Primary Vertical Gridlines* and then *Major Gridlines* (see Figure 5.57). If the horizontal gridlines

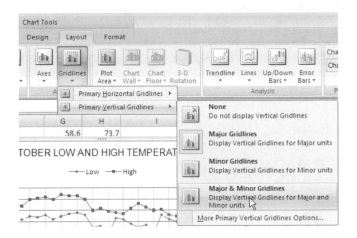

Figure 5.57
Chart gridlines

are not already present, then click the Gridline option again and select *Primary Horizontal Gridlines* and *Major Gridlines*.

2. With the chart still selected, click the selection arrow under Gridlines in the Axes group (Chart Tools Layout tab). Select *Primary Vertical Gridlines* and then *More Primary Vertical Gridlines*. The *Format Major Gridlines* box displays. Click *Line Color* on the left side of the *Format Major Gridlines* box. Choose *Solid Line* and set the Transparency to 55% (see Figure 5.58).

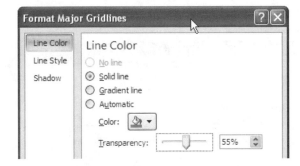

Figure 5.58
Format major
gridlines

3. Click the Line Style option on the left side of the *Format Major Gridlines* box. Set the line width to 0.75 pt and set the dash type to *Long Dash*, the third option from the bottom of the list (see Figure 5.59).

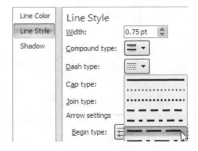

Figure 5.59
Gridline line style

Adjust Chart Background Color

To direct attention to the plot area, change the background color of the chart to light blue.

1. Click in the plot area. You can accomplish this by clicking between the major gridlines (see Figure 5.60). Be careful not to click on data series lines or mistakenly select the gridlines.
2. The Chart Tools tab becomes active. Click the Format tab and then click the selection arrow below Shape Fill (Shape Styles group). On the Shape Fill options panel, click *Olive Green, Accent3, Lighter 80%* (see Figure 5.61).

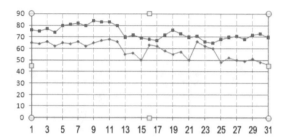

Figure 5.60
Select major gridlines

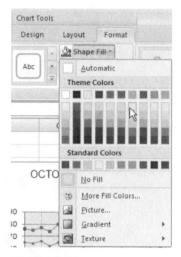

Figure 5.61
Shape Fill options

LET ME TRY: CHARTING PRESIDENTIAL DATA

In the *PresidentsByState_Chart.xlsx* file on the CD that accompanies the book, you will find a column labeled *States of Presidents* and another labeled *Number of Presidents from State*. These columns list the presidents' states of birth and the number of presidents from each state. Use this information to create the Column chart presented in this exercise.

Charting Presidents by State of Birth

1. In both the *States of Presidents* and the *Number of Presidents from State* columns, select rows 2 through 21.
2. Click the Insert tab. Click the selection arrow under Column (Charts group) and choose the 2-D Clustered Column chart.
3. Click the chart to select it. The Chart Tools tab becomes active. Click *Layout* and in the Labels group click *Legend* and then select *None*.
4. Click the title and type *Number of Presidents by State* if it is not already present.
5. Click the chart to select it. The Chart Tools tab becomes active. Click the Design tab and under Chart Styles click the More option and select *Style 45*, which should be a black background, white text, and green 3-D columns.

Saving as a Web Page

This section uses the example of sharing weather data over the Web. Suppose you and your students form school weather stations, as do five other schools throughout the country. You record the daily low and high temperatures and precipitation. You want to share the data with students at other schools to observe how weather patterns differ nationally. You can save a workbook as a Web Page (.htm; .html) or as a Single File Web Page (.mht; .mhtml), both of which can be viewed in a Web browser.

Saving a Workbook as a Web Page

The Web Page (.htm; .html) option converts the workbook to HTML and stores all associated files on your computer. Excel appends the .htm extension to the file name. For example, when saving *Weather.xlsx* as a Web Page, Excel assigns it the name *Weather.htm*. In addition, Excel creates a folder named *WeatherStation_files* that contains the HTML and graphic files associated with the workbook. You will need both the *Weather.htm* and the *Weather_files* folder for the workbook to display properly on the Web (see files on CD). When uploading the workbook to the Web, you must upload the .htm file and the folder.

Saving a Workbook as a Single File Web Page

The Single File Web Page (.mht; .mhtml) option creates a single file with the .mht extension. For example, when saving *Weather.xlsx* as a Single File Web Page, Excel assigns it the name *Weather.mht*, and it creates one file containing the workbook (see files on CD). With the Single File Web Page, you need to upload only one file to the Web server. However, this format typically produces a larger file size than the Web Page format.

Even though you save a workbook as a Web Page or a Single Web Page and can view it, the Web-formatted workbook files need to be placed on a computer server for them to be available worldwide. After saving a workbook as HTML, you need the following to make it available on the Web:

- Access to a Web server that stores and serves your Web files and graphics. Internet service providers provide this service.
- File transfer software that transfers the Web files and graphics from your computer to a server.

1. Open the *weather.xls* workbook containing the weather station data.
2. Before saving as a Web page, let's format the worksheet. If the chart is in your worksheet, position it under columns F through K beginning at row 4 so that you will be able to see the chart in the Web page.
3. Click in cell A1 and select all cells down through K35.
4. On the Home tab, click the selection arrow under Cell Styles (Styles group) and select the *Output* style (see Figure 5.62). This sets the style of the sheet.

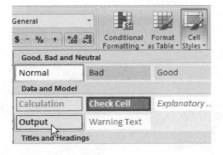

Figure 5.62
Cell styles

5. To save the weather workbook in a Web format, click the Office button and select *Save As* and then *Other Formats*. You can also just click the *Save As* option.

6. The Save As dialog box appears. Click in the *Save in* box to locate the folder where you want to save the files. In this example, you will save it to a folder titled *WeatherData* located in the Office folder on the computer's C: drive. If you do not have a folder with this name and want to create one, click the Create New Folder button on the top right (second option from right) of the Save As dialog box. When the *New Folder* box appears, enter the folder name and click *OK*.

7. *File name* specifies a file name and location to save the Web page. By default, Excel assigns a file name of .htm or .mht extension. Enter the file name of *weather.mht*. When saving a workbook in a Web format, it is preferable to remove blank spaces in the file name. The computer server may not recognize file names containing blank spaces. For example, if you are converting a workbook named *weather data.xls* to a Web format, the file should be saved as *weatherdata.mht* or *weatherdata.htm*.

8. In the *Save as* type box, select *Web Page* (*.html; *.html) (see Figure 5.63) and then click the *Selection: Sheet option* (see Figure 5.64).

9. Click the Change Title button (see Figure 5.64) and type a title in the *Set Title* box. Type *School Weather Station: October Temperature Data*.

10. With a Web browser, users can bookmark Web pages to quickly return to them without having to type (sometimes long) addresses. Internet Explorer uses the term *Favorites* to refer to bookmarks. Once you have bookmarked a

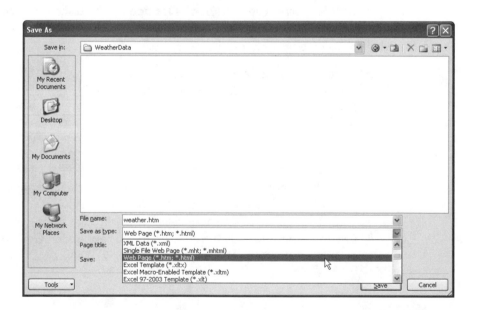

Figure 5.63
Save as

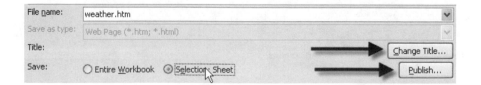

Figure 5.64
Sheet selection

page, you can select it from a list of titles and go directly to it. The page title assigned to a Web page is used as the bookmark or favorite title. For example, if you visit an interesting Web site about weather data that has an excessively long address, you could bookmark it. On subsequent visits to the site, you select it from the bookmark list to avoid retyping the address. In such cases, the page title (e.g., *School Weather Station: October Temperature Data*) is used as the bookmark, and it displays in the bookmark list.

11. Click the Publish button (see Figure 5.64) and in the *Publish as Web page* box, select *Items on Sheet 1* in the *Choose* box. *Choose:* Specifies the worksheet (e.g., Sheet 1, Sheet 2, or Sheet 3), a range of cells to be saved, or the entire workbook.

12. Make sure the file is being saved in the correct location by examining the *File name* box (see Figure 5.65). In addition, check to make sure your title displays in the *Publish as Web Page* box. If you do not see it, click the Change button and enter the title.

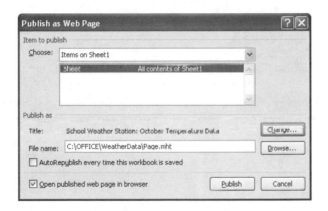

Figure 5.65
Publish as Web page

The Browse button allows you to specify a location to save the HTML file other than the one presented. Leave this option unchanged in your workbook.

13. Click *Publish.* The files and associated folder are saved to your computer. If you go to the saved location, you will see an .htm (weather.htm) file and a folder (weather_files). Notice when you select to only publish a worksheet and select *Items on Sheet1* on the *Publish as Web Page* box, Excel saves the file as a Single File Web Page (.mht).

14. Your complete Web page should look like Figure 5.66.

15. You can save files for Excel Services (on the Office button, select *Publish*) where you can specify data display options and allow others to interact with or access all or part of the data using a Web browser. However, to take advantage of these services, you need access to a computer server.

Opening the Workbook in a Web Browser

1. Open a Web browser (e.g., Netscape or Internet Explorer) to view the workbook. For this example, use Internet Explorer and press Ctrl+O (the letter O). The Open dialog box appears. If you know the location or path of your workbook, type it into the location box. If not, click *Browse*, and the Microsoft Internet Explorer dialog box appears.

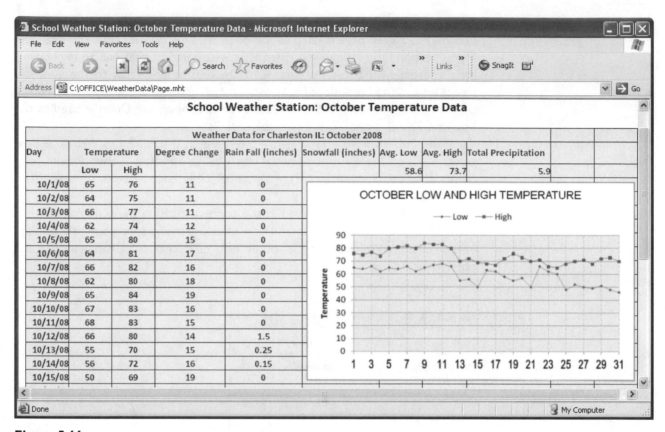

The table visible in the browser window:

| | School Weather Station: October Temperature Data | | | | | | | | |

	Weather Data for Charleston IL: October 2008								
Day	Temperature		Degree Change	Rain Fall (inches)	Snowfall (inches)	Avg. Low	Avg. High	Total Precipitation	
	Low	High				58.6	73.7	5.9	
10/1/08	65	76	11	0					
10/2/08	64	75	11	0					
10/3/08	66	77	11	0					
10/4/08	62	74	12	0					
10/5/08	65	80	15	0					
10/6/08	64	81	17	0					
10/7/08	66	82	16	0					
10/8/08	62	80	18	0					
10/9/08	65	84	19	0					
10/10/08	67	83	16	0					
10/11/08	68	83	15	0					
10/12/08	66	80	14	1.5					
10/13/08	55	70	15	0.25					
10/14/08	56	72	16	0.15					
10/15/08	50	69	19	0					

Figure 5.66
Worksheet in browser window

2. Locate the file on your computer. For this example, open the file called *weather.htm* located on the computer's C: drive within Office and in the folder called *WeatherData*. After locating the file, click *Open*. Return to the Open dialog box and click *OK*.

3. The workbook opens in the browser.

4. Keep in mind that the workbook is not on the Web even though you can view it in a Web browser. At this point, you need to transfer the HTML-formatted files to a server to make them available worldwide.

Spell Checking the Excel Workbook

1. Open the *weather.xlsx* workbook.

2. Check the workbook for spelling errors. Click the Review tab and click the Spelling button in the Proofing group. If your workbook contains spelling errors or words Excel does not recognize, then the Spelling dialog box displays (see Figure 5.67).

3. When Excel does not recognize a word, it identifies it in the *Not in Dictionary* section of the Spelling dialog box. For example, in Figure 5.67, Excel encountered a misspelling of the word *Precipitation* (*Percipitation*). Excel offers suggestions for changing the word. Clicking *Ignore Once* ignores the suggestion. Clicking *Ignore All* ignores all future instances of the word in the spell-check session. You can change the word to Excel's suggestion by clicking *Change*. *Change All* changes all future instances of the word in the spell-check session. If a word identified in

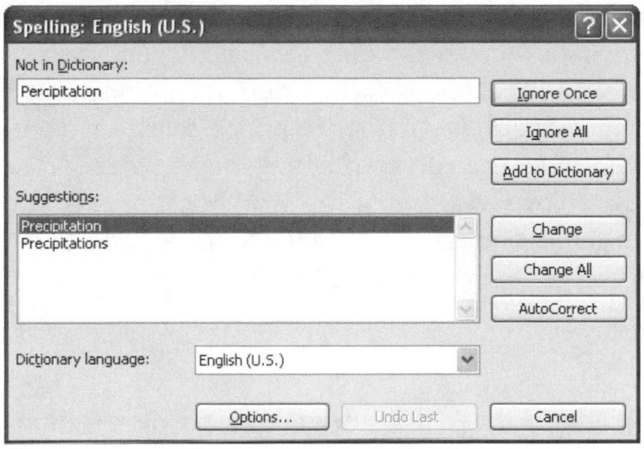

Figure 5.67
Spell check

the *Not in Dictionary* is spelled correctly and Excel does not recognize it, you can add it to Excel's dictionary by clicking *Add to Dictionary*. *AutoCorrect* adds the spelling mistake to a list of errors and automatically corrects it on subsequent occurrences. *Close* closes the Spelling dialog box.

Printing the Excel Workbook

Excel has several printing options. An entire workbook, worksheet, or selected cells within a worksheet can be printed. Printing worksheets or selections from a worksheet is particularly useful, for example, when students and teachers share and discuss their data analysis results.

1. Open the *weather.xls* workbook.
2. To print, select *Print* from the File menu, and the Print dialog box appears (see Figure 5.68).
   - *Printer Name box:* Designates a printer to print the workbook.
   - *Print range:* Specifies a range of pages to print. For this workbook example, select *All*.
   - *Copies:* Specifies the number of copies to print. Because the weather data is for the class, print 20 copies. The number of copies to print can be changed by

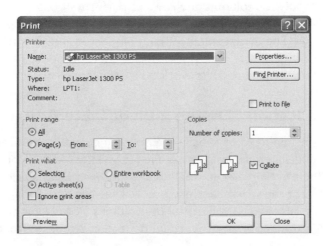

Figure 5.68
Print box

clicking the upward arrow under *Number of copies* until the appropriate number appears. With each mouse click and depending on whether the upward or the downward arrow is clicked, the number increases or decreases.

- *Print what:* Specifies whether to print a selection from a workbook, an entire workbook, or the currently active sheets. Select *Active Sheet(s).*
- *Preview:* Allows viewing of the workbook or workbook selection prior to printing. It is similar to the Print Preview option under the File menu.

3. When you are ready to print, click *OK.*

Print Preview

Prior to printing a worksheet, it is advisable to preview it in Print Preview. Often the data you enter into a worksheet extend beyond the viewing area of your computer monitor. Print Preview allows you to see what a printed copy of your worksheet will look like prior to its being printed. To preview a worksheet, click the Office button and then select *Print* and then *Print Preview.*

Show Me: PivotTable and PivotChart

PivotTable Reports and PivotChart Reports

This section explores PivotTable reports and PivotChart reports using data about presidents of the United States. Suppose you and your students are interested in examining statistical information about the presidents. Specifically, you would like to know the answers to questions such as what states had the most presidents, what was the most common occupation of the presidents, and who were the youngest and who were the oldest presidents in their first term of office. If you closely examined the *presidents.xlsx* file on the CD that contains presidential information, you could probably answer these questions, although it might take you a several minutes. However, using a PivotTable report and PivotChart report, you can glean this information from the data quickly. In this example, the data file is relatively small. As the amount of data that you have increases, the utility of PivotTables and PivotTable reports becomes even more evident.

What Are PivotTable and PivotChart Reports?

A PivotTable report allows you to quickly summarize large amounts of data dynamically and to generate easily adjustable summary tables. Without writing complex formulas, you can shift, or "pivot," columns and rows to perform in-depth and diverse analyses.

With a PivotChart report, you can generate graphical representations of data in a PivotTable report. The arrangement of data presented in a PivotChart report can be easily modified. Each PivotChart report has a corresponding PivotTable. To see how PivotTable and PivotChart reports work, you will use data about the presidents.

PivotTable Report: Define a PivotTable Range

1. To begin, you need to specify the range of data to use in the Pivot table. Open the *President_PivotTableData.xlsx* file in the Excel folder under Examples on the CD. If it is not already active, click the *President_Data* worksheet tab at the bottom left of the worksheet, and you will see the data for the presidents.
2. In this example, you will use all the columns from *Name* through *Party.* Click in cell A2 that contains the column header *Name.* With the mouse button

pressed, drag down to row 45 and right to column L so that all data from cell A2 through L45 are selected (see Figure 5.69). These are the data you will use in the PivotTable report. If you plan to add additional rows of information later, you can do so. However, after entering the data, you need to click the Refresh button, which can be found in the Data group on the Options tab under PivotTable Tools. The PivotTable Tools tab becomes active when you click in the PivotTable.

	E	F	G	H	I	J	K	L
11	68	1841	1841	68	Not Living	Soldier	Virginia	Whig
12	72	1841	1845	51	Not Living	Lawyer	Virginia	Whig
13	54	1845	1849	50	Not Living	Lawyer	North Carolina	Democratic
14	66	1849	1850	65	Not Living	Soldier	Virginia	Whig
15	74	1850	1853	50	Not Living	Lawyer	New York	Whig
16	65	1853	1857	49	Not Living	Lawyer, Public Official	New Hampshire	Democratic
17	78	1857	1861	66	Not Living	Lawyer	Pennsylvania	Democratic
18	56	1861	1865	52	Not Living	Lawyer	Kentucky	Republican
19	67	1865	1869	57	Not Living	Tailor, Public Official	North Carolina	Democratic
20	63	1869	1877	47	Not Living	Soldier	Ohio	Republican
21	71	1877	1881	55	Not Living	Lawyer	Ohio	Republican
22	50	1881	1881	50	Not Living	Teacher, Public Official	Ohio	Republican
23	57	1881	1885	52	Not Living	Lawyer	Vermont	Republican
24	69	1885	1889	46	Not Living	Lawyer	New Jersey	Democratic
25	68	1889	1893	56	Not Living	Lawyer	Ohio	Republican
26	69	1893	1897	54	Not Living	Lawyer	New Jersey	Democratic
27	58	1897	1901	54	Not Living	Lawyer	Ohio	Republican
28	61	1901	1909	43	Not Living	Author, Public Official	New York	Republican
29	73	1909	1913	52	Not Living	Lawyer, Public Official	Ohio	Republican
30	68	1913	1921	57	Not Living	Teacher, Public Official	Virginia	Democratic
31	58	1921	1923	56	Not Living	Editor, publisher	Ohio	Republican
32	61	1923	1929	51	Not Living	Lawyer	Vermont	Republican
33	90	1929	1933	55	Not Living	Engineer	Iowa	Republican
34	63	1933	1945	51	Not Living	Public Official, Lawyer	New York	Democratic
35	88	1945	1953	61	Not Living	Farmer, Public Official	Missouri	Democratic
36	79	1953	1961	63	Not Living	Soldier	Texas	Republican
37	46	1961	1963	44	Not Living	Author, Public Official	Massachusetts	Democratic
38	65	1963	1969	55	Not Living	Teacher, Public Official	Texas	Democratic
39	81	1969	1974	56	Not Living	Lawyer, Public Official	California	Republican
40	94	1974	1977	61	Not Living	Lawyer, Public Official	Nebraska	Republican
41		1977	1981	53	Living	Farmer, Public Official	Georgia	Democratic
42	93	1981	1989	70	Not Living	Actor, Public Official	Illinois	Republican
43		1989	1993	65	Living	Businessman, Public Official	Massachusetts	Republican
44		1993	2000	47	Living	Lawyer, Public Official	Arkansas	Democratic
45		2000		54	Living	Businessman, Public Official	Texas	Republican

Figure 5.69
Define data range for PivotTable

Figure 5.70
PivotTable button
on Insert tab

3. On the Ribbon, click the Insert tab. Click *PivotTable* and select the PivotTable drop-down option (see Figure 5.70). The *Create PivotTable* box appears (see Figure 5.71). *Select a table or range* is currently active. If your data existed in an external file, you would choose the *Use an external data source* option. The two options under *Choose where you want the PivotTable report to be placed* allow you to specify the location for the PivotTable. Choose the default, *New Worksheet*, and Excel creates a new worksheet and places the PivotTable within it. Click *OK*.

The worksheet presents a new PivotTable (see Figure 5.72). Excel refers to columns in your source data as Fields. Notice in this example that the column headers of your source data are listed under the *PivotTable Field List*. In addition, notice the *Drop Page Fields Here, Drop Row Fields Here, Drop Column Fields Here*, and *Data Items Here* regions of the PivotTable. If the PivotTable does not display regions and looks like Figure 5.73, right-click inside the PivotTable area and

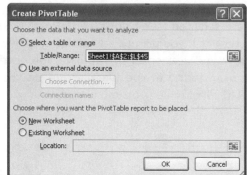

Figure 5.71
Create PivotTable box

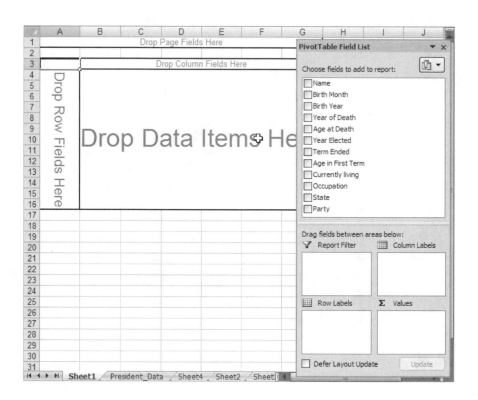

Figure 5.72
New PivotTable

Figure 5.73
New PivotTable without regions displayed

select *PivotTable options*. Click the Display tab and check the *Classic PivotTable layout (enables dragging of fields in the grid)* item and click *OK*. The regions should now be visible.

To examine the data, you can drag fields listed under PivotTable Field List and drop them on any one of the regions. You may also drag fields into any of the four areas (Report Filter, Column Labels, Row Labels, and Values) at the bottom of the PivotTable Field List. To remove a field, click inside any cell corresponding to the region, right-click, and select *Remove*. Alternatively, click the down arrow on the field item at the bottom of the PivotTable Field List and select *Remove Field*. If the PivotTable Field List gets hidden, click inside the PivotTable to make the PivotTable Tools tab active. Click the Options tab under PivotTable Tools and then click the Field List button in the Show/Hide group. Following is a short description of each region.

Drop Page Fields Here: You can filter an entire report based on the item placed in this region. For example, suppose you are interested in examining the presidents based on their occupation. When you view your data, you want to know the president's name, state of birth, party affiliation, and age in first term of office, but you want to examine this information based on occupation. In other words, when you ask to identify the presidents who were soldiers, the table should display all corresponding information for those who served as soldiers before the presidency. The PivotTable might look like Figure 5.74. To create the table, drag the *Occupation* field to the *Drop Page Fields Here* region; the *Name*, *State*, and *Party* fields would be placed in the *Drop Row Fields Here* region; and the *Age in First Term* field would be placed in the *Drop Data Items Here* region. In addition, notice that these fields are also present at the bottom of the PivotTable Field List (bottom right of Figure 5.74).

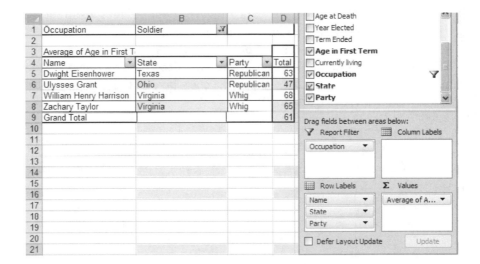

Figure 5.74
An analysis of presidents by occupation

In Figure 5.75, an icon appears to the right of the word *Soldier* (cell B1) that allows the data to be filtered based on occupation. When the icon is clicked, a list appears from which you can select the occupation of interest, then information about those presidents who served in that occupation is presented.

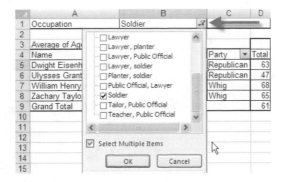

Figure 5.75
Filter data

Figure 5.76
Count of presidents
by state of birth

Drop Row Fields Here: By placing a field in this region, the data in the field are displayed as rows. In Figure 5.76, the list of states on the left side resulted from the *State* field being placed in this region.

Drop Column Fields Here: By placing a field in this region, the data in the field are displayed as columns at the top of the report.

Drop Data Items Here: In this region, place the fields for which you want to obtain subtotals. For example, suppose you are interested in the birth states of presidents and how many presidents were born in each of those states. To get a summary of these data, you could place the *State* field in the *Drop Row Fields Here* region and then place the *Names* (a listing of all present names) in the *Drop Data Items Here* region. The result is a count of presidents by state of birth (see Figure 5.76).

Presidents by Party Affiliation

1. Now that the data range is defined, let's examine the data. For the first example, assume you are interested in the total number of presidents affiliated with the various political parties since the beginning of the presidency. To examine the data in this way, drag the *Party* field to the *Drop Row Fields Here* region or into the *Row Labels* box at the bottom of the PivotTable Field List (see Figure 5.77).

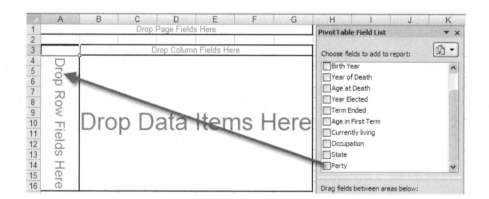

Figure 5.77
Party affiliation as
row fields

2. Drag the *Name* field into the *Drop Data Items Here* region or into the *Values* box at the bottom of the PivotTable Field List (see Figure 5.78). Your PivotTable should look similar to Figure 5.79, which shows the total number of presidents within each party. To have your PivotTable present totals, if these are not already

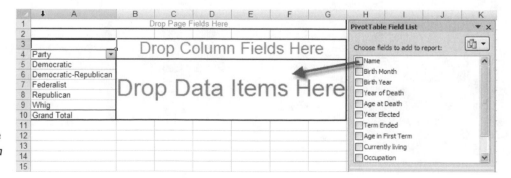

Figure 5.78
Party affiliation name
field in the *Drop Data
Items Here* region

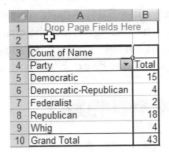

Figure 5.79
Party affiliation tallies

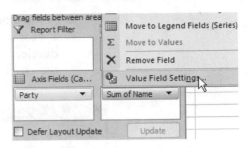

Figure 5.80
Change the Value Field settings

shown, set the Value Field settings for the *Name* field to *Count*. Click the down arrow on the *Name* field located at the bottom of the PivotTable Field List and then select *Value Field Settings* (see Figure 5.80). On the *Value Field Settings* box, select *Count* and click *OK* (see Figure 5.81).

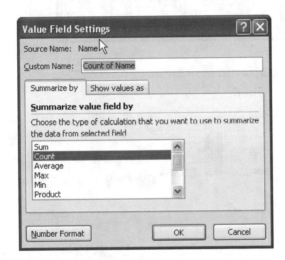

Figure 5.81
Value Field Settings box

Making a PivotChart from Party Affiliation Data

Now that the party affiliation data are summarized, let's create a chart based on these data.

1. Click anywhere inside the PivotTable, and the Ribbon should display the Pivot-Table Tools tab. Click the Options tab located under PivotTable Tools and then click the PivotChart button in the Tools group (see Figure 5.82).
2. The *Insert Chart* box displays. Click the first item under Column on the *Insert Chart* box (see Figure 5.83) and click *OK*.

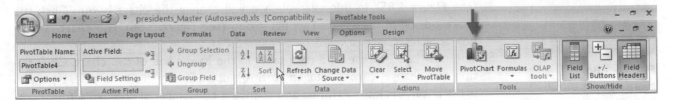

Figure 5.82
PivotTable Tools options

3. A Column chart appears (see Figure 5.84). Adjust the settings to change the appearance of the chart. To alter the settings, select the chart. If you inadvertently deselect the chart, Ribbon options change. To return to the chart options, click in the chart area, and on the Ribbon under PivotChart Tools click the Design tab.

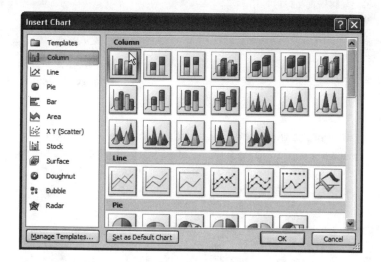

Figure 5.83
Insert Chart box

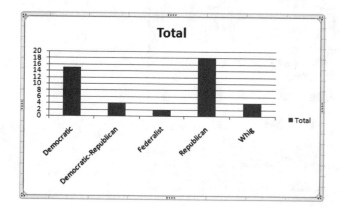

Figure 5.84
Column chart

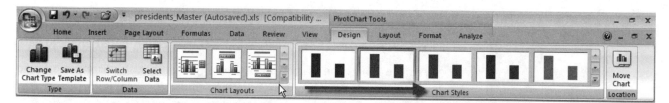

Figure 5.85
Chart Styles group

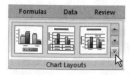

Figure 5.86
More options on Chart Layouts group

4. Change the color and style of the chart with options in the Chart Styles group (see Figure 5.85). In this example, we will change the chart layout. Click the More option in the Chart Layouts group (see Figure 5.86). The chart layouts box appears, select *Layout 5* (see Figure 5.87).
5. The new layout presents a data table in the lower half of the chart. Click the title and change it from *Total* to *Party Affiliation*. Simply click the title, type, and press Enter. Click the *Axis Title* and change it to *Number of Presidents*. Your complete chart should look like Figure 5.88. We can now select the chart, copy it, and then open Word or PowerPoint and paste it.

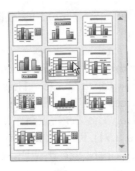

Figure 5.87
Chart Layout box

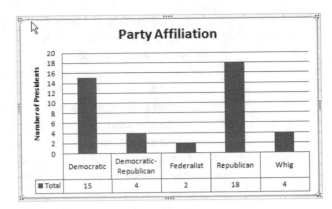

Figure 5.88
Finished column chart

Using a Formula to Calculate the Number of Years Each President Lived After His Term in Office Ended

1. Open the *President_PivotTableData.xlsx* file if it is not already opened. Define a data range as you did in the *PivotTable report: Define a PivotTable range* section. Click in cell A2 that contains the column header *Name*. With the mouse button pressed, drag down to row 45 and right to column L so that all data from cell A2 through L45 are selected (see Figure 5.69).

2. Click the Insert tab and then click the PivotTable button and select *PivotTable* to create a new PivotTable report. Place the report in a new worksheet. After Excel creates the PivotTable report, ensure that the Classic PivotTable layout is turned on.

3. Drag the *Name* field from the *PivotTable Field List* to the *Drop Row Fields Here* region.

4. Drag the *Year of Death* and the *Term Ended* fields to the *Drop Row Fields Here* region also. You can accomplish this by dragging *Year of Death* to the top of the *Row Fields* region, where the *Name* header is located in Figure 5.89. Alternatively, you can drag *Year of Death* to the *Row Labels* box at the bottom right of the PivotTable Field List (see Figure 5.89).

5. Place the *Year of Death* field first and then the *Term Ended* field so that the row fields appear in the same order as in Figure 5.89 (*Name, Term Ended*, and then

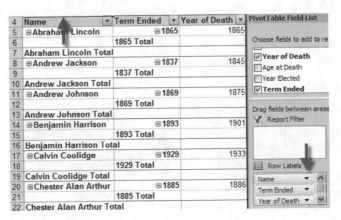

Figure 5.89
PivotTable

Year of Death). If needed, you can rearrange a field by clicking the header and dragging it to another location.

6. Notice in Figure 5.89 that an additional (Total) row appears after each name and date. You don't need the additional rows for this example, so remove them by clicking the down arrow on each field item in the *Row Labels* box (see Figure 5.89) and select *Field Settings* (see Figure 5.90). You can also access the Field Settings option by right-clicking inside the table and selecting *Field Setting*. The *Field Settings* box appears. Select the None option and click *OK* (see Figure 5.91). Repeat this step for the *Name, Term Ended,* and *Year of Death* fields. In addition, notice that the table items have small (show/hide) buttons that you do not need. Turn them off by clicking in the PivotTable area, which activates the PivotTable Tools and Options. Click the Button+/− button in the Show/Hide group. Your PivotTable should look like Figure 5.92.

7. In Figure 5.92, noticed that the word *blank* appears when there is no value for either *Term Ended* or *Year of Death*. In addition, an empty cell appears below Grover Cleveland because his two terms in office were separated by several years. It would be preferable to replace the empty cell with Cleveland's name. To do this, make the PivotTable Tools and Options tabs active by clicking in the table. On the Ribbon, click *Options* in the PivotTable group, and the *PivotTable Options* box appears. Check the item for *Merge and center with labels* and click *OK*. Your table should look like Figure 5.93.

8. To calculate the number of years each president lived after his term in office, you'll write a formula that subtracts the *Term Ended* field from the *Year of Death* field.

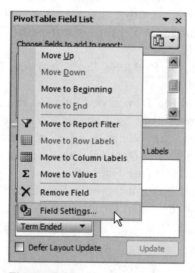

Figure 5.90
Field settings

Figure 5.91
Field Settings box

14	George Bush		1993	(blank)
15	George W. Bush	(blank)		(blank)
16	George Washington		1797	1799
17	Gerald Ford		1977	2007
18	Grover Cleveland		1889	1908
19			1897	1908
20	Harry Truman		1953	1972
21	Herbert Hoover		1933	1964
22	James Buchanan		1861	1869
23	James Carter		1981	(blank)

Figure 5.92
PivotTable without totals or buttons

9. With the PivotTable Tools and Options tabs active, click *Formulas* and select *Calculated Field* (see Figure 5.94). The *Insert Calculated Field* box displays (see Figure 5.95). In the *Name* box, type a name for the calculated field, *Years presidents lived after presidency*. In the *Formula* box, type the following formula and click *OK*:

=*IF('Term Ended'< >0,IF('Year of Death'< >0,'Year of Death'− 'Term Ended', NA()),NA())*

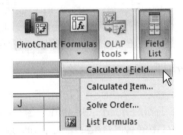

14	George Bush	1993	(blank)
15	George W. Bush	(blank)	(blank)
16	George Washington	1797	1799
17	Gerald Ford	1977	2007
18	Grover Cleveland	1889	1908
19		1897	1908
20	Harry Truman	1953	1972
21	Herbert Hoover	1933	1964
22	James Buchanan	1861	1869

Figure 5.93
Merged field

Figure 5.94
Calculated field

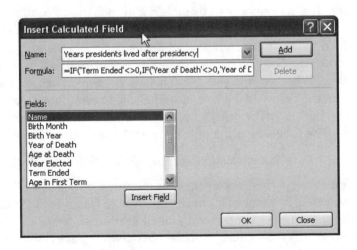

Figure 5.95
Insert Calculated
Field box

The formula contains a nested IF-then conditional statement or one IF-then statement within another. To better understand it, let's review an example. Suppose you typed the following IF-then statement into Excel's formula bar for cell B2:

=*IF(A2=95,"Good Job","Keep Trying")*

This statement has several parts: (a) the IF statement preceded by an equals sign to denote that it's an Excel formula; (b) the condition (A2=95) followed by a comma; (c) the result-if-true (*Good Job*) or, in other words, what Excel places in cell B2 if the condition turns out to be true; and (d) the result-if-false (*Keep*

Table 5.1 Outer IF-then statement

Condition	When condition is TRUE, do the following	When condition is FALSE, do the following
IF('Term Ended' < >0,	IF('Year of Death'< >0, 'Year of Death'–'Term Ended', NA()),	NA())

Trying). In the formula, the result-if-true precedes the result-if-false. The statement first checks the condition, if the content of cell A2 equals 95. If the condition is true (A2=95), then the result-if-true (*Good Job*) is placed in cell B2, the cell for which the formula was written. If cell A2 does not equal 95, then the result-if-false (*Keep Trying*) gets placed in cell B2.

Now let's go back to the presidential spreadsheet example and examine the following formula more closely.

=IF('Term Ended'< >0,IF('Year of Death'< >0,'Year of Death'–'Term Ended', NA()),NA())

In this formula, there are two IF-then statements; one is nested within the other. The following is the outer IF-then statement. The blank space in the line represents where the nested/inner IF-then should be placed:

=IF ('Term Ended'< >0 „NA())

The outer IF-then checks the condition (*Term Ended < >0*) to determine whether the current cell in the *Term Ended* field is not empty. Using this form, we can identify the empty cell associated with the current president because his term has not yet ended and the spreadsheet contains no term ending date. We need to identify the empty cell so that it is not used in the calculation. When *Term Ended < > 0* is true, or, in other words, *Term Ended* is not empty and there is a date for when the term ended, the result-if-true occurs. In the earlier example, the result-if-true was *Good Job*, but in this case the inner/nested IF-then statement gets executed. When *Term Ended < > 0* is false or *Term Ended* is empty and there is no date, the result-if-false occurs, and Excel places #N/A in the corresponding cell (see Table 5.1). The NA() function places #N/A in PivotTable to mark empty cells.

The following is the nested/inner IF-then statement:

=IF('Year of Death'< >0,'Year of Death'–'Term Ended', NA())

The inner IF-then statement gets executed only if *Term Ended < >0* is true or the cell is not empty. It checks the *Year of Death* field for empty cells because the spreadsheet contains no year of death date for presidents who are not yet deceased. When Excel locates empty cells, it places #N/A in them. You do this to exclude empty fields from calculations. The format of this IF-then statement is similar to the outer IF-then (see Table 5.2). When *Year of Death < > 0* is false or, in other words, *Year of Death* is empty, Excel places #N/A in the corresponding cell. When *Year of Death < > 0* is true or is not empty, Excel subtracts

Table 5.2 Inner/nested IF-then statement

Condition	When condition is TRUE, do the following	When condition is FALSE, do the following
IF('Year of Death'< >0,	'Year of Death'–'Term Ended',	NA())

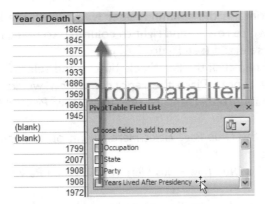

Figure 5.96
Years lived after presidency

3	Sum of Years Lived Aft			
4	Name	Term Ended	Year of Death	Total
5	Abraham Lincoln	1865	1865	0
6	Andrew Jackson	1837	1845	8
7	Andrew Johnson	1869	1875	6
8	Benjamin Harrison	1893	1901	8
9	Calvin Coolidge	1929	1933	4
10	Chester Alan Arthur	1885	1886	1
11	Dwight Eisenhower	1961	1969	8
12	Franklin Pierce	1857	1869	12
13	Franklin Roosevelt	1945	1945	0
14	George Bush	1993	(blank)	#N/A
15	George W. Bush	(blank)	(blank)	#N/A

Figure 5.97 Years lived after presidency

the value in the *Term Ended* field from the value in the *Year of Death* field, which gives the number of years lived after the term in office ended.

1. The *Years presidents lived after presidency* field appears in the PivotTable field list. Drag it to the *Drop Data Items Here* region (see Figure 5.96), and your PivotTable should look similar to Figure 5.97. You may notice a *Grand Total of-5570* at the bottom of your table. To remove this figure from the table, click in the cell containing the words *Grand Total* and then right-click and select *Remove Grand Total*.

2. To edit or delete the *Calculated* field, click inside the PivotTable to make the PivotTable Tools and Options tabs active. In the Tools group on the Ribbon, click *Formulas*, and the *Insert Calculated Field* box displays. Click the selection list arrow in the *Name* box to display a list of formulas (see Figure 5.98). Select the formula that you want to edit and then type changes in the *Formula* box. Delete the formula by clicking the Delete button.

Figure 5.98
Edit or delete a
formula

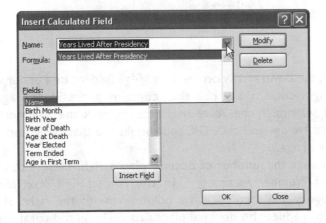

Average Age of Presidents in First Term

For this example, suppose you are interested in knowing the average age of the presidents in their first term in office and the presidents who were under the age of 50 when elected to the presidency.

1. Open the *President_PivotTableData.xlsx* file if it is not already opened. Define a data range as you did in the *PivotTable report: Define a PivotTable range* section.

Click in cell A2, which contains the column header *Name*. With the left mouse button pressed, drag down to row 45 and right to column L so that all data from cell A2 through L45 are selected (see Figure 5.69).

2. Click the Insert tab and then click the PivotTable button and select *PivotTable* to create a new PivotTable report. Place the report in a new worksheet. After Excel creates the PivotTable report, ensure that the *Classic PivotTable layout* is turned on.

3. Drag *Age in First Term* to the *Drop Page Fields Here* region or to *Report filter* on the *PivotTable Field List* box.

4. Drag the *Name* field to the *Drop Row Fields Here* region or to *Row labels* on the *PivotTable Field List* box.

5. Drag the *Age in First Term* field to the *Drop Data Items Here* region or to *Values* on the *PivotTable Field List* box.

6. Your PivotTable should look similar to Figure 5.99. Notice in the figure that the values are set to *Sum of Age*, and as a result Grover Cleveland's age is listed as 100 because he had two first terms in office. We will get the average age.

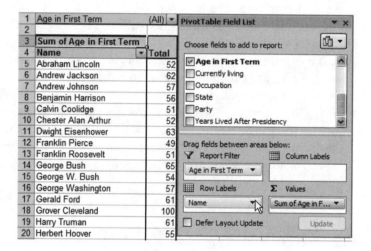

Figure 5.99
Age in first term

7. Click the down arrow on the *Sum of Age* field located under Values in Figure 5.99 or right-click in any cell that contains a president's age and select *Value Field Settings*. In the *Value Field Settings,* click the *Summarize by* tab and then select *Average* and click *OK.* You should see that the grand total is 55.4651128 years of age.

8. To reduce the number of decimal places, right-click in the *Grand Total* cell and select *Number Format . . .* In the *Format Cell* box, click *Number* under Category and then click the down arrow to the right of the *Decimal Places* box to reduce the decimal places to 1. The grand total should change to 55, indicating that the average age of all presidents in their first term in office is 55 years.

9. To determine the presidents who were under the age of 50 in their first term of office, click the down arrow at the top of the *PivotTable* in the *Page* fields region (see Figure 5.100), and the list of ages displays. Click *Select Multiple Items* and then click *All*, which will deselect all the ages. Next, click all the ages below the age of 50, and a check will appear next to the selected items. Click *OK*. Your PivotTable should look similar to Figure 5.101.

Figure 5.100
Age in first term

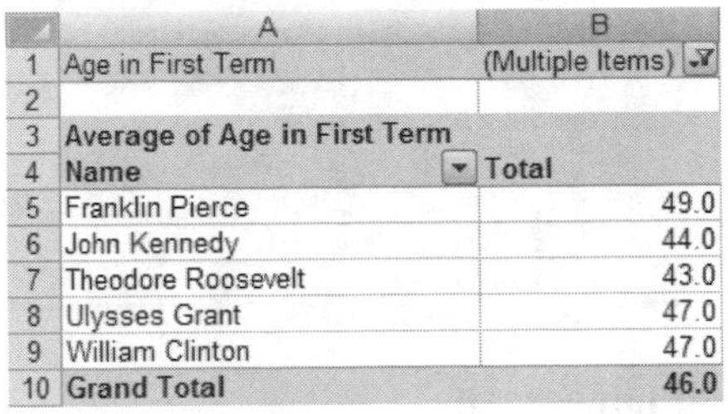

Figure 5.101
Age in first term

Use PivotTable and PivotChart to Analyze the States in Which Presidents Were Born

1. Open the *President_PivotTableData.xlsx* file if it is not already opened. Define a data range as you did in the *PivotTable report: Define a PivotTable range* section. Click in cell A2, which contains the column header *Name*. With the mouse button pressed, drag down to row 45 and right to column L so that all data from cell A2 through L45 are selected (see Figure 5.69).

2. Click the Insert tab and then click the selection arrow under the PivotTable button and select *PivotChart* to create a PivotTable with PivotChart in a new worksheet. After Excel creates the PivotTable with PivotChart, ensure that the Classic PivotTable layout is turned on.

3. Drag *State* to the *Drop Row Fields Here* region or to *Row labels* on the PivotTable Field List box.

4. Drag the *Name* field to the *Drop Data Items Here* region or to *Values* on the *PivotTable Field List* box. Ensure the value field settings are set to *Count*. On the *PivotTable Field List* box, click the selection arrow on the *Name* field (under *Values*) and select *Value Field Settings*. In the *Value Field Settings* box, click the *Summarize by* tab and then select *Count*. Click *OK*.

5. You should now have a count of the presidents born in each state (see Figure 5.102) as well as a chart depicting these results.

6. Click in the chart title and type a new title, *President Birth States*.

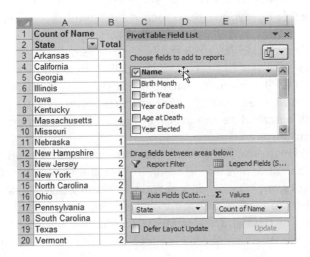

Figure 5.102
States of birth

Figure 5.103
Remove legend

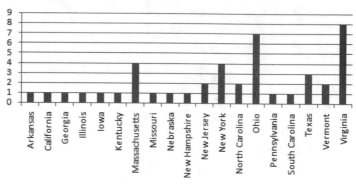

Figure 5.104
PivotChart

7. Remove the chart legend by clicking the chart to select it. The PivotChart Tools tab becomes active. Click the Layout tab. In the Labels group, click the selection arrow under Legend and select *None* (see Figure 5.103). The complete chart should look like Figure 5.104.

A CHALLENGE USING EXCEL 2007

For those who would like a challenge beyond the Let Me Try activities presented in this chapter, try the following exercises.

1. *Let's get counting.* Create a Change counting worksheet. In one column, list the amount of money that was spent. In a second column, list the amount of money that was given to the cashier. The students can enter a value in a third column for how much change should be given. A fourth column could provide feedback about whether the change amount is correct.

2. *What we eat.* Create a worksheet that tracks the amount of food students eat in the following food groups: fruits, meats, milk, grains, and junk foods. The rows of column A should list the days of the week. Label column A *Days of Week*. Make column headers for each food group starting at column B. Create a *Total* column. You will have a total of seven columns including *Days of the Week* and *Total*. Decide how you want to record the amounts (e.g., serving size) and enter those values for each food group for each day. Use the SUM function or write a formula that calculates the totals. Chart the data.

3. *Temperature.* Using Excel, record the daily high and low temperatures and precipitation for 1 month. For each day, ask students to calculate the temperature change and to record the average change in temperature for the month. Ask students to calculate the average high and low temperatures and the total precipitation.

4. *What we like to read.* Have students create reading lists. In one column (column A) list all student names and in column B list the book titles. Create columns for descriptors, such as fiction/nonfiction, mystery, science, animals, book length, time taken to read, and so on. Write descriptions for each book. Compile the data for the class and ask students to identify, among other things, the most common types of books, the number of books read, and the average length of

pages. Discuss the kind of books that were read and the kind of books that students have not yet explored.

5. *The presidents.* Create an Excel worksheet that lists all the presidents of the United States. Include the presidents' dates of birth, dates of death, states of birth, election years to office, years terms ended, and occupations. With this information, ask students to calculate the states with the most presidents, the age of each deceased president when he died, the most popular occupation other than president, and the number of presidents from each state. Finally, ask students to create a column chart that represents all states in which a president was born and the number of presidents from those states.

6. *The solar system.* Create a worksheet of data pertaining to the planets in the solar system, including their distance from the sun. Calculate the distance each planet is from one another.

7. *Study habits.* Create a study habits worksheet. For 1 month, ask students to record the number of hours they study, read, and watch television. Record this information by day of the week and date. At the end of the month, chart the data to observe trends in studying, reading, and television viewing.

8. *Showing respect.* Discuss with students what is means to show respect to others, such as treating people the way you want to be treated. Ask students to watch three of their favorite television programs. For 1 day, each student records the number of times someone in each of the programs showed respect as well as disrespect. If possible, students should record how the respect or disrespect was shown, such as someone said thank you or someone laughed at another person. Students should rate how much they like the program (e.g., on a 10-point scale). Create an Excel worksheet and enter all student data by program and by indicators of respect and disrespect. Ask students to identify the programs that have the highest indicators of respect and those with the lowest. Conduct comparisons by program and by how much students like the program. Discuss the implications of these data with students.

TYING IT ALL TOGETHER

In this chapter, you created an Excel workbook containing several worksheets. Your workbook served as an electronic weather data recorder. You organized data according to Excel's row-and-column format and formatted the worksheet layout, including font type, size, and style. Excel's formula capability and built-in functions allowed you to calculate the differences between daily high and low temperatures and precipitation averages. You explored PivotTables and charts and some of their key characteristics. You were walked through the steps of saving the file in a workbook (.xlsx) and in Web format.

REFERENCES

Grolier. (1994). *The American presidents.* Danbury, CT: Grolier.

Microsoft Corporation. (2004). *Excel specifications and limits.* Retrieved August 5, 2004, from http://office.microsoft.com/assistance/hFWS.ASPX?AssetID= HPO5199291103

CHAPTER

6 ACCESS 2007

CHAPTER OUTLINE

LEARNING OBJECTIVES

At the completion of this chapter you will be able to:
- Start a new database
- Create tables for data display
- Create forms for input of data
- Create reports of the database
- Edit the data and fields that display the data
- Create queries of the information in the database
- Print reports
- Save the database

CHAPTER OVERVIEW

This chapter provides an introduction to Access 2007. The content focuses on Access fundamentals and how to apply them to a variety of learning activities. You will create three different databases throughout this chapter, and using the databases, will create reports that provide specific information about the reports. Again using databases that are created, forms and queries will be formulated. Studying the chapter contents and working through the Let Me Try exercises will enable you to create databases suitable for many classroom learning activities.

Each of the illustrations given in this chapter may be found on the CD accompanying the text. You may follow along with the document as you go through the text by pulling it up from the CD. Also, other examples using Access may be found on the CD.

How Teachers and Students Can Use Access

Microsoft Access can be used in a variety of activities both by students and teachers in the classroom. When examining Bloom's taxonomy of cognitive levels in conjunction with the National Educational Technology Standards for Students: The Next Generation, teachers can utilize Access to accomplish instruction and, it is hoped, learning at a variety of levels and addressing multiple standards. Some examples of using Access by students could include the following:

- *Knowledge*—Students can create their own database to list information about the planets in the solar system and create reports of the data they have compiled.
- *Comprehension*—Students can compare data collected about the states in their region and summarize the information collected.
- *Application*—After reading *Sarah, Plain and Tall*, students will research and create a database collecting data about the two states that Sarah lived in.
- *Analysis*—After collecting data about the planets in the solar system, the students will compare and contrast the attributes of the planets.
- *Synthesis*—Students will collect Census Bureau data on three large cities in their area and hypothesize why populations of persons 65 or older increased or decreased in those cities.
- *Evaluation*—After reading *Vacation Under the Volcano*, students will collect data related to the Pompeii volcano eruption and evaluate if the novel is plausible.

NETS for Students*

The following activities can be accessed to address the standards:

- *Creativity and innovation*—Students demonstrate creative thinking, construct knowledge, and develop innovative products and processes using technology.
- *Communication and collaboration*—Students use digital media and environments to communicate and work collaboratively, including at a distance, to support individual learning and contribute to the learning of others.
- *Research and information fluency*—Students apply digital tools to gather, evaluate, and use information
- *Critical thinking, problem solving, and decision making*—Students use critical thinking skills to plan and conduct research, manage projects, solve problems, and make informed decisions using appropriate digital tools and resources.
- *Technology operations and concepts*—Students demonstrate a sound understanding of technology concepts, systems, and operations.

What Is New in Access

As with almost the entire 2007 Microsoft Office suite, the Ribbon replaces the menu and toolbars of the previous versions of Access. The new Access uses a new file format when saving documents that compacts the file but may not be opened in earlier versions unless saved in the earlier format.

When you open Access, the opening screen looks much different. You can still open a blank database, but with the new version you can build a new database based on Access online templates. When you create a database using the template, the database includes prebuilt tables and forms.

In past versions of Access, the database window listed all objects associated with the database, such as reports, forms, and queries; in Access 2007, the Navigation pane replaces the database window. The Navigation pane lists all objects in the currently open database and can be organized by object type, date created, and date modified.

As in the past, you may open only one database at a time. You may create multiple reports, queries, and export information to other Office suite formats, such as Word or Excel.

About Access

Access is a database program that allows you to store and manage information. Some individuals think of a database program as an electronic stack of index cards that can be sorted and reported electronically. Common databases include telephone directories or television program schedules. A database consists of objects, such as tables, forms, reports, and queries. Access allows you and your students to collect information, organize it, and report the information.

It is very important to plan your database prior to creating the file. You will need to think about what sort of data you want to collect and manage. What do you want to do with this data? What kind of reports do you want to generate with the data? Taking time in advance to plan the database will save you time when trying to create reports or queries later.

In Access, a table is a list of information organized into rows and columns. Every entry you make in a table in Access is a record, and every record appears in a row in your database. Each column in a record is a field. An example of a record would be student contact information. The fields in that record might include address, phone number, and e-mail address. The field names appear at the top of the table. A form in Access presents your table fields in a fill-in-the-blank format, allowing you or others to enter data into the database without seeing all data in the database at one time. After creating a database and entering data, you can use reports to summarize your data and generate printouts. You can use queries to sort and filter your data. For example, you can choose to view only part of your fields in a table and have them match certain criteria.

Working with Access

The primary purpose of this chapter is to introduce fundamental components and features of Access so that you may use them in productive ways. To accomplish this objective, we present several examples throughout the chapter. Although the examples are specific, the steps and procedures they present for developing databases, tables, forms, reports, and queries are generic and applicable to a variety of classroom management tasks and learning activities. As you work through the chapter's contents, substitute our examples with your own. *In addition, you can locate files that correspond to the chapter activities on the CD in the Access folder under Examples. Additional Let Me Try activities can be found on the CD in the Let Me Try Exercises folder.*

A Word About the Access Workspace

Unlike other Office products, Access requires that a database be created and saved prior to data entry. When you open the database program, you will find ribbons common to other Microsoft products; however, you are also presented with options when *Getting Started with Microsoft Access* is opened rather than a blank document, as in Word or Excel (see Figure 6.1).

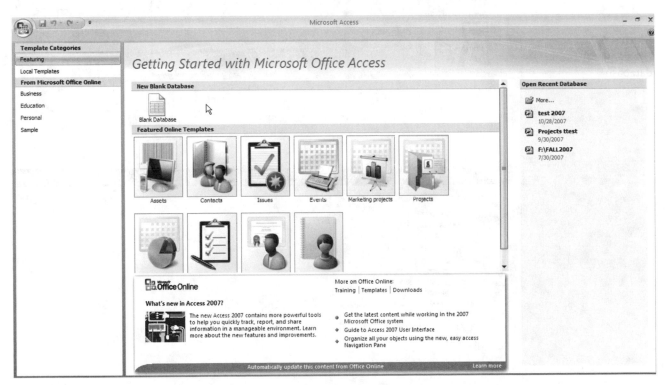

Figure 6.1
Access opening screen

There are several ways of starting a database. You may create a new blank database, open a recent database, or create a database using Featured Online Templates. When you create a database using the template, the database includes prebuilt tables and forms, reports, and queries. To give you an overview of the database, you will create a blank database. To do so, click on the Blank Database icon on the Getting Started window. You will type in the title for the database and click the Browse button to designate the exact location where the file will be saved on the computer (see Figure 6.2).

When you click on the Browse button, navigate to the folder or drive where you want to store the new file. In this example, the file will be stored on a removable disk. (see Figure 6.3).

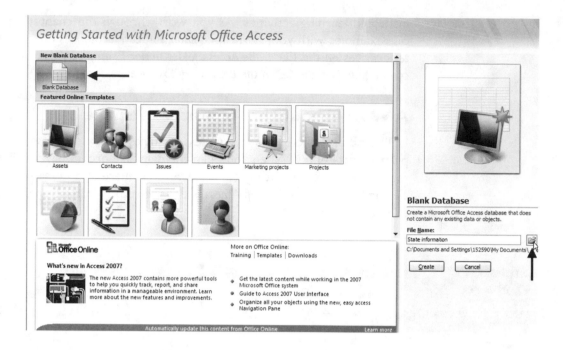

Figure 6.2
File name for blank
database

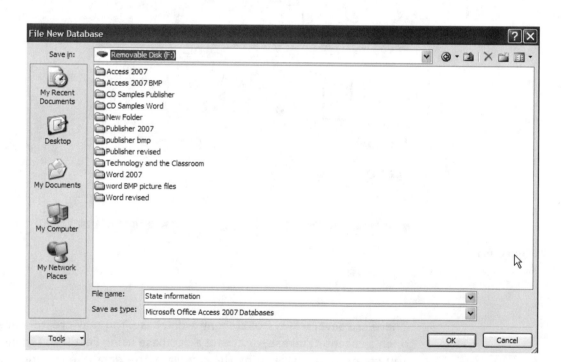

Figure 6.3
File New Database
removable disk

Show Me

1. Once you have clicked *OK* on the new file, click on the Create button on the
   Getting Started with Microsoft Access, and the software will create a database file
   with the file name indicated in the location you specified. It is a good idea to

use the browse capability when creating a database to ensure you know exactly where the file is saved so you may retrieve it at a later date. After the Create button has been clicked, a new table appears ready to input data (see Figure 6.4).

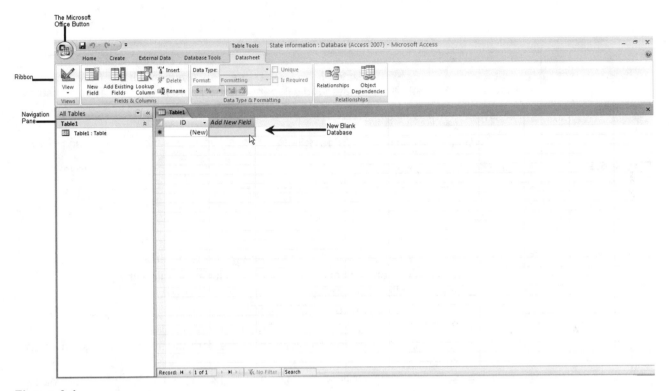

Figure 6.4
New table

2. By double-clicking on the *Add New Field* cell, you can add a label to the fields by typing in the information and pressing the Tab key. The fields you will want to add to this database include the following:
   - State
   - Capital
   - Date of statehood
   - Persons per square mile
   - Number of persons per family
   - Amusement parks
   - Fast-food restaurants
   - Toy stores

   To increase the width of the columns, place the mouse cursor between the columns at the field label and hold the left mouse button down and drag the column until it is the appropriate width (see Figure 6.5).
3. After the fields have all been identified, you can start to enter data in the respective fields. The data for this database should include the data in Figure 6.6.

   As with the other Office products, Access has a ribbon for navigation and production in the program. You will find the first tab on the Ribbon is Home.

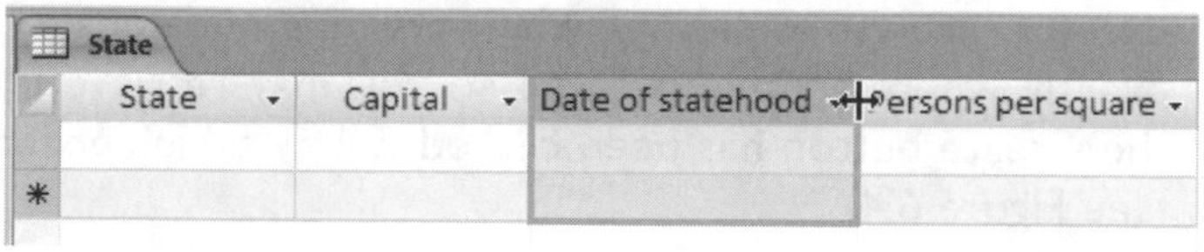

Figure 6.5
Width of column

State	Capital	Date of Statehood	Persons per square	Amusement parks	Fast food	Toy store
Pennsylvania	Harrisburg	1787	274	27	9739	459
Pennsylvania	Springfield	1818	223	14	10336	425
Colorado	Denver	1876	41	16	4262	250

Figure 6.6
Data for database

Within this tab, you will find some new options because of the structure of a database. The components of the ribbon include the following:

- Views—Allows you to see different views of the database
- Font—Allows you to modify the font, very similar to word processing
- Rich Text—Allows you to start bullets and numbered lists
- Records—Allows you to work with the data in the database, such as spell checking
- Sort and Filter—Allows you to alphabetize as well as filter and sort data
- Find—Allows you to find data, replace, and go to particular parts of the database (see Figure 6.7)

Figure 6.7
Access Home Ribbon

The next tab on the Ribbon is the Create tab. The options in this ribbon include the following:

- *Tables*—A new table can be created, templates used, or table design view shown
- *Forms*—Forms can be created: Pivot Chart and form design, among others
- *Report*—Creates a report from a wizard, report design, labels, or a blank report

■ Others include query information and macro options (see Figure 6.8)

The External Data tab on the Ribbon allows you to import information from other sources, export databases, collect data, and use SharePoint lists (see Figure 6.9). The Database Tools tab allows you to work with the database as a whole, working with macros, showing relationships among databases, analyzing information, moving data, and database tools, including encrypting databases with a password (see Figure 6.10).

Figure 6.8
Access Create tab

Figure 6.9
External Data tab

Figure 6.10
Database Tools tab

The Datasheet tab allows you to work with and modify the information in tables that have been created. View allows you to see the various views of the database; Fields & Columns allows you to add, delete, and rename columns and fields; Data Type & Formatting allows you to modify the type of data and how you format it (i.e., dollars or percentages). The Relationship component defines how data in the table are related to each other (see Figure 6.11).

4. The database created can generate a report of the information in the database for others to review. To start the process, click on the Create tab and then select *Report Wizard* (see Figure 6.12). As you create a report, you can select the table or query on which to base your report. Because you have only one

Figure 6.11
Datasheet tab

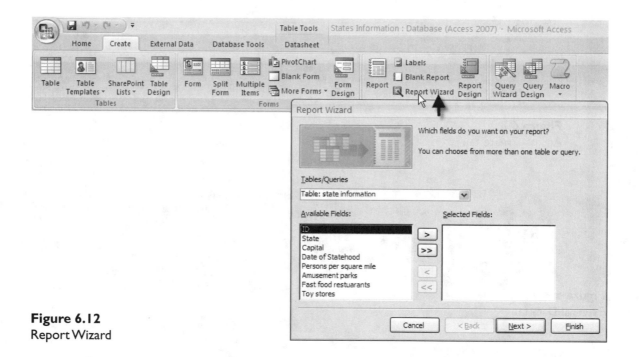

Figure 6.12
Report Wizard

report, there will be no other options to select to create a report. Select the *State, Persons per square mile, Amusement parks, Fast food restaurants*, and *Toy stores* fields.

5. After selecting the appropriate fields, click on the Next button to continue with the wizard to create the report (see Figure 6.13).

6. The Report Wizard will then ask if would like to have grouping levels and what field you would like to use. This allows you to have a particular field stand out above the rest of the information in that record. In this case, you do not want to group any of the fields, so click on the Next button (see Figure 6.14).

7. The next screen in building a report will ask what sort order you would like for your records. Select *State* from the listing, and you can select ascending or descending order from the listing. In this example, use ascending order (see Figure 6.15).

8. The next step is to select the layout of your report. In this case, you want to select *Tabular* as the layout for the report as well as *Portrait* for the orientation, making sure that there is a check in the box that adjusts the field

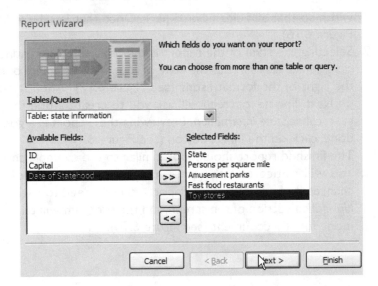

Figure 6.13
Selecting fields

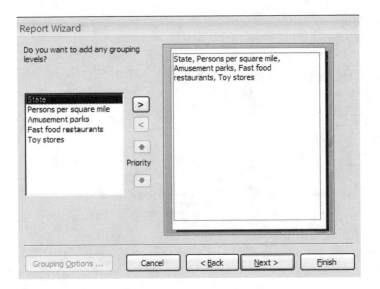

Figure 6.14
Grouping levels

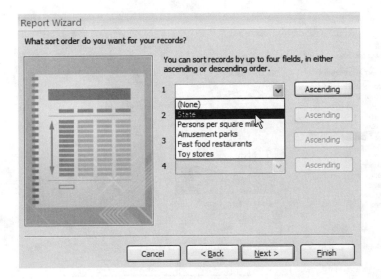

Figure 6.15
Order of records

width so that all fields fit on a page. Once that is selected, click on Next (see Figure 6.16).

9. Selecting the style of the report is the next step in creating the report. In this case, select *Concourse* as the style of report. An example of the style appears to the right of the format listing (see Figure 6.17). After selecting the style, click on *Next*. The next screen will ask you to create a title for your report. In this case, call it *state information*. Previewing the report is a good idea. Once this is done, click on the Finish button (see Figure 6.18).

10. The finished report should look similar to the example shown in Figure 6.19.

11. You will notice that the state names have been cut off. In order to make changes in the layout of the report, you will need to click on the report in the *Navigation* section of the screen, and the program will take you out of the print mode for the document (see Figure 6.20).

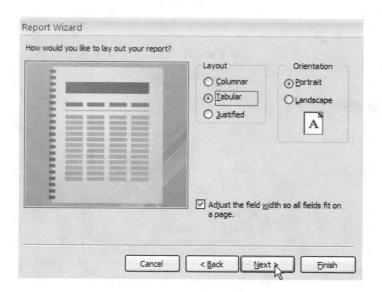

Figure 6.16
Layout of report

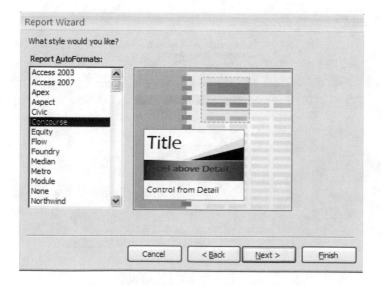

Figure 6.17
Selecting style
of report

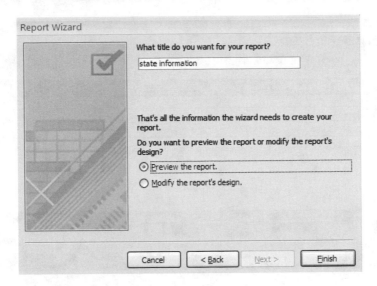

Figure 6.18
Title the report

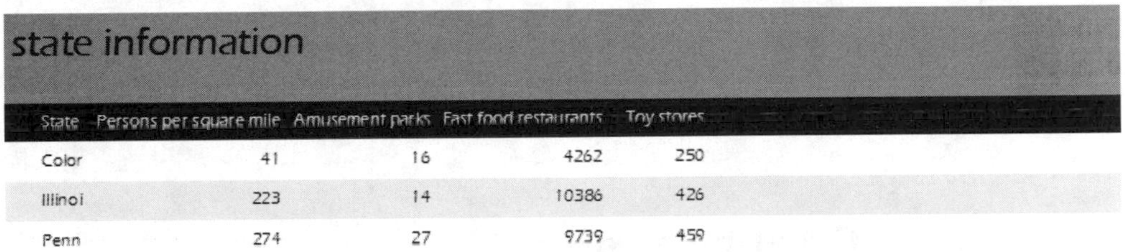

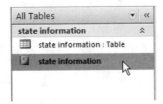

Figure 6.19
Finished report

Figure 6.20
Navigation pane

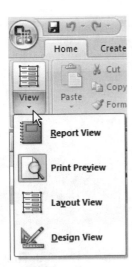

Figure 6.21
View menu

12. On the Home tab of the Ribbon, select *View* and from the pull-down menu select *Design View*. This will allow modification of the report to show the entire spelling of the state (see Figure 6.21).

13. In the design view, highlight the *State* field under Page Header and move the cursor until it turns into a double-sided arrow. At that time, hold down the left mouse button and drag the text box with *State* in it until you estimate enough space to allow for the entire state to be spelled out (see Figure 6.22).

14. After modifying the spacing, select the Report view from the View menu on the Home ribbon. The modified report should look similar to Figure 6.23.

15. You will want to save work periodically, just as a good practice. To save, click on the Office button and select *Save*.

16. To print this form click on the Office button and select Print. You will need to choose the printer connected or affiliated with your computer to print.

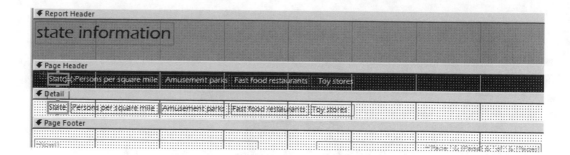

Figure 6.22
Design view

state information

State	Persons per square mile	Amusement parks	Fast food restaurants	Toy stores
Colorado	41	16	4262	250
Illinois	223	14	10386	426
Pennsylvania	274	27	9739	459

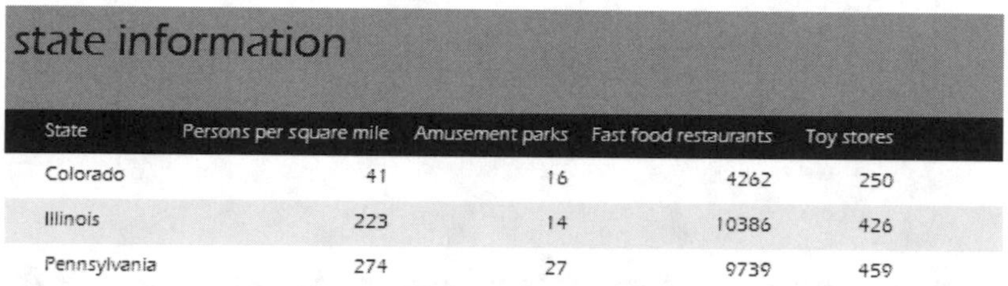

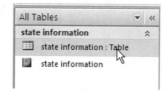

Figure 6.23
Modified report

Creating a Form

1. In the Navigation pane, open the table for State Information by double-clicking on the State Information table (see Figure 6.24).

Figure 6.24
Open a table

2. Once the table is open, click on the Create tab in the Ribbon. Within that tab, click on *Form* in order to create a form where individuals may enter data without seeing all the information at once (see Figure 6.25).

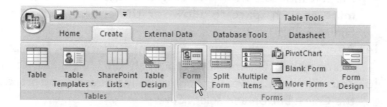

Figure 6.25
Creating a form

3. The program will create a form using the fields in the database opened. The data already in the table will appear, and the first record in the table will appear in the form (see Figure 6.26).

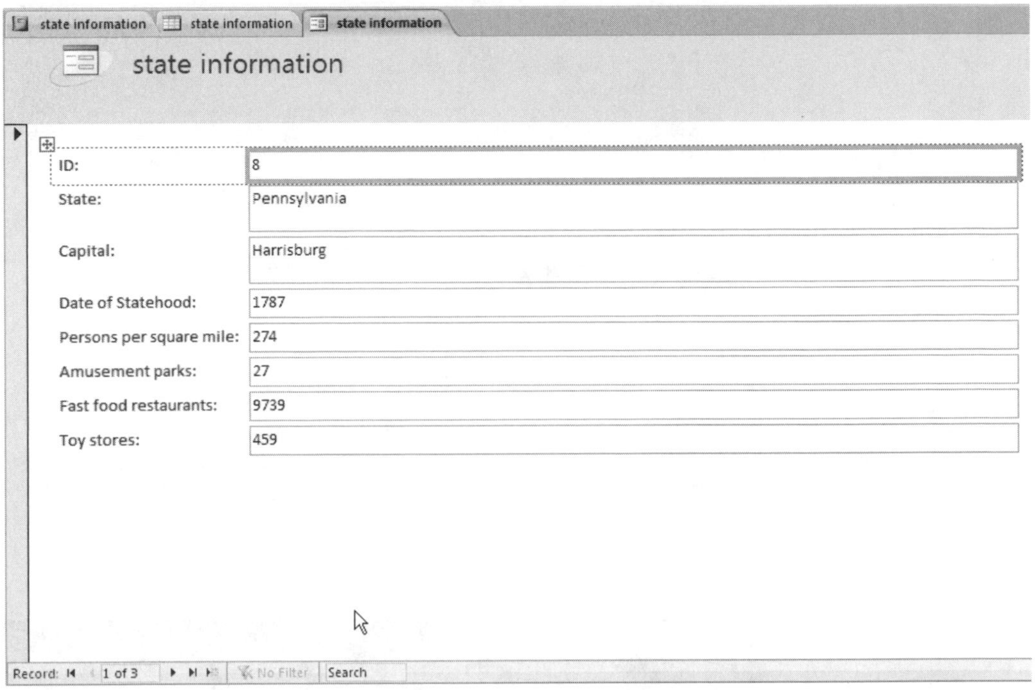

state information
state information
state information
state information
ID:
8
State:
Pennsylvania
Capital:
Harrisburg
Date of Statehood:
1787
Persons per square mile:
274
Amusement parks:
27
Fast food restaurants:
9739
Toy stores:
459
Record: 1 of 3
No Filter
Search

Figure 6.26
Form for state information

4. To go to the blank form to begin filling in new data, click on the bottom of the form on the arrow with a rectangle next to it, and that will take you to a new blank record form (see Figure 6.27).

Record: 1 of 3
No Filter
Search

Figure 6.27
New blank record

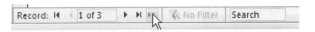

5. If you choose, you can create a form using Form Wizard and create a form that selects only certain fields in the database. To create such a form, click on *More Forms* and then select *Form Wizard* (see Figure 6.28).

Form
Split Form
Multiple Items
PivotChart
Blank Form
More Forms
Form Design
Form Wizard
Datasheet
Modal Dialog
PivotTable

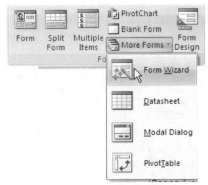

Figure 6.28
Opening Form Wizard

6. Once the Form Wizard is open, you can select the fields in which you would like to enter data using the form you are creating (see Figure 6.29).
7. By following the wizard, you will be able to create a form using only the fields you select for the database entry. The following is an example of what a form might look like based on the state information database created but using only part of the fields (see Figure 6.30).

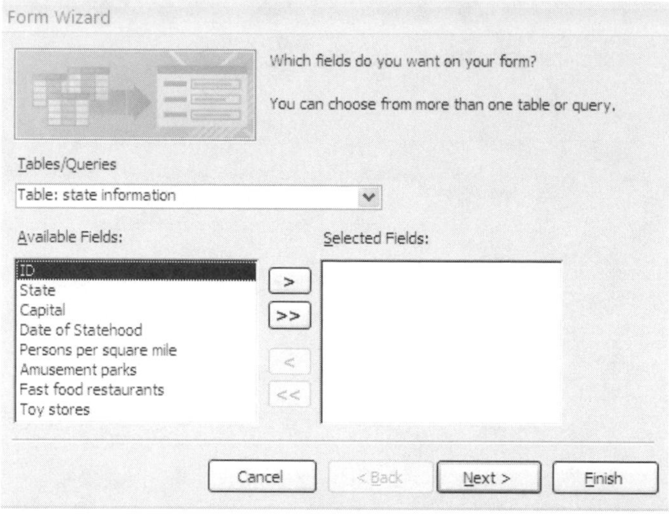

Figure 6.29
Form Wizard

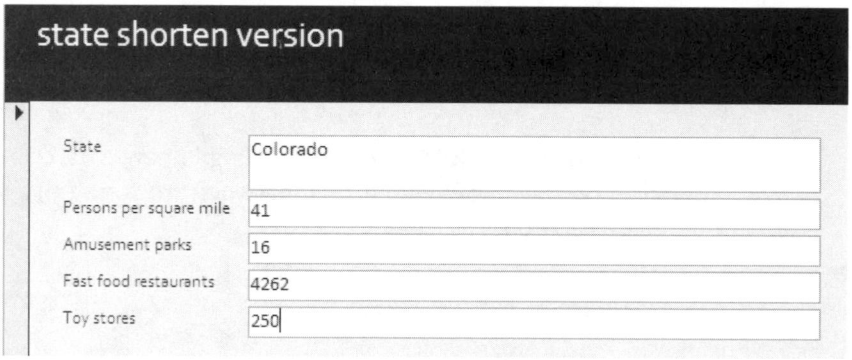

Figure 6.30
Wizard-created form

8. You will want to save work periodically, just as a good practice. To save, click on the Office button and select *Save*.
9. To close out of this database, click on the Office button and select *Close*.

LET METRY

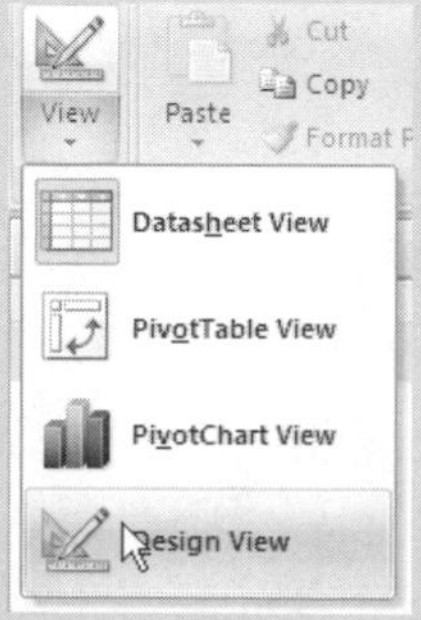

Figure 6.31
Design view

So far, you have opened Access, created a database from a blank database, created a table with data, and created a report using that data. You have also modified the spacing on the report in Design view. You now have the opportunity to create a new database from a blank database.

1. Open Access and create a new blank database.
2. Name the new database *Volcanic Activity* and browse to save it in a location where you can find it, then click on *Create*.
3. A new database table is then created ready for you to name the fields of the database.
4. Click on *Design View* under the *View* section on the Home ribbon (see Figure 6.31).

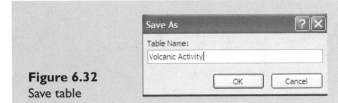

Figure 6.32
Save table

5. Before going into the Design view you are asked to save the table created. Title the table *Volcanic Activity* (see Figure 6.32) and click *OK*.

6. Once the table has been saved, the table will appear in the Design view. This view is another way of designing the database and allows you to select the type of data that goes into each field. Also, *Primary Key* is a field that is typically automatically set. The primary key is a column that is used to uniquely identify each row. You can arrow down past the primary key to the first field name that you will specify. The first field name will be *Volcano*; type that in the *Field* column, and then press the Tab Key to tab to the data type (see Figure 6.33).

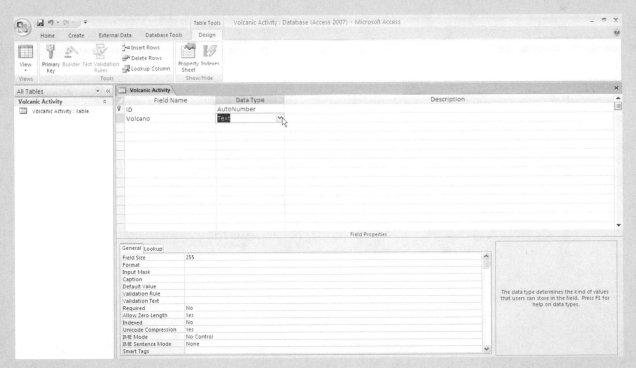

Figure 6.33
Design view

7. You will see that once you type in *Volcano* and press the Tab Key, the data type will automatically come up text and the field properties will be displayed below. This is where you may modify the field size or other properties found in the *Field Properties* section. Tab through until you are at the next field name.

8. The next field name will be named *Year Significant Eruption*, and under Data Type select *Number*. You do not want *Date/Time* because the data you have will be only in the year format (see Figure 6.34).

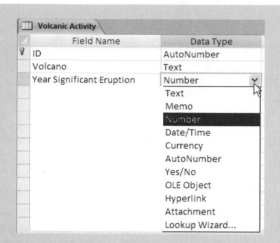

Figure 6.34
Year field

9. The finished field names and data type should look like the following (see Figure 6.35).

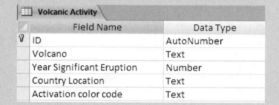

Figure 6.35
Field name and types of data

10. In order to see all the field names in the table, on the Home tab of the Ribbon, select *More* in the records section of the Ribbon and select *Column Width* (see Figure 6.36) and then select *Best Fit* (see Figure 6.37).

Figure 6.37
Best Fit

Figure 6.36
Column Width

11. The data that should be entered into the table should look like the following (see Figure 6.38).
12. Once all the data are in, you can work on sorting and filtering the records. Highlight the *Year of Significant Eruption* column and select *A to Z* in the filter section. The

Volcano	Year Significant Eruption	Country Location	Activation c
Cikurachki	2005	Russia	Orange
Kerinci	2004	Indonesia	not available
Ol Doinyo Legai	2006	Tanzania	not available
Pavlof	1997	USA, Alaksa	Orange
Arenal	2007	Costa Rica	not available
Cleveland	2006	USA, Chuginak Island,	Yellow
Karymsky	2007	Russia, Kamchatka	Orange
Kilauea	2007	USA, Hawaii	not available
Pacaya	2005	Guatemala	not available
Poas	1996	Costa Rica	not available
Rabaul	2007	New Guinea, Papua	not available
Sangay	2007	Ecuador	not available
Shiveluch	2007	Russia, Kamchatka	Orange
Soufriere Hills	2007	West Indies, Montser	4 on a 5 point s
Mount St. Helens	2007	USA	not available
Liama	2003	Chile	not available
Sakura-Jima	2007	Japan, Kyushu	not available

Figure 6.38
Data for Volcanic
Activity database

dates are now arranged in chronological order; you will notice the rest of the field followed the date as they were rearranged (see Figure 6.39).

13. In the Table view, select the Create tab of the Ribbon and select *Query Wizard*. The simple query will sort out information on the field that you specify.

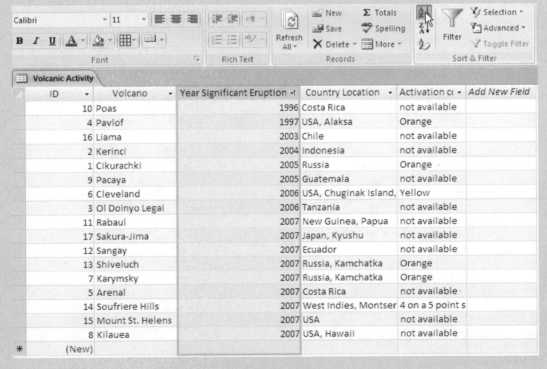

Figure 6.39
Arrange dates

Queries can be a very powerful tool, but we will just go over the basics in this illustration. Once you select *Query Wizard*, you will be asked what kind of Query Wizard you want to run; in this case, select *Simple Query Wizard* and click *OK*. You will now have an opportunity to select what table you would like to query. In this case, it is the Volcanic Activities table, and you are asked to select what field you would like to query. Select *Year Significant Eruption* and *Country Location* (see Figure 6.40). After those are selected, click on *Next*.

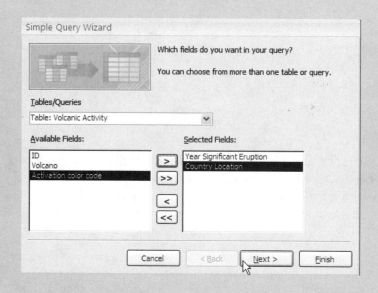

Figure 6.40
Selecting query
fields

Country Location	Year Significant Eruption
Russia	2005
Indonesia	2004
Tanzania	2006
USA, Alaksa	1997
Costa Rica	2007
USA, Chuginak Island,	2006
Russia, Kamchatka	2007
USA, Hawaii	2007
Guatemala	2005
Costa Rica	1996
New Guinea, Papua	2007
Ecuador	2007
Russia, Kamchatka	2007
West Indies, Montser	2007
USA	2007
Chile	2003
Japan, Kyushu	2007

Figure 6.41
Finished query

14. The wizard will ask whether you would like a detailed or a summary query. In this case, you want a detailed summary. Click on *Next*. You will then be asked to title the query; use the title *Volcanic Activity Query* and open the query to view the information and click on *Finish*. The completed query should show only the fields selected (see Figure 6.41). You can create a report of the query if you wish and follow the steps for creating a report, as outlined earlier in this chapter.
15. You will want to save work periodically, just as a good practice. To save, click on the Office button and select *Save*.
16. To close out of this database, select the Office button and select *Close*.

Show Me

Creating a Database Using a Template

Access 2007 has online templates that allow you to have databases created with forms and reports already created for you. If you do not have access to the Internet, you will need to click on *Local Templates* under Template Categories. To start the process, click on the Student template; name the database *Students in My Class* and browse to make sure you know where the database is being saved, and click on *Create* (see Figure 6.42).

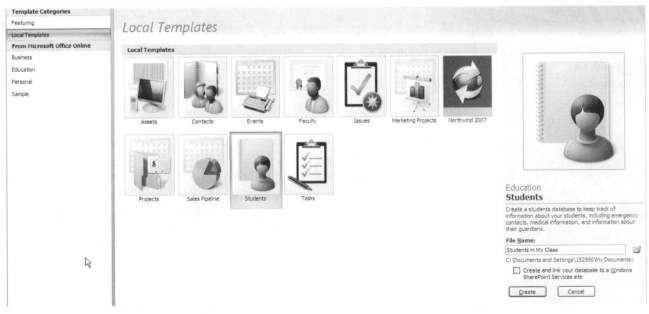

Figure 6.42
Using a template

Once you click on *Create*, Microsoft Office downloads or prepares the database for your use, creating a table, forms, and reports of the database created (see Figure 6.43).

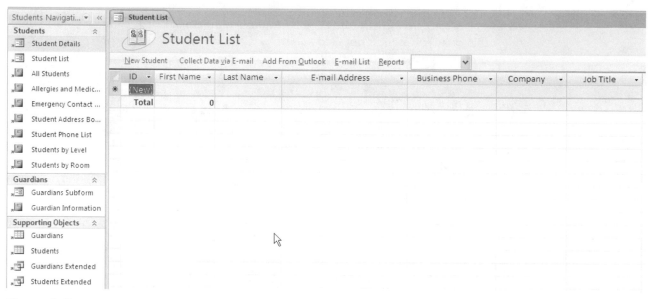

Figure 6.43
Template created database

When the template is downloaded, you have ways of entering data also included in the template. You can access these by clicking on the titles above the table on the Student List. In this example, select *New Student* (see Figure 6.44).

Figure 6.44
Data input

By clicking on *New Student*, a form appears to input data. Include the following data in the forms for these students (see Figure 6.45).

Now explore the forms, reports, and materials already created that have been populated once data have been placed in the database. You will want to save work periodically, just as a good practice. To save, click on the Office button and select *Save*. To close out of this database, select the Office button and select *Close*.

Last Name	First Name	E-mail Address	Level	Room	Date of	Home Phone	Mobile	Address	City	Sta	ZIP/Post
Aster	Helen	Aster@ ourschool.com	8th Grade	2148	5/5/1997	531-8836		449 Green	Charleston	IL	61912
Beckett	LeRoy	lbeckett@myschool.us	7th Grade	2148	6/5/1997	531-4618	531-4619	18 Chad Drive	Ashmore	IL	61920
Birch	Anthony	abirch@my school.us	Freshman	2146	7/5/1996	531-2330	531-2331	159 Chestnut	Asmore	IL	61020
Bonzi	Rebecca	rbonzi@myschool.k12.us	7th Grade	2148	3/5/1997	531-4775	531-1000	760 Court	Mattoon	IL	61738
Campbell	Kelly	kcampbell@ourschool.il.	8th Grade	2147	1/30/1996	531-5483	531-3311	936 Oak	Charleston	IL	61912
Gong	Lori	lgong@myschool.net	7th Grade	2148	6/5/1997	531-2511	531-2568	718 Lincoln Ave	Charleston	IL	61912
Kay	Monica	mkay@myschool.net	Freshman	2146	4/5/1996	531-2411	531-2103	214 Madison	Ashmore	IL	61920
Lando	Joy	jlando@myschool.k12.us	7th Grade	2148	4/5/1997	531-9832	531-9833	410 Orchard La	Charleston	IL	61912
Lawyer	Livingston	llawyer@myschoo.us	Freshman	2146	8/5/1996	531-5249	531-5348	1440 18th Stree	Charleston	IL	61929
Montalto	Juan	jmontalto@myschool.ne	Freshman	2146	9/30/1996	531-3195	531-8927	144 Ashby	Ashmore	IL	61920

Figure 6.45
Student data

LET ME TRY

Mail Merge

Databases can be used to insert information into letters that you write using Word, perhaps to personalize a letter. In order to perform the Mail Merge function in Word, you will be using the database you just developed: Students in My Class.

1. Open Microsoft Word and a new blank document.
2. Select the Mailings tab and select *Start Mail Merge* and select from the listing *Step by Step Mail Merge Wizard* (see Figure 6.46).

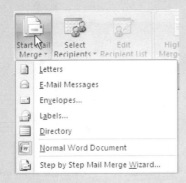

Figure 6.46
Starting a mail merge

3. The Mail Merge Wizard pane will appear along the right side of the Word document. Select *Letters* from the listing of documents you want to work on. At the very bottom of the pane, you will have directions as what to do next in the mail merge by clicking *Next: Starting document* and then an action. To proceed with this action, click on the directions, and you will go to the next step in the wizard (see Figure 6.47).
4. After clicking on *Next: Starting document*, the next pane of the wizard will appear; select *Use the current document* from the list and then click on *Select recipients* at the bottom of the pane (see Figure 6.48).
5. In the next pane, you will want to select *Use an existing list* and then click on *Browse* to find the database that you created (see Figure 6.49).
6. Once you select *Browse*, you will need to remember where you placed the file for Students in My Class.
7. The database is selected from the source by highlighting it and then clicking on *Open* (see Figure 6.50).
8. Once you open the database, it will give you several items to choose from. In this case, you will want to select *Students* in the table format (see Figure 6.51).
9. After selecting the table, you will be asked to select mail merge recipients. In this case, you want to select all recipients; you will note they all have a checkmark in front of the last name to deselect individuals. Click on the box and remove the checkmark. You can also refine the recipient list by sorting or finding duplicates in the list. In this case, just click on *OK* (see Figure 6.52).
10. The next step in the wizard is to write the letter; you will want to insert an address block. To do so, click on *Address block* (see Figure 6.53).

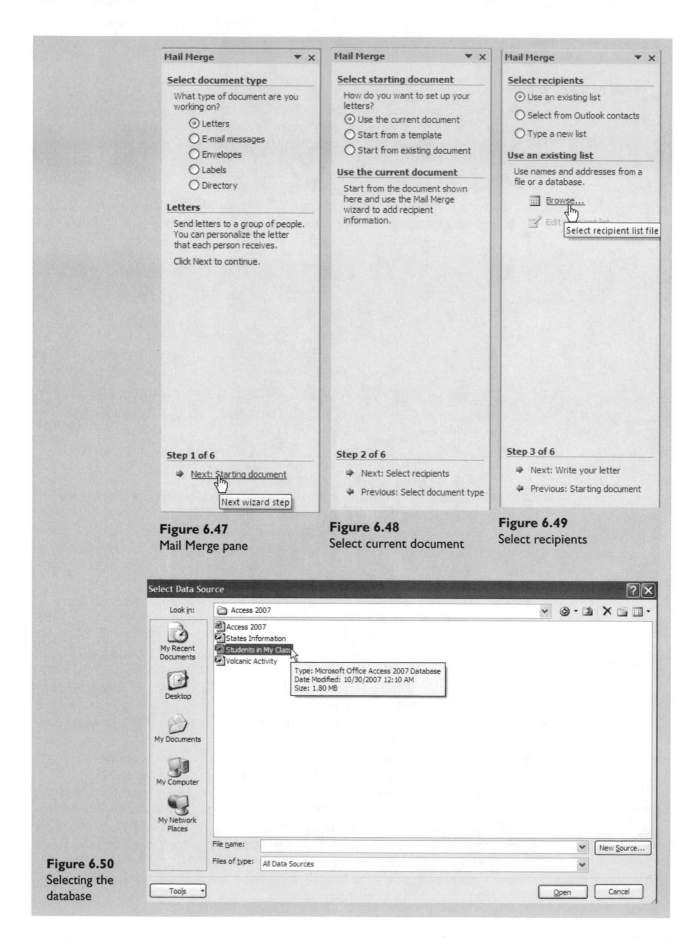

Figure 6.47
Mail Merge pane

Figure 6.48
Select current document

Figure 6.49
Select recipients

Figure 6.50
Selecting the
database

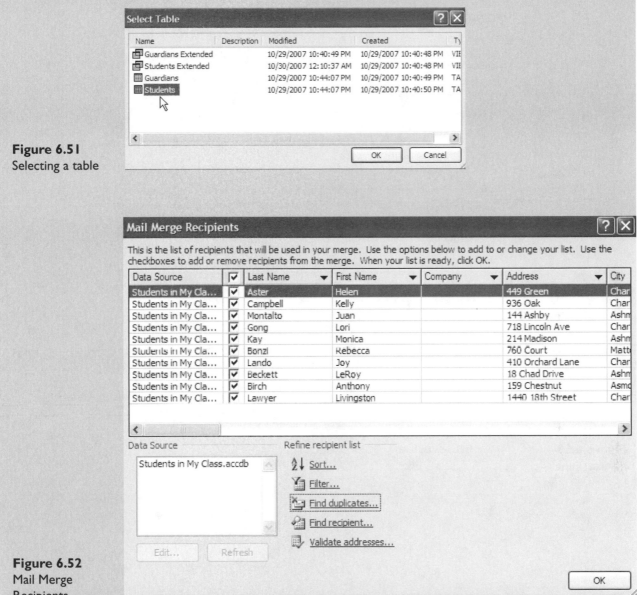

Figure 6.51
Selecting a table

Figure 6.52
Mail Merge
Recipients

11. The address block will give you options of what the address will look like and give you a preview of the address. You will notice that there is no state noted in the address previewed, which means the field needs to be matched with the database. Click on *Match Fields* (see Figure 6.54).

12. The matching fields will allow you to match the address component with the field in the database. Select *State/Province* from the list provided and click *OK* (see Figure 6.55).

13. Press Enter three times and then insert the greeting line from the listing and press Enter again. The body of the letter should look like the following figure (see Figure 6.56). The e-mail address is also a component that you want in the letter; click on *More items*.

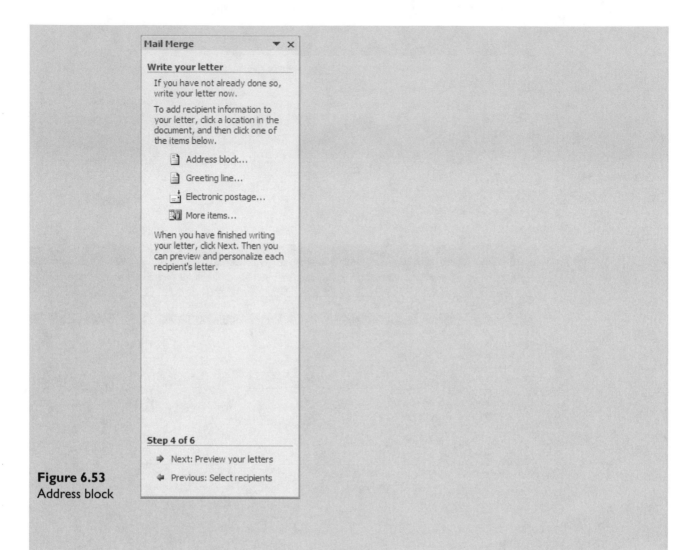

Figure 6.53
Address block

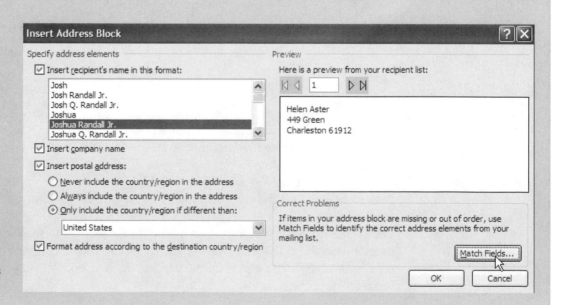

Figure 6.54
Specify address
elements

Match Fields   [?][X]

In order to use special features, Mail Merge needs to know which fields in your recipient list match to the required fields. Use the drop-down list to select the appropriate recipient list field for each address field component

Required for Address Block

First Name	First Name
Last Name	Last Name
Suffix	(not matched)
Company	Company
Address 1	Address
Address 2	(not matched)
City	City
State	(not matched)
Postal Code	ZIP/Postal Code
Country or Region	Country/Region

Optional information

Unique Identifier	ID

Use the drop-down lists to choose the field from your database that corresponds to the address information Mail Merge expects (listed on the left.)

☐ Remember this matching for this set of data sources on this computer

[OK]   [Cancel]

Figure 6.55
Matching fields

Figure 6.56
Writing the letter

14. From the *More items* list, select *E-mail Address* (see Figure 6.57) and click on *Insert*. Then click on *Cancel* in order to go back to the letter.

15. Continue writing the letter until complete and then click on *Next: Preview your letters* in the wizard page (see Figure 6.58).

16. The information in the first record of the database will be presented in your letter. Once that is done, you may click on *Next: Complete the merge*. This will create letters for each of the recipients in the database (see Figure 6.59)

17. To print your letters, click on *Print* in the Wizard pane and select the printer associated with your computer. You can at that time elect how many of the mail-merged letters you would like to print (see Figure 6.60).

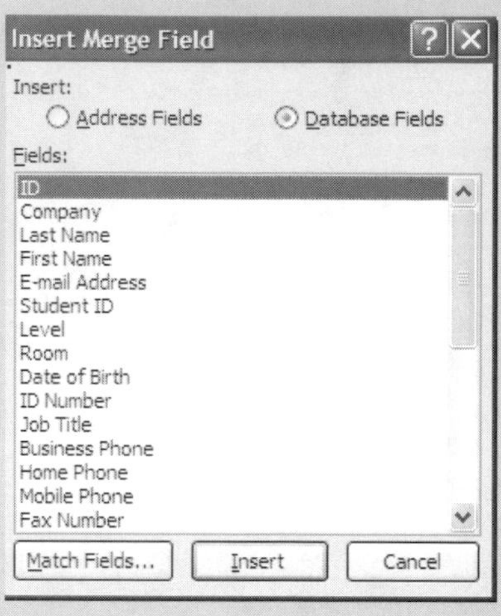

Insert Merge Field

Insert:
- ○ Address Fields ◉ Database Fields

Fields:

> ID
> Company
> Last Name
> First Name
> E-mail Address
> Student ID
> Level
> Room
> Date of Birth
> ID Number
> Job Title
> Business Phone
> Home Phone
> Mobile Phone
> Fax Number

[Match Fields...] [Insert] [Cancel]

Figure 6.57
Insert Merge Field

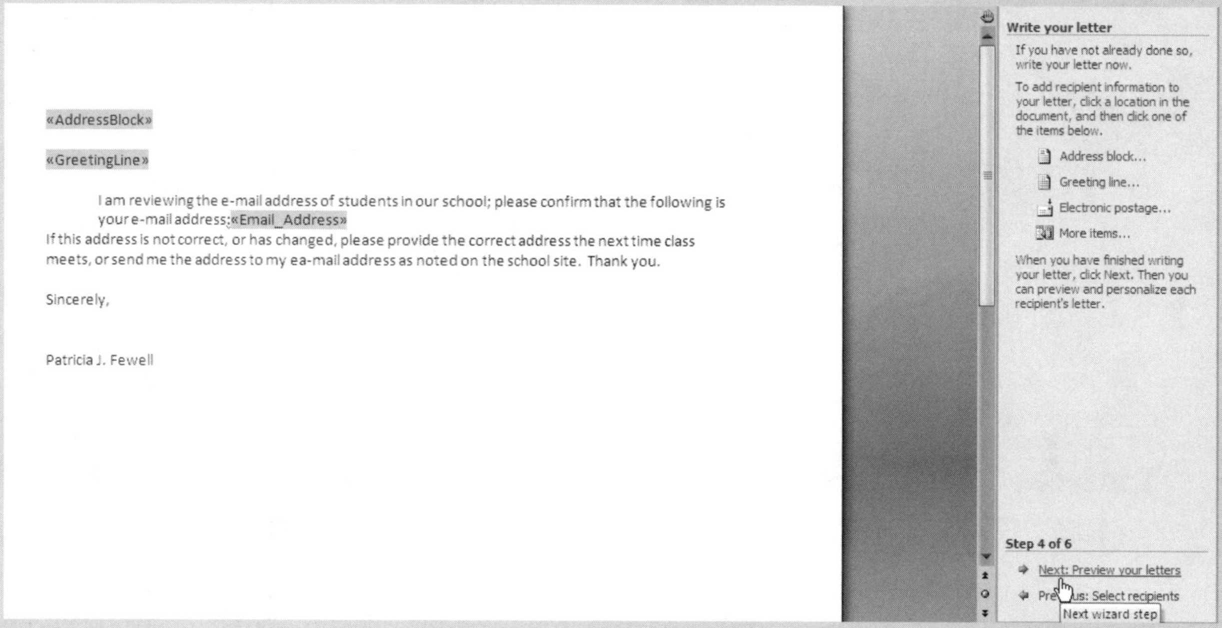

«AddressBlock»

«GreetingLine»

I am reviewing the e-mail address of students in our school; please confirm that the following is your e-mail address: «Email_Address»
If this address is not correct, or has changed, please provide the correct address the next time class meets, or send me the address to my ea-mail address as noted on the school site. Thank you.

Sincerely,

Patricia J. Fewell

Write your letter

If you have not already done so, write your letter now.

To add recipient information to your letter, click a location in the document, and then click one of the items below.

- Address block...
- Greeting line...
- Electronic postage...
- More items...

When you have finished writing your letter, click Next. Then you can preview and personalize each recipient's letter.

Step 4 of 6

→ Next: Preview your letters
← Previous: Select recipients

Next wizard step

Figure 6.58
Preview your letters

18. At this time, it would be a good idea to click on the Microsoft Office button and select *Save* to save the document in the appropriate storage item associated with your computer (i.e., My Documents).

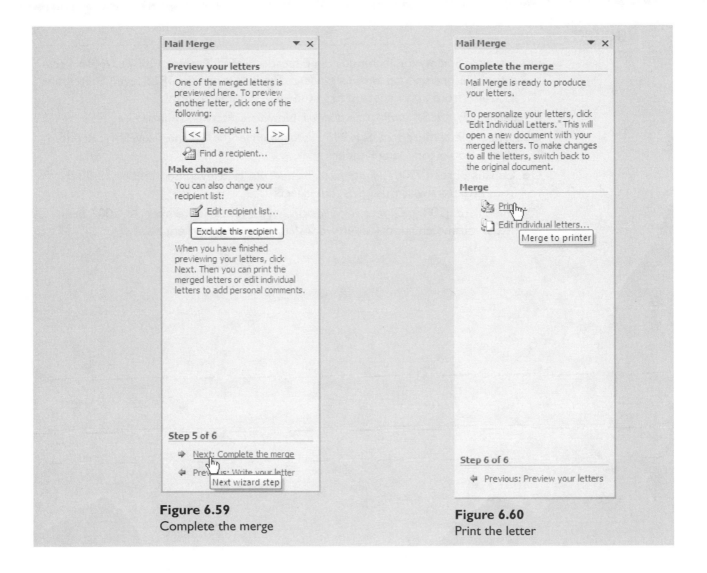

Figure 6.59
Complete the merge

Figure 6.60
Print the letter

A CHALLENGE USING ACCESS 2007

For those of you who would like a challenge beyond the Let Me Try activities presented in this chapter, try the following exercises.

1. Create a database about the characters of a book you have recently read. Fields could include character name, gender, characteristics, and role in the book.
2. Create a database of all the plants that are in and around the school building, including the common name, scientific name, where these plants may be found, and descriptions of the plants.

TYING IT ALL TOGETHER

In this chapter, you created three Access databases. You produced tables, forms, reports, queries, and mail merges from these databases. All these objects were saved to a data source. The reports and mail merge were printed.

REFERENCES

International Society for Technology in Education NETS Project. (2007). *National educational technology standards for students: The next generation.* Retrieved September 21, 2007, from http://cnets.iste.rg/students/s_standards.html

MacLachlan, P. (1985). *Sarah, plain and tall.* New York: HarperCollins.

Osborne, M. P., & Murdocca, S. (1998). *Vacation under the volcano.* New York: Random House Books for Young Readers.

U.S. Census Bureau. (2007). *State facts for students.* Retrieved September 28, 2007, from http://www.census.gov/schools/facts

Volcanic Word. (2007). *Current volcanic activity.* Retrieved September 28, 2007, from http://volcano.und.nodak.edu/vwdocs/current_volcs/current.html

CHAPTER OUTLINE

LEARNING OBJECTIVES

At the completion of this chapter you will be able to:

- Display a summary of the current day using Outlook Today
- Send an e-mail message
- Check incoming e-mail messages
- Construct a calendar
- Create an address book using Contacts
- Create several reminder notes
- Delete unwanted items in folders

CHAPTER OVERVIEW

This chapter provides an introduction to Outlook 2007. The content focuses on the fundamentals of using the tools in the Outlook program and applying them to a variety of learning activities. When you open Outlook, you will notice the Inbox, Calendar, Contacts, Tasks, Notes, and Journal. These are the features that you will most likely use and are examined in the chapter. The Show Me section presents instructions on using many of these features so that you feel comfortable using the calendar to schedule events, sending e-mail to students and parents, and creating a task list for yourself and your students. Several Let Me Try student-oriented exercises give specific examples and step-by-step instructions for using Outlook 2007 to accomplish a variety of learning activities. Studying the chapter content and working through the Let Me Try exercises will enable you to use several of the tools found in the program.

How Teachers and Students Can Use Outlook

Microsoft Outlook differs in many respects from the other Office products because it is not primarily a materials development or analysis tool. However, it can be used in innovative ways to support various educational activities that benefit students and teachers. Following are a few examples of how Outlook can be used to support instruction reflective of types of learning outcomes and the National Educational Technology Standards for Students. Looking first at types of learning, the following items identify ways Outlook can be used by students:

- *Knowledge*—(a) Students can create a contact list of all important people in a particular area of study and note key facts about specific individuals. (b) Students can create a contact list of historical figures. The contact list could include titles, addresses, first and last names, employment, and so on. (c) Students can create a calendar of key historical dates and the events that took place at a particular time in history.
- *Comprehension*—(a) Using an e-mail account set up by the teacher, students can compose a fictitious e-mail to a famous historical figure (e.g., Abraham Lincoln). The e-mail could relate to the student's understanding of an important issue taking place at that period in time. Students could explore such issues as what to write in the e-mail and how to write it.
- *Application*—(a) Students can e-mail pen pals from other countries and explain important precepts of our form of government and political system.
- *Analysis*—(a) Students can e-mail pen pals from other countries and explore and discuss political and cultural similarities and differences.

NETS for Students*

Applications of Outlook to educational activities could address the following:

- Communication and collaboration—Students use mediated materials to communicate and engage with one another and to support each other's learning.
- Research and information fluency—Students apply digital tools to gather, evaluate, and use information.

*Reprinted with permission from *National Educational Technology Standards for Students, Second Edition*, © 2007, ISTE® (International Society for Technology in Education), www.iste.org. All rights reserved.

About Outlook

Outlook is an electronic management system that enables you to keep a calendar, send and receive e-mail, create a list of activities, and maintain an address book. In many ways, Outlook is an electronic day planner.

As a teacher, you can use Outlook for a variety of activities in your classroom. It will help you keep track of appointments with parents, faculty meetings, and state testing dates. You can use it to indicate your classroom activities for parents and students.

Working with Outlook

The primary purpose of this chapter is to help you become familiar with the fundamental components and features of Outlook 2007 so that you will use them in productive ways in your classes and with students. To accomplish this objective, we present several examples that will help you learn the components of Outlook and apply them to your teaching and learning activities. Although the examples here may be specific, the steps and procedures are generic and applicable to a variety of classroom management tasks and learning activities. As you work through the chapter's content, substitute our examples with your own.

A Word About the Outlook Workspace

Unlike other Office programs, Outlook has essentially five different tools that allow you to create calendars and lists of things to do, make appointment lists, send and receive e-mail, and create electronic sticky notes. You have folders that are automatically set up as your personal folders along the left side of the screen (see Figure 7.1). These folders include the following:

- Calendar—Your personal calendar
- Contacts—Personal contacts

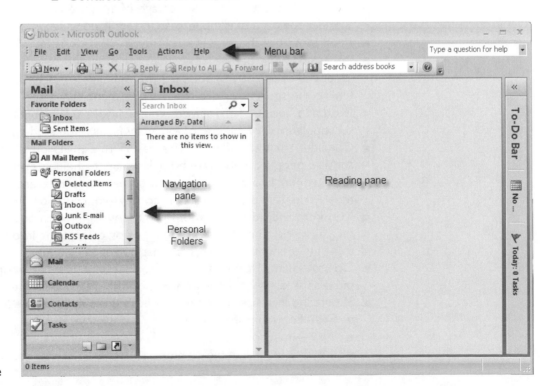

Figure 7.1
Outlook workspace

- Deleted items—Items you have deleted are stored until permanently deleted
- Drafts—Saved e-mail messages you have not finished are stored here temporarily
- Inbox—Where all incoming mail comes in
- Junk e-mail—Mail you have designated as junk e-mail is stored here
- Notes—Notes to yourself can be stored here
- Outbox—Mail waiting to be sent is kept here until it is mailed
- Sent Items—Messages sent out are saved here
- Tasks—Your to-do list
- Search Folders—Contain results of searches you have conducted in your personal folders

The Outlook folders do not correspond to folders on your hard drive; their contents are not individual files.

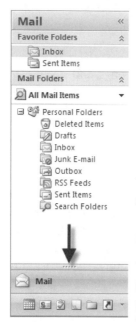

Figure 7.2
Navigation pane

Using the Navigation Pane

The Folder list is really one pane of the Navigation pane. You may modify the size of the Navigation pane by clicking and dragging the thin bar. If you drag it up to shrink the pane, you will see larger buttons on the Navigation pane. If you drag it down, the buttons are replaced by small icons at the bottom of the Navigation pane (see Figure 7.2).

E-Mail Netiquette

Using the Internet for e-mail is unique and, in many ways, differs from sending handwritten notes, talking on the telephone, or talking face-to-face. Keep the following in mind as you compose e-mail messages:

- Do not compose an e-mail message of all uppercase letters. In the electronic world, a message of all uppercase letters is considered shouting.
- Keep messages short.
- Remember that people other than the intended recipient may read the message. The recipient may forward the message to individuals unknown to you. Unlike the spoken word, e-mail is permanent.
- Read and become familiar with your school's acceptable use policy. There may be stipulations for the use of e-mail by faculty and students.
- Consider the tone of your messages. With e-mail, you are not personally present, so people cannot note body language to help interpret what you are saying. You may know how you want someone to interpret a message, but you must write it in the manner that conveys your intended meaning.
- Know the individuals to whom you are writing when possible. If you are chatting, lurk (watch in the background) prior to entering into the conversation.
- E-mail is the written word; grammar and spelling count.
- Do not "flame" other individuals. "Flaming" is what people do when they express strongly held opinions without holding back any emotion.
- Shorthand language used by some individuals includes the following:
  - FYI—For your information
  - IMO—In my opinion
  - IMHO—In my humble opinion

- BTW—By the way
- LOL—Laugh out loud
- FWIW—For what it's worth

Show Me

The Inbox

1. To use e-mail in Outlook, open Outlook 2007. The first time you open Outlook, a wizard appears to help you set it up. Click the Start button on the Windows taskbar. On the Start menu, move the mouse pointer over *All Programs*, and the Programs submenu appears. Move the mouse over *Microsoft Office*, and the Microsoft Office submenu appears. Click *Microsoft Outlook* to open the program. *Note:* Depending on how you installed Outlook 2007, the menu items for it may be located in various locations on the Start menu.

2. To read an e-mail message, click on *Mail* along the Navigation pane. Click *Inbox* to view the messages you have received. As you click on the message you would like to read from the Inbox, the message will appear in the Reading pane. All messages in your Inbox will be displayed in the Message pane (center pane), and the current message you have selected will be displayed in the Display pane on the right (see Figure 7.3).

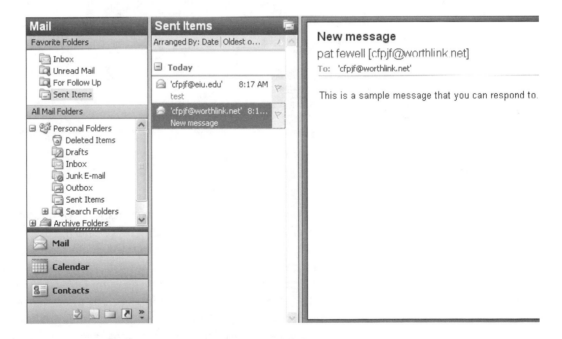

Figure 7.3
Display pane

3. You can double-click on the message to have it appear in the Read pane. You have the ability to forward, reply, reply to all, or delete messages.

Sending E-Mail

1. To send a message, you must know the e-mail address of the individual you want to contact. *There are netiquette issues you should be aware of when sending e-mail messages as mentioned previously in this chapter.*

2. To send an e-mail, select *New* from the File menu and then select *Mail Message* (see Figure 7.4).

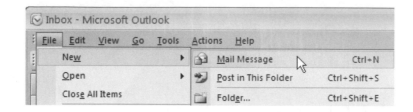

Figure 7.4
Mail message

3. The screen shown in Figure 7.5 will appear. Type the e-mail address of the person to whom you are sending the message in the space next to the *To* line.
4. If you want to send a message to more than one individual, separate each e-mail address with a semicolon (;).
5. To send a courtesy copy of the e-mail to an individual, type that address in the *Cc* space.
6. E-mail messages should have a subject so that the recipient knows what the message is about. Type a subject for the message in the *Subject* line.
7. In the empty screen below the *Subject* line, type your e-mail message (see Figure 7.5).

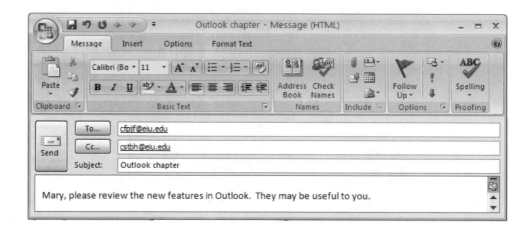

Figure 7.5
Message screen

8. When sending a message, you can rank its level of importance to provide the recipient an indication of how quickly he or she needs to attend to it. In addition, you can flag the message for follow-up. These features are available on the Message tab of the Ribbon in the Options group (see Figure 7.6). In addition, by clicking the Options tab and selecting *Delay Delivery* or *Direct Replies to* in the More Options group, you can rank the importance of the message, set its sensitivity (Normal, Personal, Private, Confidential) and delivery options, and request a response from the recipient (see Figure 7.7).

Figure 7.6
Options group

9. Files can be attached to e-mail messages. Attachments may include documents, pictures, and video or audio clips. Keep in mind that to read the attached file, the recipient must have the appropriate software installed on his or her computer.

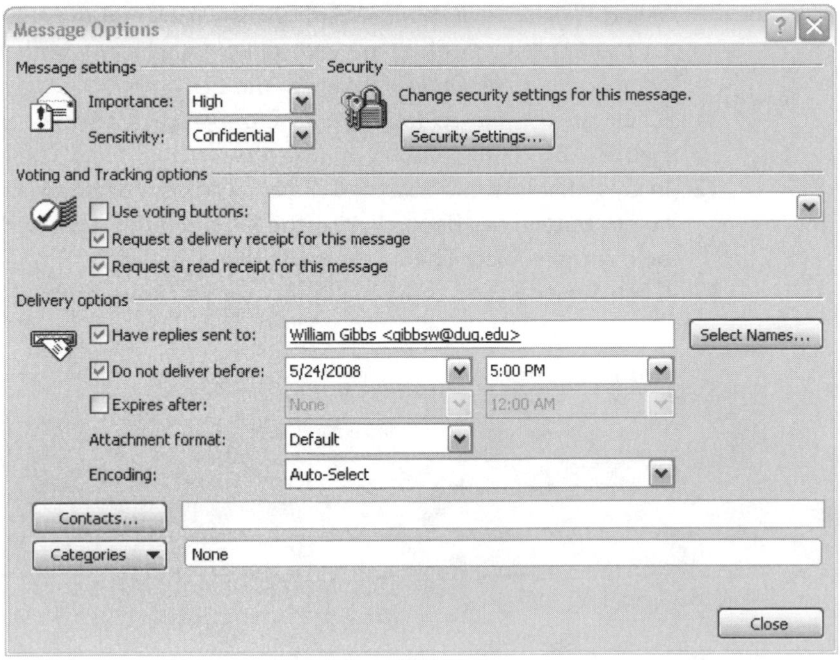

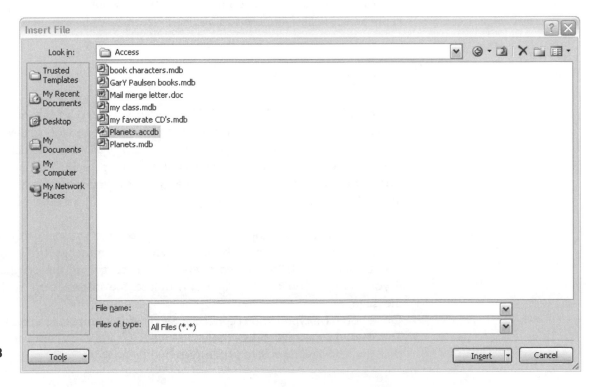

Figure 7.7
Message options

Files can be attached to e-mail messages in several ways. On the Message window, click the Insert tab and then click *Attach File* (the paper clip icon) in the Include group, or on the Message tab in the Include group click *Attach File* (see Figure 7.6).

10. After clicking on *Attach File,* the Insert File window displays for you to indicate the file path to your attachment. Select files that are on any of the drives to which you have access. In Figure 7.8, the attachment is on the C: drive, and it is

Figure 7.8
Insert file

called *Planets.accdb. You* can find *"Planets.accdb"* in the Access folder in *"Examples"* on the CD. You can also practice sending attachments with the *"Hershey and chip"* photograph in the Outlook folder on the CD.

11. Click on the file to highlight it. Double-click the file or click on *Insert* (see Figure 7.8).

12. In this example, the attached file is an Access database titled *Planets.* Once the Insert button has been clicked, the file becomes attached and its name appears below the subject line of the e-mail (see Figure 7.9).

13. Click *Send* to send the e-mail message you have created with the attachment.

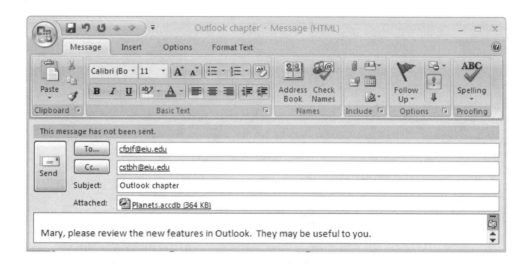

Figure 7.9
Attachment

Replying to and Forwarding Messages

1. When you receive messages, you may want to reply to them. Click *Inbox* under Personal Folders and select a message from your Inbox to which you want to reply. Select *Reply* from the toolbar (see Figure 7.10).

Figure 7.10
Reply option

2. You could also select *Reply to all.* By doing so, you send a reply not only to the individual who sent you the message but also to anyone who received the original message. In this example, you selected *Reply to all.* Once you click on *Reply to all,* your e-mail message will look similar to the screen shown in Figure 7.11. The e-mail address of the individual who originally wrote your message appears in the *To* line, and the subject is filled as an *RE* (the title of the original message).

3. The cursor appears at the beginning of the text, and you can reply with a copy of your original message at the end of your new message. In Figure 7.11, the text beginning with *"Mary, please review . . ."* is text from the original message. If you choose, you can highlight and delete the information in the original message.

4. Once you have typed your reply, click *Send,* and the message is on its way.

5. To forward a message, select the e-mail message and then click *Forward.* Notice that the attached item also gets forwarded (see Figure 7.12).

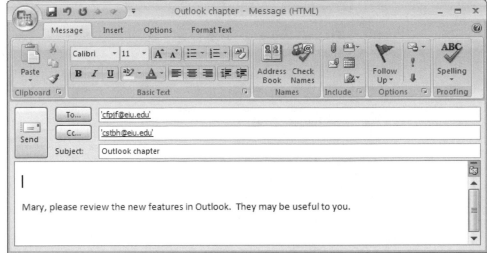

Figure 7.11
Replying to a message

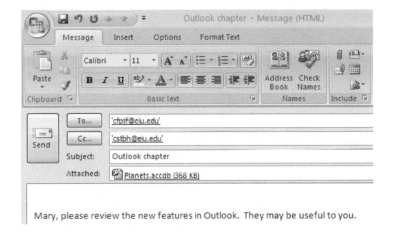

Figure 7.12
Forwarding attachment

Printing E-Mail Messages

1. To print an e-mail message, select the message and click on the Printer icon (see Figure 7.13).

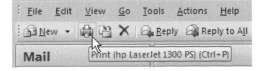

Figure 7.13
Printing a message

2. Or you can select *File* from the Outlook toolbar and then select *Print* (see Figure 7.14).

Deleting Messages

1. To delete a message, highlight the message on the Inbox screen and then click the Delete icon (see Figure 7.15) or press Ctrl+D.

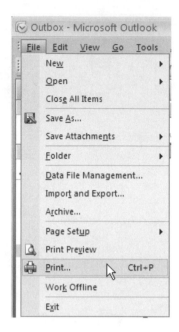

Figure 7.14
Print menu item

Figure 7.15
Delete message

2. Periodically, you will want to delete messages in the Deleted Items folder. Material remains in the Deleted Items folder until you empty the folder. All items you delete from Outlook are collected in this folder, including e-mail messages, calendar appointments, contacts, tasks, and notes.

3. To empty the Deleted Items folder, select *Tools* on the toolbar, then select *Empty "Deleted Items" Folder* (see Figure 7.16).

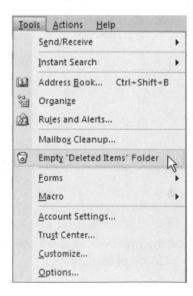

Figure 7.16
Empty Deleted Items folder

LET ME TRY

So far, you opened Outlook 2007 and created and sent an e-mail message. You responded to an e-mail and reviewed how to forward a message.

Suppose you and your students are studying the federal government. After reviewing what might be included in an appropriate e-mail, have the students write out e-mail messages for your review. Prepare the messages for e-mail and then send them. Some of the e-mail addresses they could use are the following:

President: president@whitehouse.gov
Vice President: vice.president@whitehouse.gov
First Lady: first.lady@whitehouse.gov

These addresses are good for practice because the students will receive an almost immediate response. These e-mail addresses provide robot responses that acknowledge receipt of an e-mail message and indicate that it will be addressed at a later time. Emphasize that it is a federal offense to make threats by e-mail and that their e-mail messages will be taken very seriously.

Sending E-Mail to the President

1. Open Outlook.
2. Click *Inbox*.
3. Click *New*.
4. Type in the e-mail address for the president: president@whitehouse.gov.
5. Type an appropriate subject for your e-mail.
6. Type your e-mail message and sign it.
7. Click *Send*, and your message is on its way.

Calendar

1. The Calendar is another component of Outlook that can be very helpful for scheduling events. You can view the calendar as a day, a work week, a full week, or a month. To display the Calendar tool, click on the Calendar icon on the Navigation pane (see Figure 7.17).
2. To view the different calendar formats, select the views along the toolbar or select the View menu and then select the style of calendar you wish to use (see Figure 7.18).
3. Select a 1-day calendar from the View menu item. The daily appointment displays appointments for the current day. To add an item to the calendar for the day shown, click on the appropriate time and type the information needed, then press Enter (see Figure 7.19).
4. Once the appointment has been entered, double-click the appointment, and the Appointment window will appear so that you may modify it by specifying the duration of the event and adding notes. To open the Appointment window, you may also select an appointment and press Enter, and the window opens.
5. To display another day of the month, click the drop-down menu next to *Start Time*.
6. Delete an appointment by clicking the Delete icon (it looks like an X) on the Appointment tab (Actions group). You may also delete an appointment by clicking on the item in the calendar view and pressing Delete.

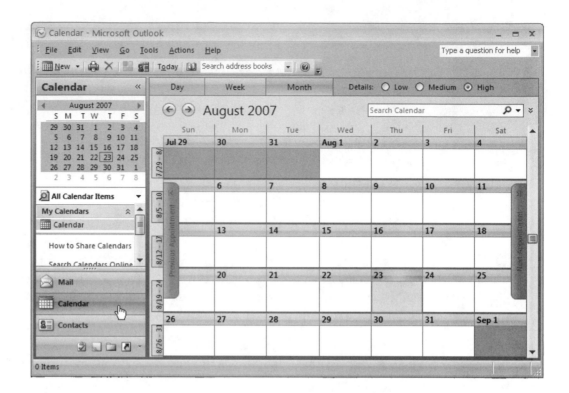

Figure 7.17
Calendar

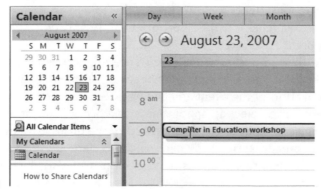

Figure 7.18
Calendar views

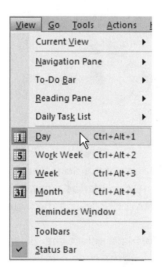

Figure 7.19
Enter an appointment

7. When you are done, click *Save & Close* in the Actions group on the Appointment tab (see Figure 7.20).

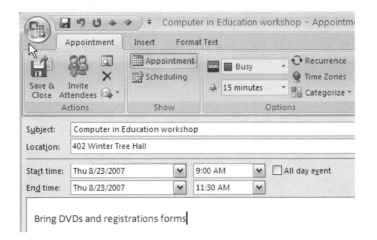

Figure 7.20
Appointment tab

8. To display another day of the month, click the drop-down menu next to *Start Time*.

9. To delete an appointment, highlight the appointment and click on the Delete icon or press Delete on the keyboard.

LET ME TRY

So far you have made an appointment, modified that appointment, and selected another date. Students can keep their own appointment calendars for class assignments and other activities in which they participate during the school year. Let's set up a day in the student calendar.

1. Open Outlook.
2. Click on *Calendar*.
3. Click on a date 2 weeks from today.
4. Click on the *9:00* A.M. box.
5. Type in *History test*.
6. Click on the *12:00* box and type *Meet Joan for lunch*.
7. Scroll down the times using the bar along the side of the date until you reach 3:00.
8. Click on *3:00* and drag the mouse to *4:30*; type in *Debate practice*, then press Enter.

Contacts

Outlook Contacts allows you to keep information about friends, family members, colleagues, and students' parents or guardians.

1. Click *Contacts* on the Outlook Navigation pane (see Figure 7.21).
2. If this is your first contact, a screen appears allowing you to double-click on the area to create a new contact. You may also click *New* on the toolbar (see Figure 7.22).
3. To create a new contact, type information into the Contact display window (see Figure 7.23).
4. Under Addresses, select *Home, Business,* or *Other* and identify a preferred mailing address.

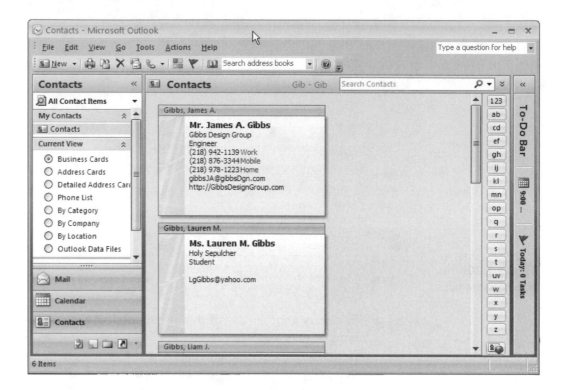

Figure 7.21
Contacts

Figure 7.22
New contact

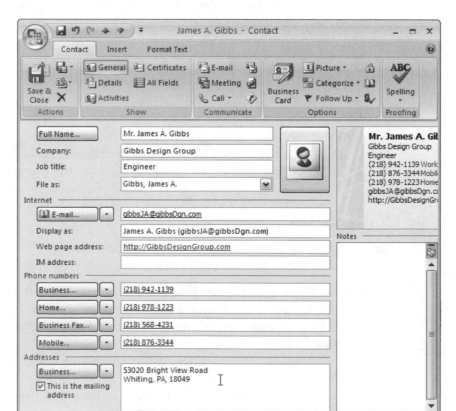

Figure 7.23
Create new contact

5. Each of the fields with an arrow allows for selection of different titles to the field.
6. Once you have typed in the fields, save the contact by clicking *Save & Close* on the Contact tab in the Actions group.
7. If you click on *Save & Close,* the window you were just typing in (the individual contact) closes, and the list of contacts appears. You can double-click contact to open and edit the individual contact information screen (see Figure 7.24).

Figure 7.24
Contact information
screen

8. When viewing an individual contact, the options on the Contact tab in the Actions group enable you to save and close, create a new contact, print, flag the contact for further follow-up, e-mail the contact, and autodial for phone or fax (see Figure 7.25).

Figure 7.25
Contact tab

9. Click on a contact to select it (see Figure 7.24). Click *Actions* on the Outlook taskbar. A menu drops down that allows you to create a new contact, draft a message to the contact, and send an e-mail message, among other things.
10. Select *Create* and then *New Message to Contact* (see Figure 7.26). This launches the message window where you can type your message. Notice that the e-mail address of the contact is automatically placed in the *To* line (see Figure 7.27).

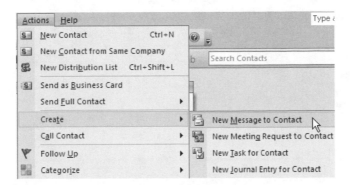

Figure 7.26
New message
to contact

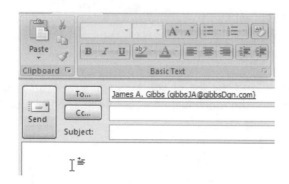

Figure 7.27
E-mail address
to contact

LET ME TRY

So far you have opened Contacts and entered data for one contact. Select one of your students and enter data for that individual. Then write a letter to that student's parents or guardians.

1. Click on *New Contact.*
2. The Contact window appears.
3. Click in an area and type the contact's information that is pertinent to you and/or your class.
4. Click *Save & Close.*
5. The contact information you just typed will appear in the Contact list.
6. Select Contact and then click *Actions.*
7. Click on *Create* and then *New Message to Contact.*
8. Type a message to your contact and send the message if you are connected to the Internet.

Tasks

Tasks allow you to create an electronic to-do list, including due dates for tasks.

1. Click on the Tasks icon from the Navigation pane. The Task window will appear.
2. On the left side of the window, click *Simple List* under Current View (see Figure 7.28). Begin to type your task in the *Click here to add a new task* box. Press the Tab key to move to *Due Date.* Click the drop list arrow to the right of *Due Date* to select a date and then press Enter.

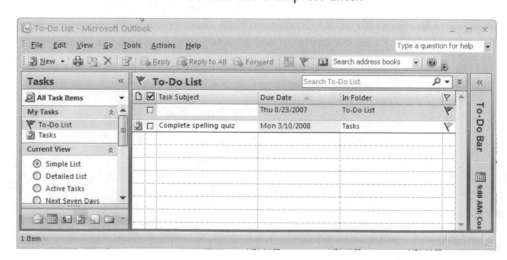

Figure 7.28
To-Do List

3. After completing a task, click on the box beside the task to mark it as complete. A line appears through the task to note that the task has been completed (see Figure 7.29).

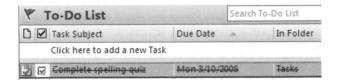

Figure 7.29
Completed items

4. To delete a task, click on the checked box next to the item that you want to delete. Click *Delete* on the screen or press Delete.

LET ME TRY

So far you have seen how to make a task list. Now you can make a list for your own use.

1. Open Outlook 2007.
2. Click on the Tasks icon.
3. Select *Click here to add a new Task*.
4. Add your own tasks, including due dates. You may want to begin with committee assignments that have due dates.
5. Click the Print icon on the toolbar to print your task list.

Notes

1. Outlook Notes are equivalent to sticky notes that you make for yourself and have on or around your desk.
2. Click on the Notes icon. A window appears, and you can type the note (see Figure 7.30).
3. Select *New* to create a new note. A window appears, and you can type the note. The date and time appear at the bottom of the new note (see Figure 7.31).
4. Type the note in the window. When you are finished, click the X in the upper-right corner of the window to close the note.
5. To delete a note, select it and then press Delete or click on the delete icon on the toolbar.
6. To open a note after you have created it, double-click on it.

LET ME TRY

So far you have seen how to make notes within the program. Now you can make notes for your own use.

1. Open Outlook.
2. Click on *Notes*.
3. Click on the New Notes icon on the taskbar.
4. Add your own notes.

Figure 7.30
Notes

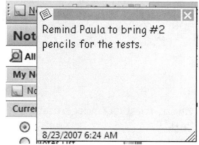

Figure 7.31
New note

Journal

1. Select *Journal* from the icons on the Navigation pane. If you do not see the Journal option, click the list arrow at the bottom of the Navigation pane (see Figure 7.32). The Journal in Outlook might be similar to a journal you may keep in your office. Students can use it to record activities that take place during a long-term project.

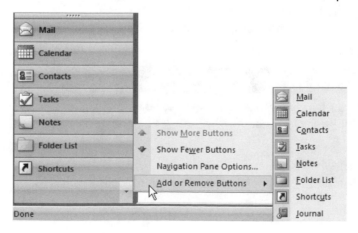

Figure 7.32
Journal

2. The first time you open Outlook Journal, the screen shown in Figure 7.33 appears. The options allow you to keep track of the contacts or records associated with a student, a particular meeting, or even a thematic unit you may be working on if you have associated contacts. If you do not want to set journal associations with contacts, do not check any of these boxes; simply click *OK*.

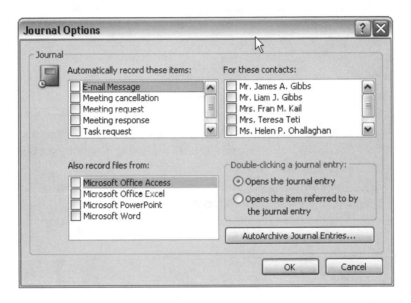

Figure 7.33
Journal options

3. To begin a new journal entry, select *Actions* from the toolbar, then select New *Journal Entry* (see Figure 7.34).

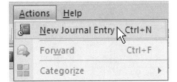

Figure 7.34
New Journal Entry

4. After clicking on *New Journal Entry,* a window appears and allows you to place information about activities that have taken place today (or any day) by selecting the appropriate date on the calendar in the window (see Figure 7.35).

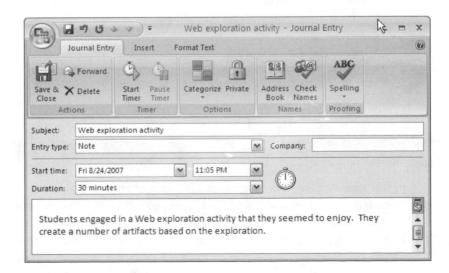

Figure 7.35
Journal Entry

5. After entering all the data you need for the journal entry, click *Save & Close* in the Actions group of the Journal Entry tab. This closes the entry, and the entry then appears under the date on the Journal calendar (see Figure 7.36).

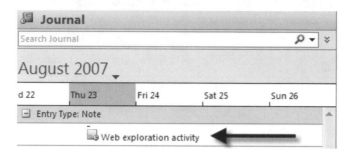

Figure 7.36
Journal Entry

6. Clicking on the Journal entry with a plus beside it allows you to see the information in the journal. Double-clicking the entry takes you to the original Journal entry, where you can edit it.
7. You can print out the calendar document or the individual Journal entries by clicking on the Printer icon on the toolbar.
8. The calendar can be viewed for today, 1 day, 1 week, or 1 month (see Figure 7.37).

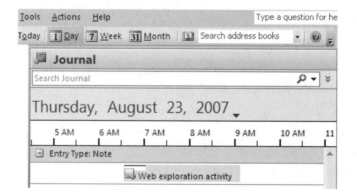

Figure 7.37
Journal Entry and
calendar

A CHALLENGE USING OUTLOOK 2007

For those who would like a challenge beyond the Let Me Try activities presented in this chapter, try the following exercises.
1. Send an e-mail with an attachment.
2. In the address book of the Inbox, create a group for students working together on a project.
3. Have your students create a calendar for appointments, including holidays or official days, and print the calendar.
4. Have your students create a task list for a character in a story they are reading.

TYING IT ALL TOGETHER

In this chapter, we have examined the parts of an electronic date keeper. You created a calendar, a list of contacts, and a list of tasks, and worked with e-mail messages. By using all these tools in conjunction with other components of Microsoft Office, you will be able to maintain your calendar. Your students also will be able to keep information that can be updated, and tasks may be assigned or e-mail messages sent directly to the class.

CHAPTER OUTLINE

LEARNING OBJECTIVES

At the completion of this chapter you will be able to:

- Start a document from a Publisher template
- Navigate the Publisher workspace
- Resize a text box in a publication
- Add a frame or artwork to a document
- Cut, copy, and paste in a document
- Preview a document for printing
- Create a new blank Publisher document
- Indentify Publisher Design Sets
- Print a publication
- Save a publication

CHAPTER OVERVIEW

This chapter provides an introduction to Publisher 2007. The content focuses on Publisher fundamentals and how to apply them to a variety of learning activities. Using the examples of developing a brochure, the chapter's Show Me section presents instructions on how to use many of Publisher 2007 tools for creating, editing, and manipulating information within a Publisher document. The Let Me Try student-oriented exercise provides specific examples of step-by-step instructions for using Publisher 2007 in learning activities. In addition to the Let Me Try activities, the Challenge section provides stimulating projects for practicing Publisher 2007. Each one of the illustrations in this chapter may be found within the Publisher folder inside Example on the CD accompanying the book. You may follow along with the document as you go through the text by pulling it up from the CD. In addition, other examples using Publisher may be found on the CD.

How Teachers and Students Can Use Publisher

Microsoft Publisher can be used in a variety of activities both by students and by teachers in the classroom. When examining Bloom's taxonomy of cognitive levels in conjunction with the National Educational Technology Standards for Students: The Next Generation, teachers can utilize Publisher to accomplish instruction and learning at a variety of levels and addressing multiple standards. Looking first at the cognitive levels, some examples of using Publisher by students could include the following:

- *Knowledge*—(a) Students can create flash cards to use in memorization using the business card template or the postcard template. (b) Students can select a brochure template and list the 50 states and capitals adding appropriate clip art. (c) Students can create their own "dictionary" of words found in their reading that they do not know, and define them by using a catalog template or newsletter template.
- *Comprehension*—After reading a book such as *Hatchet* by Gary Paulsen, students can create a book report using the newsletter template. Students can use the postcard template to create a postcard of one of their favorite characters from a book.
- *Application*—Students can create a brochure describing a location of a book or a region of the world they learned about in a class by doing further research. Students can prepare a flier that would illustrate the concepts behind the life cycle of a spider.
- *Analysis*—Students will use a newsletter format to compare and contrast the main characters in two books such as Brian in *Hatchet* and Sam in *My Side of the Mountain*. After reading *Way Down Yonder*, students will analyze what the similes and metaphors in the book could mean, such as "cool as a cucumber," and create a brochure for the class.
- *Synthesis*—Students will write and illustrate a short story (or poem) and prepare illustrations for the story using the newsletter template. Students will design and create an advertisement for one of the inventions they have invented, or students will create a "healthy" menu for a restaurant they are hypothetically establishing using the menu template.
- *Evaluation*—Students will create a rubric for evaluating newsletters that have been created by companies and organizations to improve their (the students') creations (using a flier template or a template imported from Word) and apply those rubrics providing criticism for the newsletters in written form. Students will create a brochure comparing and contrasting videos they have seen in class, using a brochure template and using their comparison to recommend what video to see and why.

NETS for Students*

Publisher activities include the following:

- *Creativity and innovation*—Students demonstrate creative thinking, construct knowledge, and develop innovative products and processes using technology.
- *Communication and collaboration*—Students use digital media and environments to communicate and work collaboratively, including at a distance, to support individual learning and contribute to the learning of others.
- *Research and information fluency*—Students apply digital tools to gather, evaluate, and use information.
- *Critical thinking, problem solving, and decision-making*—Students use critical thinking skills to plan and conduct research, manage projects, solve problems, and make informed decisions using appropriate digital tools and resources.
- *Technology operations and concepts*—Students demonstrate a sound understanding of technology concepts, systems, and operations.

What Is New in Publisher 2007

Publisher uses the standard toolbar, but the opening screen has changed from the 2003 version of Publisher. When you enter your personal information into Publisher 2007, the program applies the information to every template and, new in this edition, shows the data in the template before you select it. You can search Publisher templates. A new task pane called Publisher Tasks shows often-used features in this program. With a download, you can convert publications to PDF files created in Publisher, allowing for a wider audience to review or receive the documents created. There is an enhanced Design Checker that identifies and fixes design errors.

About Publisher

Publisher is a computer application that allows individuals to create, customize, and publish materials. The program may be considered desktop publishing software. Publisher allows you to create a variety of materials. As you open the program, the opening screen shows you file folders with Popular Publication Types as icons that you may click on or a listing of Publication Types along the left side of the page. The Popular Publication Types include the following:

Blank Page Sizes
Brochures
Business Cards
Calendars
E-Mail
Flyers
Greeting Cards
Imported Word Documents
Labels
Newsletters
Postcards
Web Sites

The listing along the left of the screen is even longer. By clicking on the file folder, template options appear. The items listed allow you to place your own materials within a template that has been designed and included in the program. Similar to Word, you are rolling an "electronic piece of paper" on the screen. With the click of a mouse, you can create a professional looking product either in print (a newsletter) or electronically (a Web page). The finished product may be saved on a memory device, printed on paper, or sent electronically over the Internet. As a teacher who knows how to use Publisher, you can produce all types of interesting materials and facilitate student production of materials.

Working with Publisher

Opening Publisher 2007

To create a publisher document, you need to open Publisher 2007. Click the Start button on the Windows taskbar, move the mouse pointer over *Programs*, and the Programs submenu appears. Move the mouse pointer over *Microsoft Office*, and the Microsoft Office submenu appears. Click *Microsoft Office,* and the Microsoft Office submenu appears (see Figure 8.1).

Click *Microsoft Office Publisher 2007*, and Publisher 2007 opens (see Figure 8.2).

For this illustration, click on the Brochure icon (the other templates work on the same premise as the brochure). Once the icon has been clicked, a screen of brochure options will appear. You will notice that you can search templates as part of this screen. A thumbnail sketch of the brochure appears along the right side of

Figure 8.1
Opening Publisher

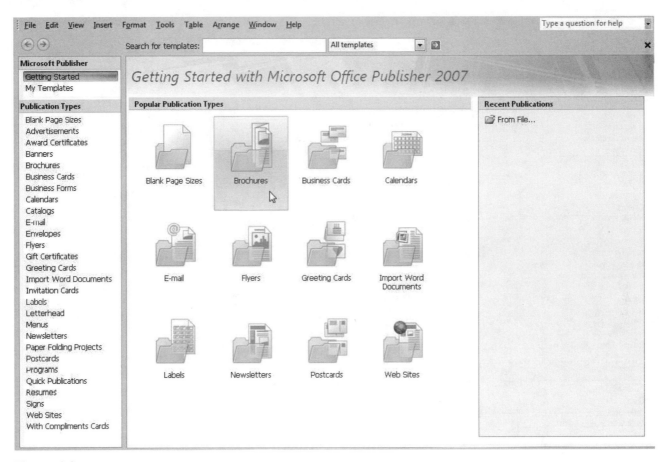

Figure 8.2
Opening screen of Publisher

the screen as well as panes that allow you to customize and change options within the brochure selected. Select the first brochure style for this illustration (see Figure 8.3).

The Brochure screen will appear, allowing you to modify information, and the Publisher workspace will appear (see Figure 8.4).

There are several work areas in Publisher that may look different from other Microsoft Office programs. The page icons will indicate what page of the document you are working on if the template you select has multiple pages and allows you to switch between pages in a publication. The Connect Textboxes portion of the toolbar allows you to create and work with connected text boxes for text flow. Publisher utilizes the toolbar similar to the 2003 version of this product. Within the workspace, several panes appear within the screen (see Figure 8.5).

Show Me

Developing the Brochure

1. As an example of the type of project that a student could develop, you will create a book report on *A Year Down Yonder* by Richard Peck. For an example of the completed project, see "Down Yonder brochure" on the CD. This project will take multiple steps. To give you an idea of what the finished results will look like, Figure 8.6 shows the front of the brochure and Figure 8.7 the inside of the brochure.

Figure 8.3
Brochure template screen

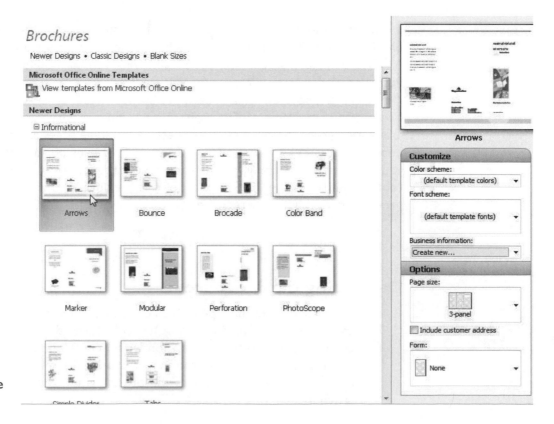

Figure 8.4
Selecting a brochure
style

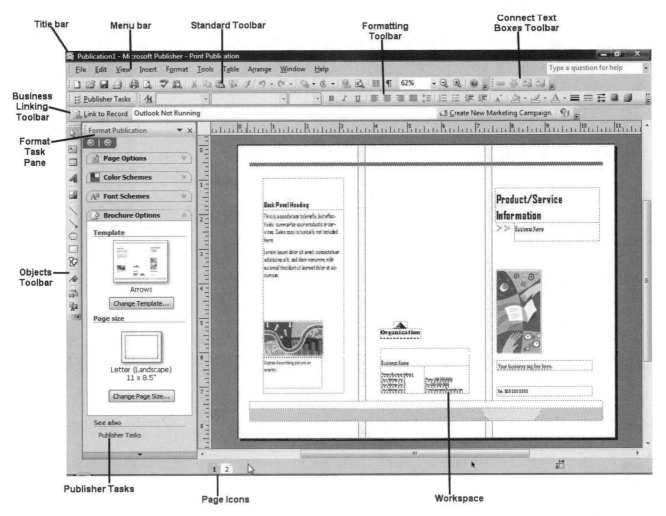

Figure 8.5
Publisher workspace

2. To begin creating this brochure, open Publisher. To do so, click the mouse pointer on the Start button, click *Programs*, move the mouse pointer over *Microsoft Office*, and click *Microsoft Publisher 2007*.

3. The first screen will allow you to select the type of publication you want to create. In this case, you want to create a brochure. Do so by clicking on the Brochures file folder. The Select Brochure Template screen will then appear. You will notice at the top of the screen that you can search the templates. Also, the templates are categorized by Newer Designs, Classic Designs, and Blank Sizes (see Figure 8.8). In this illustration, you want to use Newer Designs.

4. In this case, you want to use the Simple Divider template in the third row of the designs. Click on this design, and the thumbnail of the document will appear in the pane along the right side of the screen. In the Customize pane, you will enter business information on this screen as well, which will allow for that information to be automatically placed in the template (see Figure 8.9).

5. Pull down the arrow next to *Create new*, and a new window will appear, allowing you to enter new business information. Type in your information and click on *Save* (see Figure 8.10).

About the Author Richard Peck

Richard Peck grew up in Decatur, Illinois, and now lives in New York City. Mr. Peck taught junior high school and high school English. He has won the Margaret A. Edwards Award for lifetime achievement in young adult literature. Richard Peck does not have a computer, he types his manuscripts on a typewriter. Other books he has published include: *A Long Way from Chicago* a prequel to this book), *Strays like Us, The Great Interactive Dream Machine,* and *Voices After Midnight* to name a few.

Author of over twenty-five novels

A Year Down Yonder... A Report

PRARIELAND SCHOOL

1001 Raab Raod
Normal, IL 61761

Phone: 555-555-5555
Fax: 555-555-5555
E-mail: sschertz@normal.net

Winner of the 2001 Newbery Medal

Figure 8.6
Front of the brochure

Characters in the book

Character	Description
Grandma Dowdel	The Grandma that lives in rural Illinois
Mary Alice	A fifteen year old sent to live with her Grandmother
Bootsie	Mary Alice's cat
Joe	Mary Alice's brother who is two years older
Mr. Fluke	The principal of the school
Mildred Burdick	A girl at school that threatens Mary Alice
Miss Butler	The school teacher
Old Man Nyquist	A retired farmer that lives in town
Arnold Green	The lodger at Grandma's
Maxine Patch	The postmistress
Royce McNabb	A boy in school and the man Mary Alice marries

ABOUT THE STORY

Mary Alice has visited Grandma Dowdle in the summer time with her brother, but because her father has lost his job she is sent to live with Grandma for the school year. Mary Alice and her cat Bootsie make the journey. The story chronicles Mary Alice's year at Grandma's house. Mary Alice lives in Chicago and has to take the Wabash Railroad's Blue Bird Train from Dearborn Station to Grandma's small rural town on the eastern side of Illinois. The story talks about the school year as Mary Alice tries to fit in at school. Halloween is a big even in the town and how Grandma enjoys and takes part in the Halloween activities. About Armistice Day and how the community and Grandma helped folks in ted with a "turkey shoot". The Christmas celebration and the winter activities that Grandma does to have cash money is vividly described. The boarder that Grandma takes in to have additional money and the activities that takes place around him. As the school year ends the tornado appears and what happens to the community during the storm is told.

ABOUT THE TIME

The story takes place during the recession of 1937, better known as the Depression. The Depression affected numerous people thought out the United States. Many individuals lost jobs and there was wide spread unemployment.

PRARIELAND SCHOOL

1001 Raab Raod
Normal, IL 61761

Phone: 555-555-5555
Fax: 555-555-5555
E-mail: sschertz@normal.net

Figure 8.7
Inside of the brochure

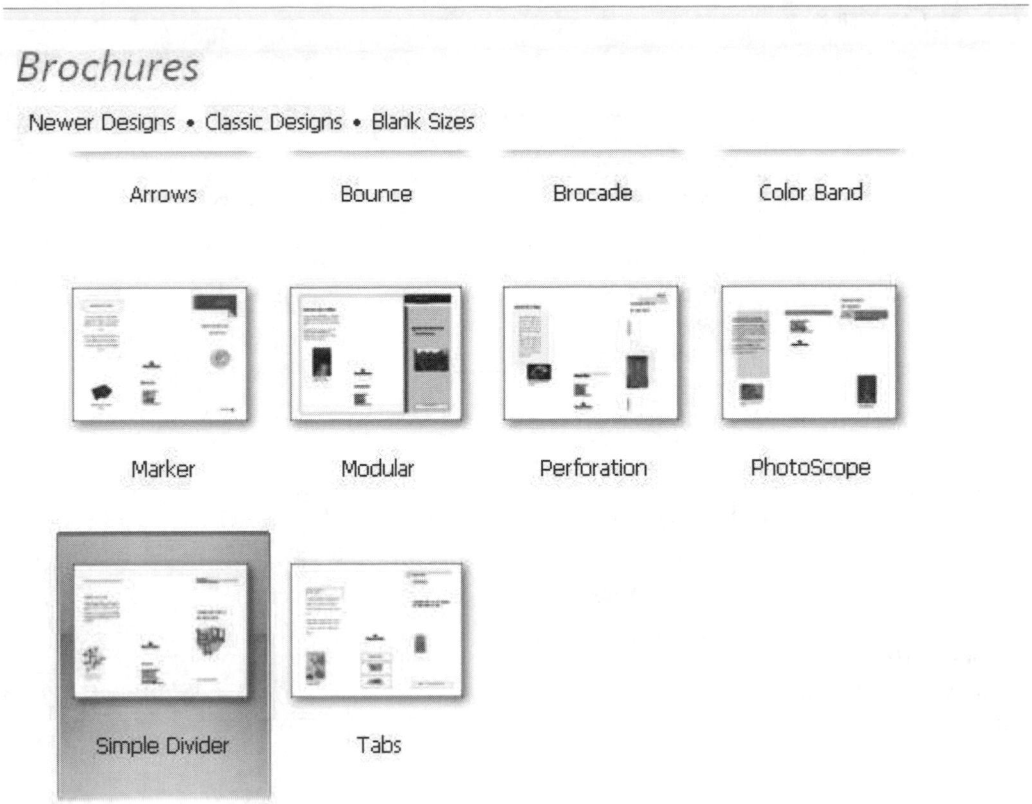

Brochures
Newer Designs • Classic Designs • Blank Sizes
Arrows
Bounce
Brocade
Color Band
Marker
Modular
Perforation
PhotoScope
Simple Divider
Tabs

Figure 8.8
Design categories of brochures

Simple Divider
Customize
Color scheme:
(default template colors)
Font scheme:
(default template fonts)
Business information:
Create new...
Options
Page size:
3-panel
Include customer address
Form:
None

Figure 8.9
Business information

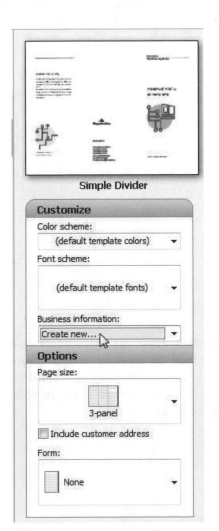

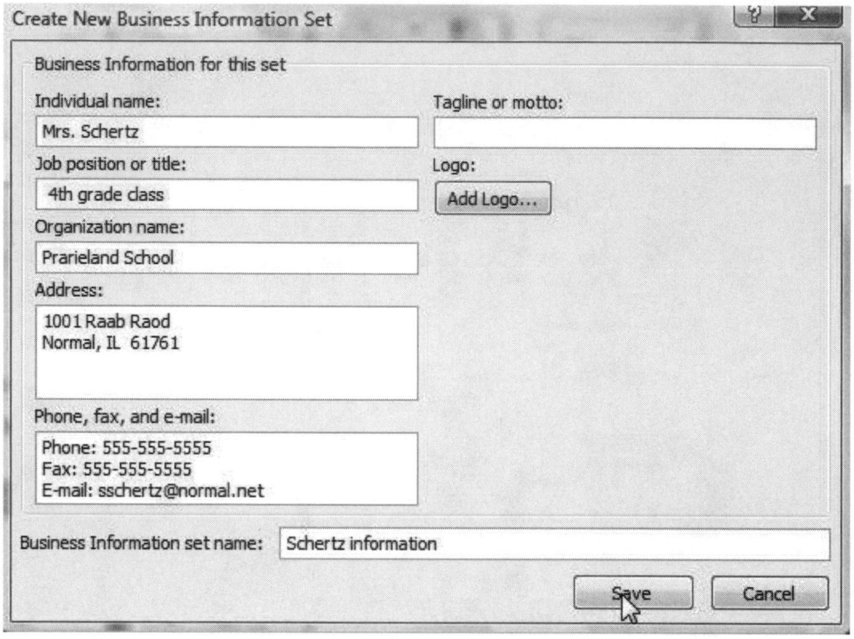

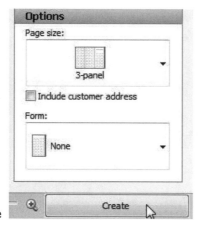

Figure 8.10
Business Information
Set

6. Once the information has been saved, click on *Create* to start creating your brochure using the template selected (see Figure 8.11).

Figure 8.11
Creating the brochure

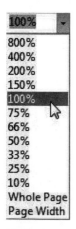

7. You will notice on the template that the business information that was typed in now appears in the brochure. To work on the brochure, it easier to increase the view size. Select the Zoom icon from the standard toolbar and increase the size to 100% (see Figure 8.12), or you may want to zoom in using the buttons on the toolbar (see Figure 8.13).

Figure 8.12
Zooming view size

Figure 8.13
Zoom-in and Zoom-out icons

8. You will notice that the individual design elements are noted by a dotted line box around them. You can modify and/or move any of this information as you create the brochure. The title of the brochure will be "A Year Down Yonder . . . A Report." Highlight the title of the brochure; you will note that the text box is activated. Press the Backspace key; this will erase the "Product/Service Information" wording and allow you to type in the title (see Figure 8.14). Resize the text box by clicking on one of the clear circles at the bottom of the box, holding the mouse button down and dragging up so that the box fits the text.

Figure 8.14
Title of the brochure

9. You will notice that as you type the title in the text box, there is a green circle above the text box. This allows you to rotate the text in the text box. Once you place the mouse pointer over the green circle, a curved arrow will appear. After typing in the title, rotate the text just slightly to give an angular effect to the text (see Figure 8.15).

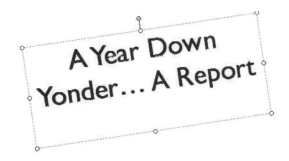

Figure 8.15
Rotating the text

Importing Graphics

10. As you look at the front of the brochure, you will want to replace the picture on the front of the brochure with something that relates to the content of *A Year Down Yonder*. You may use scanned pictures that students have drawn, pictures from a digital camera, or clip art. If you are using art from a source on the Internet, make sure that the graphic is in the public domain, or you will need to obtain permission to use someone else's artwork. In this case, you are going to use clip art. Click on the current clip art selection to activate the box. Then select *Insert* from the toolbar and select *Picture* from the menu and then *Clip Art* from that menu (see Figure 8.16).

11. As in other programs in Microsoft Office, you may use the clip art that comes with the program, or, when connected to the Internet, you may search the Microsoft Office Clip Art Web site for additional pictures. Searching for train clip art while connected to the Web will produce a number of pictures. Select the designated picture and click on it, and it will insert itself into the box that has been activated (see Figure 8.17).

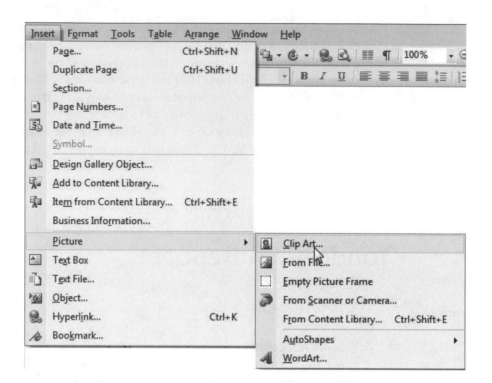

Figure 8.16
Inserting clip art

Figure 8.17
Selecting clip art

12. You will want to make the graphic larger. To make the image a little larger, click on the picture to activate the "handles" around the picture. Select the upper right-hand circle and hold down the Shift key on the keyboard, at the same time draging the mouse to the upper section of the page and to the right. This allows the picture to be resized in proportion rather than in only one direction (see Figure 8.18).

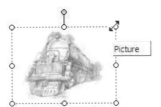

Figure 8.18
Resizing the picture

13. The next item on the front of the brochure is the telephone number. You do not want a telephone number present on the front of the brochure. Using the mouse arrow, highlight the current text and press Delete. Type *Winner of the 2001 Newbery Medal* in the text box. By clicking on *Print Preview* on the standard toolbar, the brochure should look similar to Figure 8.19.

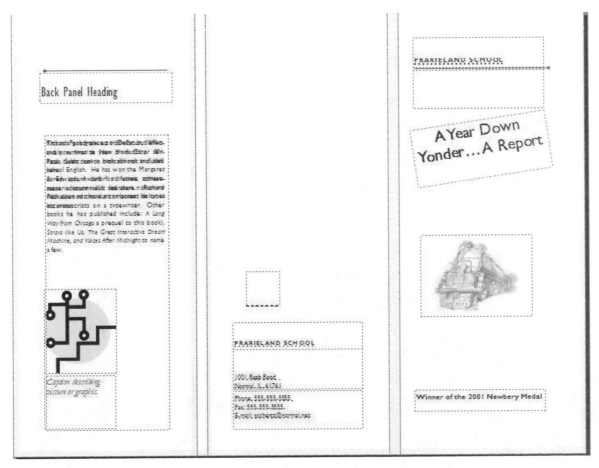

Figure 8.19
Back panel of the brochure

Adding Content to the Brochure

14. The template is set up so that you can add content where text boxes are indicated or create your own text box. On page 1 of the brochure, highlight the words "Back Panel Heading" and type in *About the Author: Richard Peck*. Resize the text box in the same fashion as the front title by clicking on the text box and dragging the circle toward the top of the page to make the text box smaller (see Figure 8.20).

Figure 8.20
Resizing text box

15. Click on the text box below "About the Author Richard Peck" and write a short paragraph about the author. You may want to use the information presented in the text or do your own research and create your own paragraph.

16. As you have previously done, click on *Clip Art* on the back panel to activate the box. Select *Insert Clip Art*, and in Search for: type *man*. Select the appropriate picture, and the picture will be placed in the box because it was activated (see Figure 8.21). You may have to resize the picture to fit the space. Be aware of

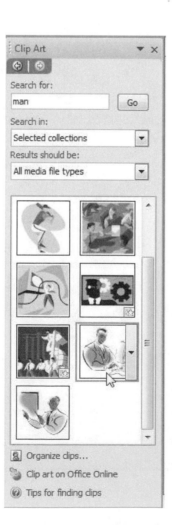

Figure 8.21
Selecting clip art

Figure 8.22
Caption box for
clip art

the margins for the brochures (shown as a dotted line around the brochure), making sure to keep the picture within the designated space.

17. To add a caption below the picture, click to activate the box and type in *Author of over twenty-five novels* (see Figure 8.22).

18. Select *Print Preview* from the standard toolbar to view the outside of the brochure as you have completed it thus far. This will allow you to see what it will look like prior to printing a copy (see Figure 8.23).

19. To save the brochure, click on *File* on the toolbar and select *Save As*. The first time you save a document, you will need to designate where you want to save it (i.e., removable disk F) and name the document and click on *Save* when completed (see Figure 8.24). You will see that you can save the document in a variety of formats. For this illustration, save the document as a Publisher file.

20. To start on the second page or the inside of the brochure, click on the Page 2 icon at the bottom of the workspace (see Figure 8.25).

21. You now can see the inside, or page 2, of the brochure. To place information in the brochure, you will start on the leftmost column. In that column, you are going to create a table listing the characters in *A Year Down Yonder*. In the text box containing *Main Inside Heading*, highlight the text and type in *Characters in the book* (see Figure 8.26).

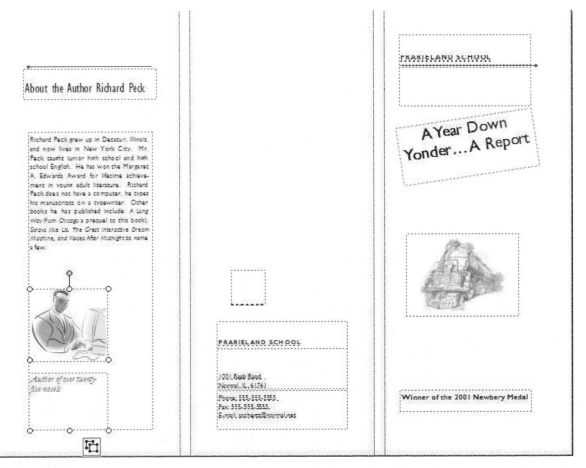

Figure 8.23
Brochure back panel

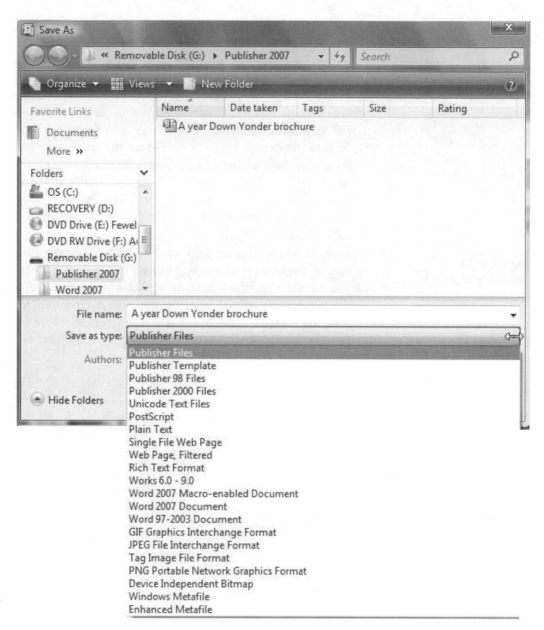

Figure 8.24
Saving the document as a Publisher file

22. In order to make space, you will need to delete the information in this column first. Click on each text box and picture box and press Delete to remove the items in the column. The text box will remain—you will have to click on one of the handles to activate the box and then press Delete to remove the text box.

23. Click on *Table* from the toolbar and select *Insert* from the menu and then *Table* again from the second menu (see Figure 8.27).

Figure 8.25
Selecting page 2 of the brochure

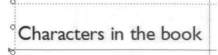

Figure 8.26
Text box

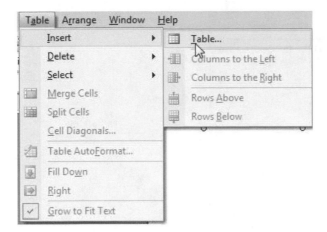

Figure 8.27
Inserting a table

24. Create the chart with 12 rows and two columns. Select List 3 from the choices of table formats. An illustration of the table format will be displayed in the right side of this pane (see Figure 8.28).

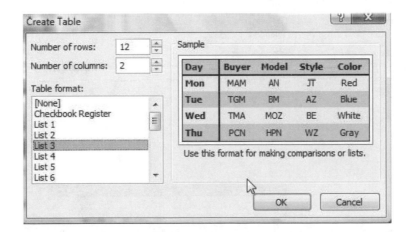

Figure 8.28
Table formats

25. Resize the table to fit in the panel of the brochure and so it is below the title *Characters* in the book. After typing in the characters, the table should look like the following (see Figure 8.29).
26. Columns 2 and 3 of the second page will include information about the story and the time frame in which the story takes place. The two secondary headings would be 1. About the Story and 2. About the time. As you write the paragraphs, delete the graphic in the middle of the second column by clicking on the graphic to activate the picture box and press Delete.
27. Insert a clip art picture at the bottom of the second column. As you add pictures, you may want to format the text around the picture. To do this, click on the right mouse button when on the picture and select *Format Picture* from the pull-down menu that appears (see Figure 8.30).
28. Select the Layout tab on the Format Picture window that pops up once you have made your selection. Select the tight wrapping style, allowing text and pictures to wrap around the format (see Figure 8.31).

Character	Description
Grandma Dowdel	The Grandma that lives in rural Illinois
Mary Alice	A fifteen year old sent to live with her Grandmother
Bootsie	Mary Alice's cat
Joe	Mary Alice's brother who is two years older
Mr. Fluke	The principal of the school
Mildred Burdick	A girl at school that threatens Mary Al-ice
Miss Butler	The school teacher
Old Man Nyquist	A retired farmer that lives in town
Arnold Green	The lodger at Grandma's
Maxine Patch	The postmistress
Royce McNabb	A boy in school and the man Mary Alice

Figure 8.29
Finished table with characters

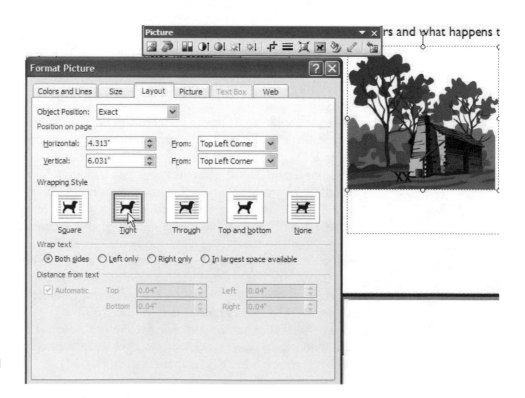

Figure 8.30
Format text around picture

cash money is vividly described. The boarder that Grandma takes in to have additional money and the activities that take place around him. As the school year ends the tornado appears and what happens to the community during the storm is told.

Figure 8.31
Tight text wrap around picture

29. The finished second page of the brochure might look like the illustration in Figure 8.32.

Characters in the book

Character	Description
Grandma Dowdel	The Grandma that lives in rural Illinois
Mary Alice	A fifteen year old sent to live with her Grandmother
Bootsie	Mary Alice's cat
Joe	Mary Alice's brother who is two years older
Mr. Fluke	The principal of the school
Mildred Burdick	A girl at school that threatens Mary Alice
Miss Butler	The school teacher
Old Man Nyquist	A retired farmer that lives in town
Arnold Green	The lodger at Grandma's
Maxine Patch	The postmistress
Royce McNabb	A boy in school and the man Mary Alice marries

ABOUT THE STORY

Mary Alice has visited Grandma Dowdle in the summer time with her brother, but because her father has lost his job she is sent to live with Grandma for the school year. Mary Alice and her cat Bootsie make the journey. The story chronicles Mary Alice's year at Grandma's house. Mary Alice lives in Chicago and has to take the Wabash Railroad's Blue Bird Train from Dearborn Station to Grandma's small rural town on the eastern side of Illinois. The story talks about the school year as Mary Alice tries to fit in at school. Halloween is a big even in the town and how Grandma enjoys and takes part in the Halloween activities. About Armistice Day and how the community and Grandma helped folks in ted with a "turkey shoot". The Christmas celebration and the winter activities that Grandma does to have cash money is vividly described. The boarder that Grandma takes in to have additional money and the activities that takes place around him. As the school year ends the tornado appears and what happens to the community during the storm is told.

ABOUT THE TIME

The story takes place during the recession of 1937, better known as the Depression. The Depression affected numerous people thought out the United States. Many individuals lost jobs and there was wide spread unemployment.

PRARIELAND SCHOOL

1001 Raab Raod
Normal, IL 61761

Phone: 555-555-5555
Fax: 555-555-5555
E-mail: sschertz@normal.net

Figure 8.32
Second page of brochure

30. You have finished the brochure, and you should save your work by clicking on *File* and then *Save*.
31. To print your brochure, select the Printer icon from the standard toolbar. Or you may select *Print* under the File menu if there is a specific printer that you want the document to be printed on.

Checking Your Publication for Design Problems

1. The Design Checker will find problems such as an image partially off the page or an empty text box. The Design Checker will not catch every flaw, but it might identify some that you did not catch. It is always a good idea not only to proof the materials and run a spell check and a grammar check but to have someone else proof the documents as well.
2. Check on *Tools* and select *Design Checker* (see Figure 8.33).
3. The software will prepare a report that indicates where it finds problems (see Figure 8.34).
4. You can select *Go to this Item* to go to the item where there is difficulty; each identified item has a pull-down menu that will allow you to do so. In that case, the text box or frame for the picture is made active (see Figure 8.34).
5. When you finish reviewing the design problems, close the Design Checker and save your document if you made any changes.

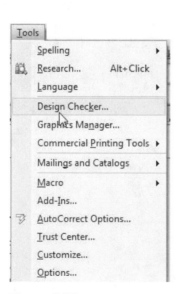

Figure 8.33
Design Checker

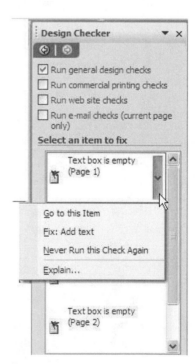

Figure 8.34
Select item to fix

LET ME TRY

You have created a brochure and utilized many of the tools available in Publisher. Web pages are (or can be) inventive information sources that students create as part of a research activity or final class project. Web pages do not have to be posted to the Internet but can be used on CD or thumb drive to allow users to have visual information that may be linked to particular Web sites if the computer on which the Publisher document is opened is connected to the Internet.

You will construct a Web page for the book *Way Down Yonder*. To see the finished product, go to "Down Yonder Web page" on the CD in the Publisher file.

As you start your own Web site or Web page, it is a good idea to talk with your technology coordinator to identify the naming protocols for the Web pages in your organization. If you are creating your own beginning Web page to be posted to the Internet, many times the naming protocol is to call the first page of a Web site *index*.

1. Open Microsoft Publisher.
2. On the Opening screen, select the Web Sites folder by clicking on it.
3. Select the first template on the screen for this project, "Arrows."
4. A pop-up window will appear to design the number of links and Web pages for this site. There is a graphic illustrator on the screen that shows the links (see Figure 8.35). The links will indicate Web pages that link from the opening Home page.
5. By clicking *OK* on the Web Site Builder, the Home page and linking pages are created using the template selected (see Figure 8.36).
6. As with the other Publisher documents, you can insert text in the area identified and replace the graphics with clip art or other pictures. First change the business name and business tag line to *Mrs. Schertz's 4th Grade Class* (for the business

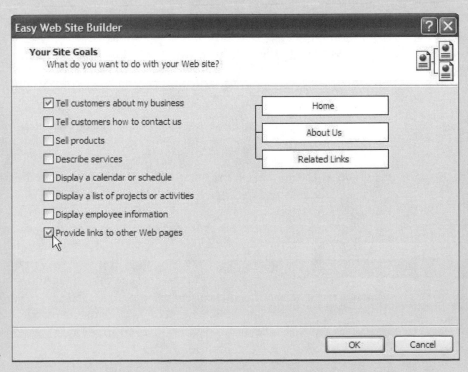

Figure 8.35
Easy Web Site Builder

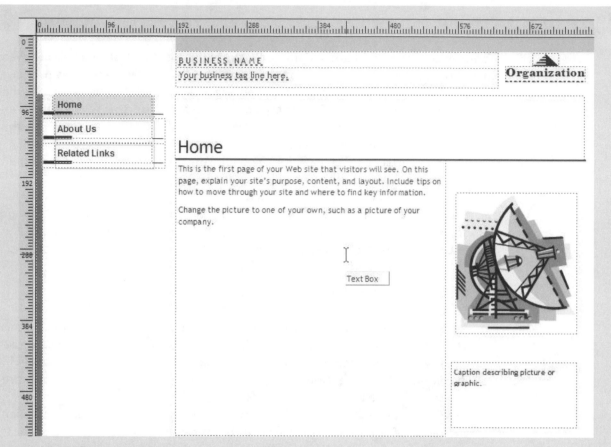

Figure 8.36
Home page created

name), *Home of the Cougars* (as the business tagline), and *Unit #5* (as the organization title).

7. For Home, type in the title of the book: *A Year Down Yonder*.

8. For the information about the Home page, type in the following:

    This web site is to provide information about the book and additional information about the topics addressed by the book as well as links to additional web sites that you can read on your own about that time, history, author, and topics found in this book.

9. Scroll down the Web page and add the contact information on the Web page to include *Prairieland School, 1001 Raab Road, Normal, Illinois 61761*.

10. Type in *About the Book*, replacing *About Us* on the link to the second page of the Web site. This provides a link to the second page of the Web site.

11. The Home Web page should look something like Figure 8.37.

12. Click on *Page 2* at the bottom of the workspace to show the second page in the Web site.

13. Open the *A Year Down Yonder* brochure. You will copy information from one document to another without having to retype. After opening the brochure, select the second page. Highlight the entire section of "About the story" by clicking and dragging the mouse pointer over the sentences (see Figure 8.38).

14. Once the text is highlighted, select *Copy* from the Edit page on the toolbar. Once that is complete, close out the brochure.

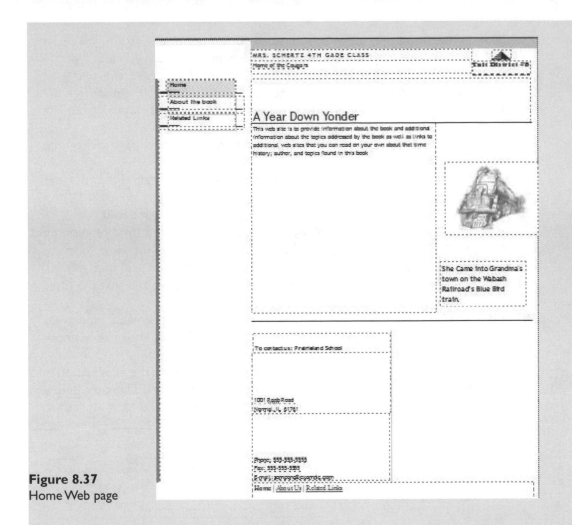

Figure 8.37
Home Web page

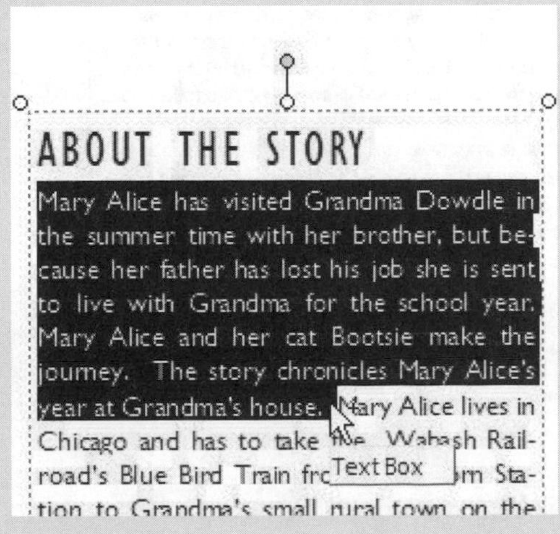

Figure 8.38
Copy from brochure

15. Click on the Web page on the toolbar at the bottom of the page. On the *About the Book* Web page (page 2) in the text box page below where you just typed in *About the story,* highlight the text and press Delete to erase the text that appeared in the template. Once that text is gone, make sure your cursor is in the text box and select *Edit* and *Paste.* This will paste the text copied from the brochure into the Web page (see Figure 8.39).

16. Insert clip art by inserting the train that was used in the front page and on the brochure.

17. The caption on the clip art below the train image will be "A train ride and a year to grow."

18. The finished page 2 of the Web site should look similar to Figure 8.40.

19. Select page 3 from the bottom of the workspace to select the third page of the Web site. This page is a listing of other Web sites and how the sites relate to the book. Note that Web sites are not necessarily permanent and that you will have to periodically check to see if the hyperlink is still active and that the topic of the page is still appropriate.

20. In the text box under Related Links, highlight the current information and press Delete, then type "The following web sites provide additional information about topics addressed in the book *A Year Down Yonder*" in the text box.

21. In the next text box labeled *Web site* or *page name 1,* highlight the information in that box and press Delete and type *The New Deal Network.* The text below should be typed in as follows: *A database of photographs and texts (speeches,*

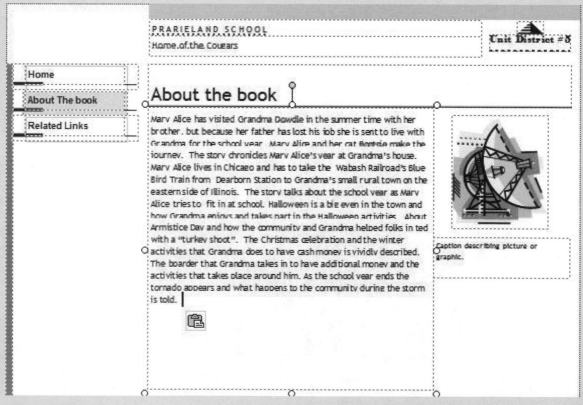

Figure 8.39
Web page 2

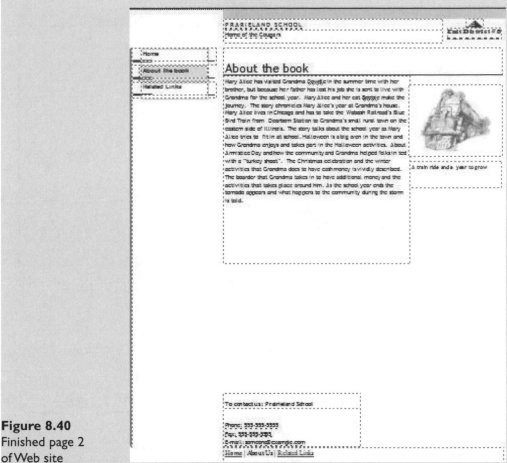

Figure 8.40
Finished page 2
of Web site

Figure 8.41
Hyperlink icon

letters, and other historic documents from the New Deal period). Sponsored by the Franklin and Eleanor Roosevelt Institute.

22. You now want to create a hyperlink to this Web page. The URL address for the page is http://newdeal.feri.org. As you create links to Web pages, you can open the Web pages. Copy the address from the address space on the browser by highlighting the address first, then press Ctrl+C. This copies the address onto the Clipboard, and it may be pasted into text or into the box on the hyperlink page, allowing for fewer mistakes in typing addresses for Web pages.

23. Highlight the text *New Deal Network* and click on the hyperlink icon on the toolbar (see Figure 8.41).

24. The Insert Hyperlink pane will appear. You are linking to an existing Web page, and that icon should be activated. You will notice there is a space for text to display, but because you have already typed in the text and highlighted it to be hyperlinked, it is not active. Paste or type in the address for the Web page in the Address page and click *Insert* (see Figure 8.42).

25. Fill in the remaining Web page boxes on this page with Web pages and descriptions of those pages. The finished product would look similar to Figure 8.43.

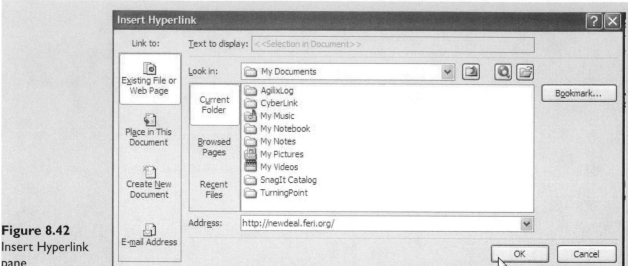

Figure 8.42
Insert Hyperlink
pane

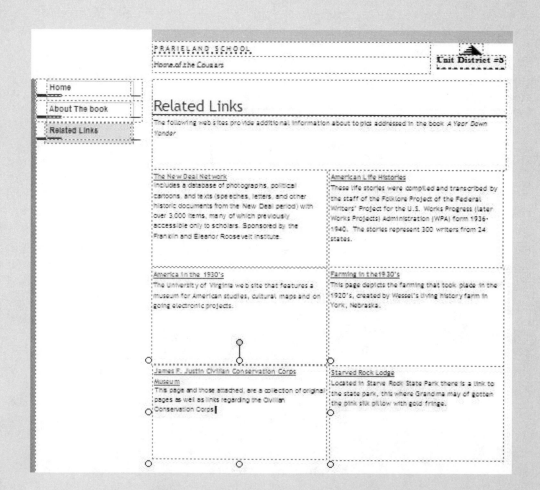

Figure 8.43
Finished Related
Links page

LET ME TRY, AGAIN

1. Select a postcard template to create a postcard that Mary Alice might have sent home during her year with Grandma Dowel.
2. Open Publisher and from the template folders select *Postcards*.
3. Select the Arrows postcard.
4. There are two pages to the postcard. Page 1 is the "front" of the postcard, and page 2 is the address block for the addresses (return and who is receiving the postcard). You will focus on the front of the postcard.
5. Replace the business name by highlighting and pressing Delete. Type in *Dear Folks*.
6. Replace *Product/Service Information* with *Halloween in Town* and resize the text box around the type to make it fit closer.
7. Type in the following information in the box below *Dear Folks: Uprooted privies, buggies on bell towers, and Grandma making glue were just part of Halloween here. We made pumpkin pies. The pies were wonderful! Halloween is definitely different here than in the city!*
8. Select and delete the Organization logo.
9. Select and delete the Business tagline text boxes (erasing information on that side of the postcard).
10. Select clip art to go on the postcard. Once the art is selected and placed on the postcard, you may want to have the art "behind" the type on the postcard. To do that, select *Arrange* from the toolbar and then *Order* from the pull-down menu. Make sure the art is selected (that the circular handles are showing) and select "Send to back" from the pull-down menu (see Figure 8.44).
11. The front of the postcard is now finished and should look something like Figure 8.45.

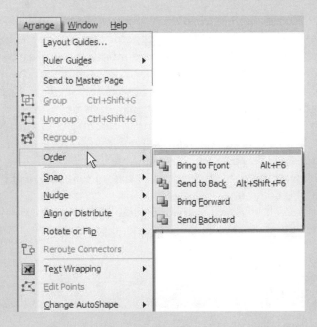

Figure 8.44
Order items
on page

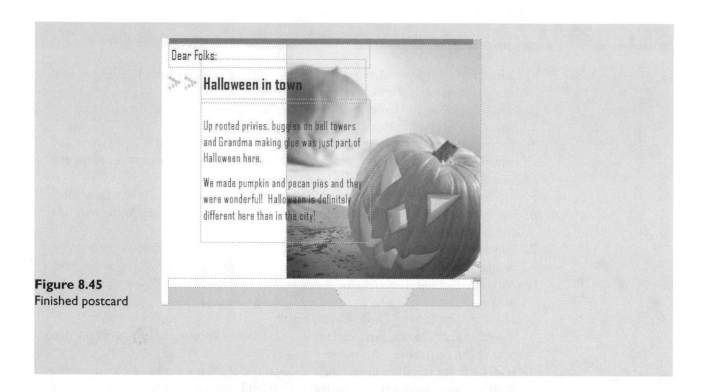

Figure 8.45
Finished postcard

A CHALLENGE USING PUBLISHER 2007

For those who would like a challenge beyond the Let Me Try activities presented in the chapter, try one of the following exercises:

1. Have students create a newsletter to let their parents and others know what they have been learning and what activities they are interested in learning about.
2. Have students create their own résumé or the résumé of a famous individual.
3. Create a letterhead for the class. Let students design the logo using Publisher.
4. Create a calendar of activities for the month that indicates the various historical activities that may have taken place on each day of the month.
5. Create award certificates for science fairs, history fairs, or good behavior.
6. Have students create a menu that may have been used at a historical event, such as the banquet after the signing of the Magna Charta.
7. Create business cards for famous people in history, sciences, or literature to allow students to research these individuals.
8. Create invitation cards for events at school that you might want to invite parents or the community to attend.
9. Create a Web site that provides additional information for a thematic unit that may be presented in class or added to as the class researches particular topics.

TYING IT ALL TOGETHER

In this chapter, you created a brochure using a template about the book *A Year Down Yonder* and a Web site also related to the book. You created a postcard from the main character in *A Year Down Yonder*. You saved publications and printed out the documents created. Publisher provides a variety of publication options, both print and nonprint. Although this chapter presented many of the fundamentals to help you get started, there are numerous other components of Publisher 2007 for you to explore.

REFERENCES

Bloom, B. (ED.). (1956). *Taxonomy of educational objectives.* New York: David McKay.

Peck, R. (2000). *A year down yonder.* New York: Puffin Books.

INTEGRATING OFFICE 2007

CHAPTER OUTLINE

LEARNING OBJECTIVES

At the completion of this chapter you will be able to:

- Copy and paste text from a Word document to a PowerPoint slide
- Place an Excel worksheet into a Word document and a PowerPoint slideshow
- Edit an Excel chart in a Word document and a PowerPoint slideshow
- Embed an Excel worksheet into a Word document
- Link an Excel worksheet to a Word document and a PowerPoint slideshow
- Embed a PowerPoint slide into a Word document
- Run a PowerPoint slideshow from a Word document
- Create contacts in Outlook and export them to Access
- Place Access data into a PowerPoint slide

CHAPTER OVERVIEW

Each Office application has a unique purpose and function. The ability to integrate their functionality expands one's capacity to efficiently design and produce materials and to incorporate diverse informational sources and media. Given this capability, it is fitting that an entire chapter of this text should be devoted to approaches to integrating these products. In the Show Me section, you will find instruction on how to develop materials that incorporate PowerPoint slides, Word documents, Excel worksheets, Outlook data, and Access data. The examples presented are only a few of the many options for developing materials. The Let Me Try exercises give step-by-step instructions for quickly accomplishing tasks related to the Show Me section. *In addition, you can locate files that correspond to the chapter activities on the accompanying CD in the Integration folder under Examples. Specifically, you will find a Project log worksheet, a sample proposal, and a proposal slideshow.*

About Integrating the Office Products

As you work with Office, you will undoubtedly encounter situations where you need files or portions of a file created with one application in a file that you created with another application. You may even need to work with one file and from it update, open, or run another file in a different application. For instance, suppose you use Word to create a class newsletter in which you highlight a student project, such as a PowerPoint slideshow illustrating the student's artwork. In Word, you provide a text description of the project as well as illustrations of the slideshow. Because PowerPoint and Word integrate so easily, you are able to select slides from PowerPoint and place them in the newsletter. In addition, if you show colleagues the newsletter you created in Word and they want to view the student project in more depth, you can click on the slide illustration and run the PowerPoint slideshow.

Integrating files across the Office products is extremely useful as you construct teaching and learning materials. It broadens the possibilities for the types of materials you can make and the efficiency with which you can produce them.

Have you ever created a chart and placed it into a document that you planned to distribute to your class of 35 students? Minutes before the class and seconds before clicking the Print button, you notice an error in the chart. Depending on how you made the chart, you may need to open an application, alter chart text and numeric values, prepare the chart for a word processor, and then place and format it. These tasks can be time consuming. Alternatively, by creating the document with Word and the chart with Excel and then linking them, you could quickly modify numeric values in Excel, which would automatically update the Word document and make it ready for printing.

The previously mentioned illustration and the examples throughout the chapter present a few approaches to integrating Office programs. As your familiarity with Office deepens, you will no doubt discover inventive ways to employ its integrative capabilities to create interesting and engaging classroom materials and activities.

Working with the Office Products

Suppose you are teaching a basic computer class and assign students to research a topic of interest that relates to an issue discussed in class. Students must create a multimedia project to present their research. You designate teams comprised of three or four individuals. Each team must write a proposal that provides an overview of the topic, a rationale for why it is important to develop the project, project objectives, ideas about how the project will look when it is finished, a projected time line, and a budget. Since it is important for students to document their work progress, you ask them to maintain a project journal in which they write details about the development process. At a minimum, each time the team works on the project, a team member records the date, time, how much time was spent working, the tasks or what was accomplished, and any thoughts about how the project is progressing.

Over a 4-month period, teams must deliver two 15-minute class presentations. The first, a project proposal presentation, provides an overview of the topic proposal, the development plan, and work already accomplished. During the presentation, teams seek feedback from the class about how to improve the project. After this presentation, teams spend time collecting additional information and materials and developing the project. At the second presentation, teams present the finished multimedia project. When the assignment is complete, students complete a self-evaluation consisting of a written summary of what they learned, an overall evaluation of the finished project, and an assessment of how well members worked together. Your classroom is equipped with a computer and projector so that teams can project their projects onto a screen for the entire class to see.

This chapter focuses on developing materials for the project proposal and the proposal presentation. Using files on the CD that have already been prepared in Word, PowerPoint, Excel, and Access, you will add material to the project proposal and the proposal presentation. The files needed for this activity are on the CD in the Integration folder under Examples. Although the content used here is specific to creating a project proposal and slideshow, the steps and procedures are generic and applicable to a variety of teaching and learning tasks.

Show Me

This Show Me section is divided into five segments. The first segment presents the following:

- Making a project journal-log in Excel
- Copying and pasting text from Word to PowerPoint
- Inserting PowerPoint slides into Word—copy and paste
- Dragging and dropping a slide
- Inserting objects

Let us suppose that team 1 chooses to create a PowerPoint slideshow that informs the class about how to create Web pages and transfer them to a Web server. The project will also present information about the HyperText Markup Language (HTML). Using an Excel worksheet, team 1 begins by creating a project journal-log (see Figure 9.1).

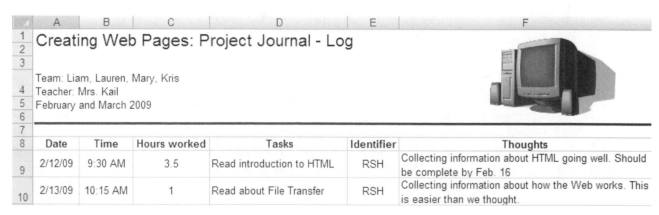

Figure 9.1
Journal-log sample

A sample project log (Project Log_Complete.xlsx) can be found on the CD in the Integration folder under Examples. Members set up columns for date, time, hours worked, tasks, and thoughts. Corresponding to the tasks column, they create a column named *Identifier* in which they place codes to help them identify task types. The identifiers are *RSH* for research, *DEV* for development, *ADM* for administrative, and *OTH* for other. When they enter task descriptions, they identify them by one of the four identifiers to help members determine the amount of time spent on different types of tasks.

After making the project journal-log, team 1 creates several PowerPoint slides representative of the finished project. The members also begin developing a project proposal that contains the following sections: title page, table of contents, project summary, project rationale, project objectives, creative strategy (what the project will be like when finished), project time line, and budget. They will use the proposal to guide their development of the PowerPoint slideshow to be delivered at the first (proposal) presentation. That slideshow will include a title slide, project objectives, sample screens (creative strategy), and time line. In addition, they intend to place slides from the PowerPoint slideshow into the Creative Strategy section of the proposal to illustrate to the teacher (or readers of the proposal) what the finished slideshow will look like.

Copying and Pasting Text from Word to PowerPoint

The members of team 1 developed several sections of the project proposal in Word. They also created several sample screens in PowerPoint. In this example, we will use text from the Objectives section of the proposal to add to a PowerPoint slide.

1. Open the *ProposalSlideShow.pptx* PowerPoint file on the CD in the Integration folder under Examples and click on the first slide.
2. Click the New Slide button or select *New Slide* from the Home tab.
3. Set the slide layout to Title and Content.
4. Open the *Proposal.docx* Word file in the Integration folder.
5. Locate the Objectives section of the proposal and select the word *Objectives*.
6. Click the Copy button on the Home tab or press Ctrl+C.
7. Go back to PowerPoint and click in the Title box (*Click to add title*) of the slide you just inserted. Click the Paste button, and the title text should appear (see Figure 9.2). If you copied the Return character after the word *Objectives*, an additional line/space may appear under the title. You can delete it by pressing the Backspace key.
8. Return to Word. Below the Objectives section heading, there are three objectives. Select them and then go back to PowerPoint.
9. Click in the text box (*Click to add text*) and click the Paste button. The bulleted items should appear (see Figure 9.3).

Figure 9.2
Objectives text

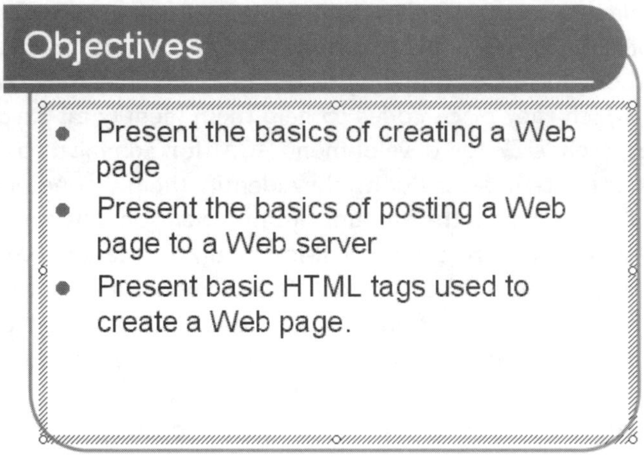

Objectives

- Present the basics of creating a Web page
- Present the basics of posting a Web page to a Web server
- Present basic HTML tags used to create a Web page.

Figure 9.3
Complete slide

Inserting PowerPoint Slides into Word—Copy and Paste

In this section, you will place two slides from PowerPoint into the Creative Strategy section of the proposal. There are several ways to place PowerPoint slides into Word. The easiest method is to copy the slide from PowerPoint and paste it into Word. A slide placed in Word is referred to as a *slide object.*

1. Open the PowerPoint slideshow. In this example, you will open a file named *ProposalSlideShow.pptx.* In the PowerPoint workspace, select the Normal view (select *Normal* from the View tab) and display the slide pane (Figure 9.4).

2. In this example, you want to copy the first slide and insert it into Word. In PowerPoint, click *slide 1* and then click the Copy button (or select *Copy* on the Home tab or press Ctrl+C).

3. Open Word and place the cursor where you would like to insert the PowerPoint slide. You will position both slides in the Creative Strategy section of the proposal. The first slide will go after the sentence *"After the title slide, it will present the objectives of the presentation and information about where the class can view the presentation online."* You will position the second slide at the end of the section.

4. With the cursor positioned after the words " . . . *presentation online,"* click the Paste button or press Ctrl+V, and the slide (slide object) will appear (see Figure 9.5).

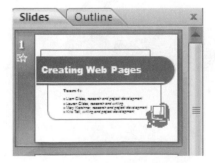

Figure 9.4
Slide pane here

Creative strategy (what the project will be like when finished)

Our presentation will open with a title slide that has music playing. After the title slide, it will present the objectives of the presentation and information about where the class can view the presentation online.

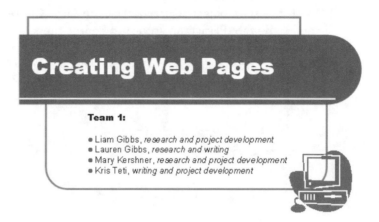

Figure 9.5
Slide pasted

5. Format the slide object by right-clicking on it in Word and select *Format Object* (see Figure 9.6), and the *Format Object* box appears (see Figure 9.7). In this case, you will resize the slide object to 70% of its original size.
6. Click the Size tab and type *70* in the *Height* box. If the *Lock aspect ratio* box is checked, then the width will automatically adjust. Click *OK,* and the slide should be smaller.

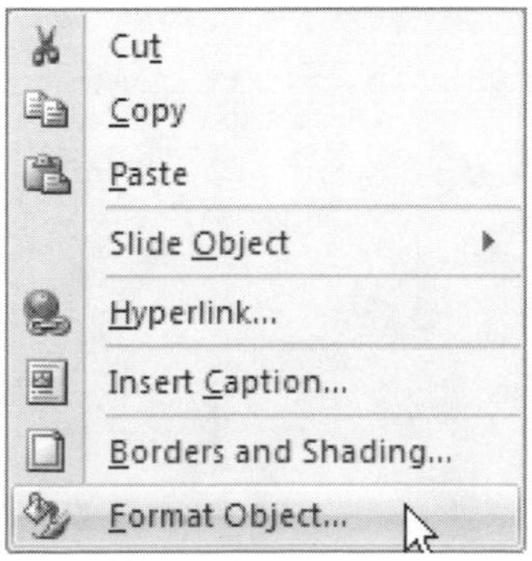

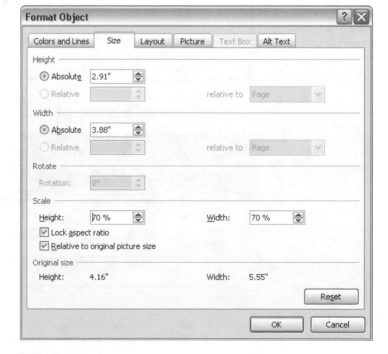

Figure 9.6
Format Object menu item

Figure 9.7
Format Object box

7. Place a border around the slide to set it apart from the text. Right-click on the slide and select *Border and Shading,* and the *Borders* box appears (see Figure 9.8). Click the Borders tab. In the Preview section of the *Borders* box, click the sides of the small image that displays or click the buttons at the left and bottom of the image. Click *OK.*

8. With the slide object selected, click the Align Center icon (see Figure 9.9) on the Home tab (Paragraph group) to center the slide on the page.

9. The slide should look like Figure 9.10.

10. Place the second slide object into Word. Go back to PowerPoint and click on *slide 3* in the slide pane or select one of the slides titled *Storage: Online.*

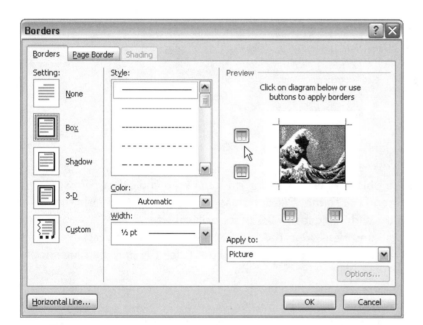

Figure 9.8
Borders box

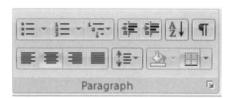

Figure 9.9
Align center

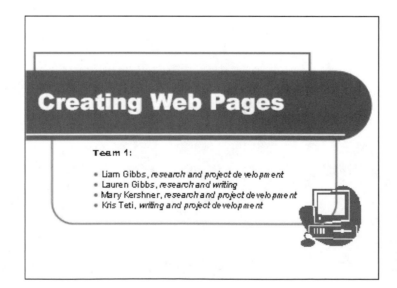

Figure 9.10
Complete slide

11. Select *Copy* from the Home tab or press Ctrl+C.
12. Go back to Word and position the cursor where you would like to place the slide. In this example, you will place it at the end of the Creative Strategy section of the project proposal on the empty line after the sentence *"The presentation will end with a black slide."*
13. Select *Paste* on the Home tab or press Ctrl+V, and the slide object appears.
14. Resize the slide to 70% of its original size.
15. Place a border around the slide to separate it from the text and center align it.
16. You can edit the slide object by right-clicking on it and selecting *Edit* from the Slide Object menu item (see Figure 9.11). In the edit mode, some of the functions on Word's Ribbon change to correspond to functions available on PowerPoint's Ribbon so that you may modify the slide layout, design, and color schemes (see Figure 9.12). You can add and modify clip art, text, and shapes as well as modify the background.

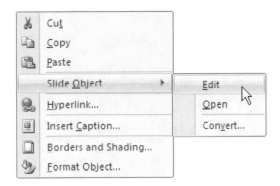

Figure 9.11
Slide Object
menu item

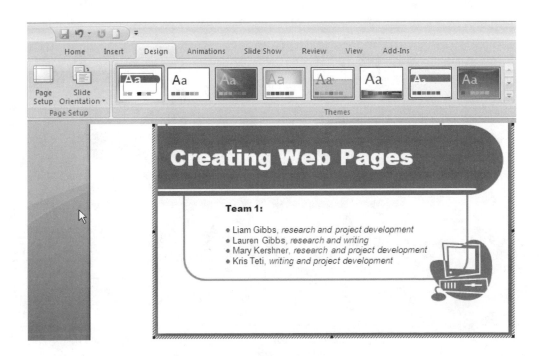

Figure 9.12
Themes

17. Click anywhere outside the slide area to exit the Edit mode. You can also edit the slide in PowerPoint. Right-click on the slide object in the Word document and then select *Open* from the Slide Object menu item. Diagonal lines appear through the slide, and PowerPoint opens with the single slide in it. As you edit the slide in PowerPoint, the changes display in the slide object that you placed in Word. To save the slide as a PowerPoint file, select *Save As* from the Office button. This saves the slide as a PowerPoint presentation. As you modify the slide, you do not affect the original PowerPoint file. You will notice that when you choose to edit a slide in PowerPoint, PowerPoint's New Slide button on the Home tab is inactive. This is because you are working with a single slide object, and additional slides cannot be added. To add slides to the PowerPoint file, you need to convert it from a slide object to a presentation object.

18. To convert the slide object, go to the slide in your Word document, right-click on it, and select *Convert.* from the Slide Object menu item (see Figure 9.13). The *Convert* box appears (see Figure 9.14).

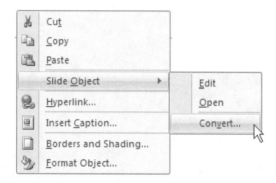

Figure 9.13
Convert slide object

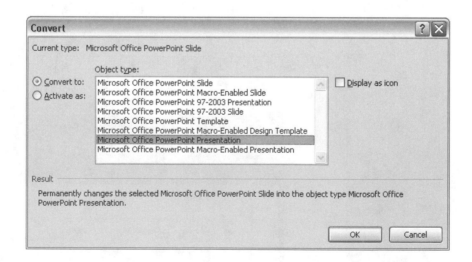

Figure 9.14
Convert box

19. Click the *Convert to:* button and then select *Microsoft PowerPoint Presentation*.

20. Click *OK*. The object is now a presentation into which you can add slides. For example, if you are in Word and right-click on the Presentation object and

select *Open* from the Presentation Object menu item, the file opens in PowerPoint. When in PowerPoint, you can add slides by clicking the New Slide button or selecting *Insert New Slide* from the Insert menu.

21. Once a slide object is converted to a presentation, you can run the PowerPoint slideshow from Word by double-clicking the object or by right-clicking on it and selecting *Show* from the Presentation Object menu item (Figure 9.15).

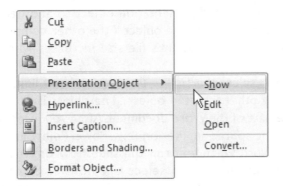

Figure 9.15
Show presentation object

Inserting a Presentation Object and Converting It to a Slide Object

Another method of placing a slide into Word is to use *Object* on the Insert tab.

1. Position the cursor at the location in Word where you want the slide to appear. Select *Object* from the Insert tab (Text group), and the *Object* box appears (see Figure 9.16).
2. Click the Create from File tab. You will notice on the *Object* box (Figure 9.16) that there is a *Link to file* option. When you insert a presentation

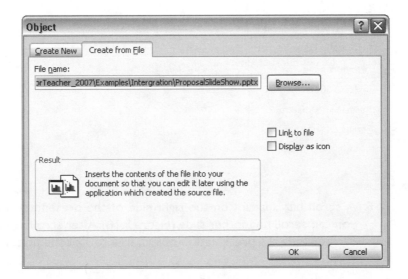

Figure 9.16
Object box

object (or any other inserted object) without selecting *Link to file,* a copy of the object embeds into the file. For example, if you insert a PowerPoint presentation titled *Presentation 1* into Word, Word embeds a copy of that file. Any changes that you make to the file embedded in Word will not affect the original file, *Presentation 1.* Likewise, when you edit the original file (e.g., *Presentation 1*), you do not affect the copy embedded in Word. Since an object becomes part of the document, it is available as you move the document from computer to computer. For instance, if you move a Word document containing an embedded presentation object to another computer, you can run the slideshow and edit the object if the other computer has PowerPoint. Keep in mind that a document's file size increases when you insert/embed an object.

When you select the *Link to file* option, Word links to the presentation object (or any other inserted object). The object is not embedded—it does not become part of the Word document. After you insert a linked object, you can work in the source application (e.g., PowerPoint), and the changes will be reflected in Word when you run the slideshow or when you right-click on the presentation object and select *Update Link.* Since Word links to the object, you must remember to move the linked file with the Word file when you move the Word document from one computer to another. If you move only the Word document, the linked object (e.g., PowerPoint slideshow) will not run from Word.

3. Click the Browse button, and the Browse window displays. Locate the PowerPoint file that contains the slide you want to insert.
4. Single-click on the file (*ProposalSlideShow.pptx*) to select it and click the Insert button on the Browse window.
5. Click *OK.* The first slide of the PowerPoint file displays. In this example, you opened a PowerPoint file named *ProposalSlideShow.pptx* that has several slides. If you want to display a slide other than the first slide, right-click on the presentation object and select *Edit* from the Presentation Object menu item (Figure 9.17).

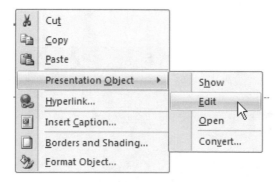

Figure 9.17
Edit presentation object

6. A scroll bar appears on the right side of the presentation object with which you can scroll to another slide (Figure 9.18). After scrolling to the desired slide, click outside the presentation object area to exit the edit mode.

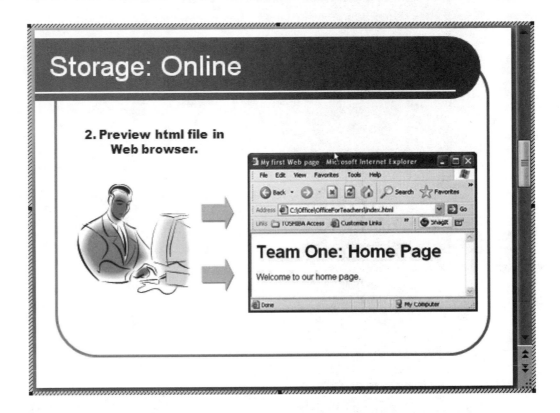

Figure 9.18
Edit mode

At this point, the presentation object is actually a PowerPoint file that, when double-clicked, will display the slides in the slideshow. Assuming that you do not need to run the PowerPoint slideshow and want to place only one slide into Word, you must convert the presentation object to a slide.

7. Right-click on the presentation object and select *Convert* from the Presentation Object menu item (see Figure 9.19).

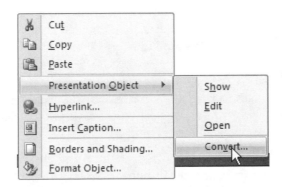

Figure 9.19
Convert object

8. When the *Convert* box displays, click the *Convert to:* option and then click *Microsoft PowerPoint Slide* under *Object type* (see Figure 9.20). Click *OK*. The presentation object is now a single slide rather than a PowerPoint presentation file.

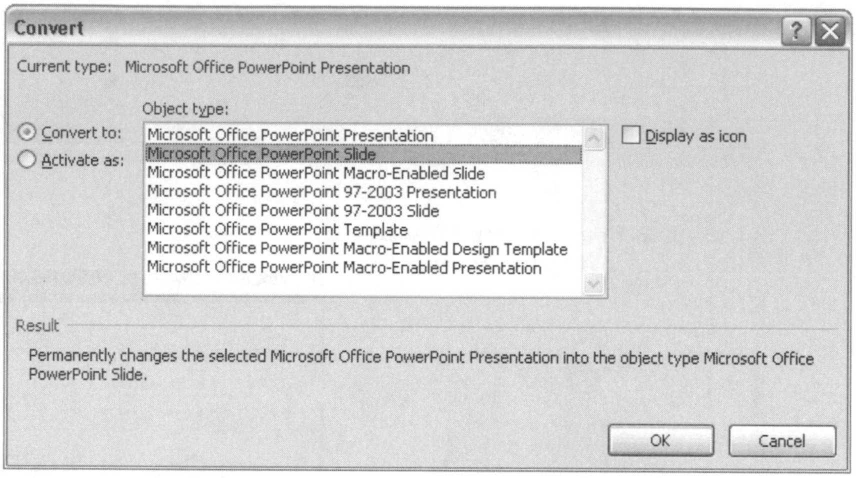

Figure 9.20
Convert box

LET ME TRY

Inserting a Linked Presentation Object

Suppose that you (the teacher) review team 1's proposal prior to the first presentation. You really like the formatting and the slide illustrations within in the document. You ask the group to share the proposal with the class. Team 1 plans to use a computer and projector for the presentation so that everything appearing on the computer can be projected onto a large screen. As a result, the group members decide to insert a presentation object to illustrate what the final project will look like. They can then show the proposal and run their PowerPoint slideshow from Word. During the presentation, the members open up their proposal in Word and discuss the formatting and some key points about the project. When presenting the section containing slide illustrations (the presentation object), they double-click on the object and the slideshow runs, without exiting Word or opening PowerPoint. When they are ready to exit the slideshow, the presenter presses the Esc key, and the presentation resumes from the Word document.

The insert object method is an appropriate choice for placing a PowerPoint file into Word. In this example, team 1 can display the PowerPoint slideshow from Word without exiting Word or opening PowerPoint.

1. To insert a PowerPoint file into Word, position the cursor at the location in Word where you want the slide to appear. Select *Object* from the Insert tab (Text group), and the *Object* box appears (see Figure 9.21).
2. Click the Create from File tab.
3. Click the Browse button, and the Browse window displays. Locate the PowerPoint file that contains the slide you want to insert. In this example, you will insert a PowerPoint file named *ProposalSlideShow.pptx*. Single-click on the *ProposalSlideShow.pptx* file to select it and then click the Insert button on the Browse window.

Figure 9.21
Object box

4. Click the *Link to file* option on the *Object* box. This enables you to modify the PowerPoint file after inserting it into Word. The changes that you make to the PowerPoint file will be reflected in the inserted object.
5. Click *OK*. The first slide of the PowerPoint file displays.

Running the Linked Presentation Object

6. Run the slideshow by double-clicking on it or by right-clicking on the Linked Presentation object or selecting *Show Link* from the Linked Presentation Object menu item. To exit the slideshow and return to Word, press the Esc key.

Pasting an Excel Worksheet into a Word Document and a PowerPoint Slideshow

This second Show Me section presents the following:

- Copying and pasting the journal-log from Excel into Word and formatting it
- Copying and pasting the journal-log from Excel into a PowerPoint slideshow and formatting it

In developing the projected time line section of the project proposal, team 1 plans to include a sample of the project log. The sample will illustrate the work that the team has completed, and it will help justify the budget and projected completion date the team has set. In addition, the team will create a chart that illustrates the time that the members have spent on specific project tasks. You will place these materials in the PowerPoint slideshow.

1. To paste a section of the project log into Word, open the Excel file. In this example, you will open a file named *Project Log.xlsx* on the CD. Team 1 would like to show the work that has been completed so far on the project, which is represented in columns A through F and in rows 8 through 19.
2. Click in column A at row 8 and, while holding the left mouse button down, drag downward and to the right to column F at row 19. The contents of the worksheet should now be selected (see Figure 9.22).

7						
8	**Date**	**Time**	**Hours worked**	**Tasks**	**Identifier**	**Thoughts**
9	2/12/09	9:30 AM	3.5	Read introduction to HTML	RSH	Collecting information about HTML going well. Should be complete by Feb. 16
10	2/13/04	10:15 AM	1	Read about File Transfer	RSH	Collecting information about how the Web works. This is easier than we thought.
11	2/14/09	2:30 PM	2	Team met and exchanged information about HTML and FTP	RSH	Team members seem to be working well together. Need to get information about Web graphics. Kris and Liam disagree about what needs to be presented and who is going to type proposal.
12	2/14/09	1:15 PM	4	Gather URLs that provide information about Web page design and HTML. Reviewed each page and collected relevant information and shared it with team.	RSH	There are many resources available. It's a bit overwhelming trying to narrow down the information. Liam will help me go through the sites again to determine what we need to include.
13	2/16/09	9:30 AM	1.5	Created first draft of proposal	DEV	Two of us meet and discussed the main topics. Lauren agreed to write the first draft and she will send it to each member for their reactions.
14	2/17/09	12:30 PM	3	Proposal review meeting	DEV	The team met to review the draft proposal. Liam will re-work the goals and objectives, creative ideas and time line section.
15	2/18/09	4:00 PM	3.5	Proposal revision	DEV	The team members had comments on the revised proposal. Lauren will make the revisions and send them to the members by tomorrow.

Figure 9.22
Select worksheet content

3. Click the Copy button on the Home tab or select press Ctrl+C.
4. Position the cursor at the location in Word where you want to place the worksheet. In this example, you will place it after the first paragraph in the *Project timeline* section of the proposal (see "Proposal.docx" on the CD).
5. Click the Paste button or press Ctrl+V. The worksheet appears in the Word document as a table. Once the worksheet is placed into Word, it can be modified as a Word table. In this example, the worksheet table extends beyond the border of the Word document (see Figure 9.23).
6. To adjust the table, click inside of it and under the Table Tools tab click the Layout tab. In the Cell Size group of the Layout tab, select *AutoFit* and then *AutoFit Window* (see Figure 9.24).

Project timeline

Phase I: Research (February 2009)

During the planning stage, we will establish team-meeting dates. We will conduct an in-depth review of the hypertext markup language, FTP, and Web page creation techniques. The information gathered during this review will enable us to write a draft of the project proposal.

Date	Time	Hours worked	Tasks	Identifier	Thoughts
2/12/09	9:30 AM	3.5	Read introduction to HTML	RSH	Collecting information about HTML g Should be complete by Feb. 16
2/13/04	10:15 AM	1	Read about File Transfer	RSH	Collecting information about how the This is easier than we thought.
2/14/09	2:30 PM	2	Team met and exchanged information about HTML and FTP	RSH	Team members seem to be working together. Need to get information ab graphics. Kris and Liam disagree ab needs to be presented and who is go proposal.

Figure 9.23
Pasted worksheet

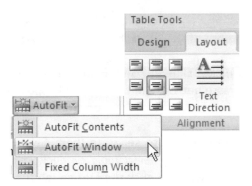

Figure 9.24
AutoFit

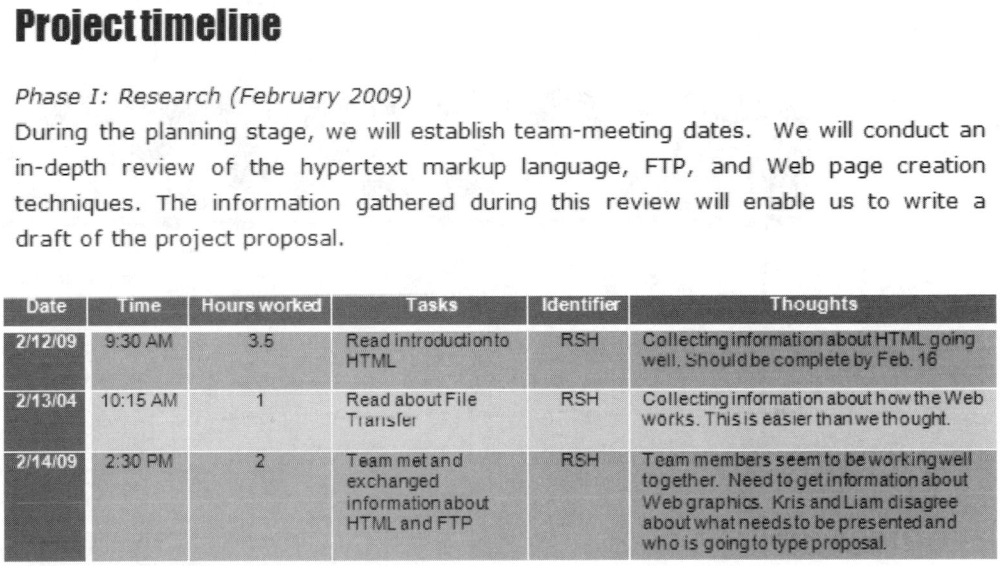

Project timeline

Phase I: Research (February 2009)

During the planning stage, we will establish team-meeting dates. We will conduct an in-depth review of the hypertext markup language, FTP, and Web page creation techniques. The information gathered during this review will enable us to write a draft of the project proposal.

Date	Time	Hours worked	Tasks	Identifier	Thoughts
2/12/09	9:30 AM	3.5	Read introduction to HTML	RSH	Collecting information about HTML going well. Should be complete by Feb. 16
2/13/04	10:15 AM	1	Read about File Transfer	RSH	Collecting information about how the Web works. This is easier than we thought.
2/14/09	2:30 PM	2	Team met and exchanged information about HTML and FTP	RSH	Team members seem to be working well together. Need to get information about Web graphics. Kris and Liam disagree about what needs to be presented and who is going to type proposal.

Figure 9.25
Table styles

7. Click the Design tab (under Table Tools) and in the Table Styles group select a style for the table. In Figure 9.25, the *Medium Grid 3-Accent 1* is used.
8. Set the font style and font size by clicking in the table, click the *Layout* tab (under Table Tools), and then choose *Select Table* from the Select option in the Table group. This action selects the table text. With the text selected, make the Home tab active and set the font to Arial and the size to 8 points.

Copying and Pasting a Worksheet into PowerPoint

You will now add the journal-log sample to PowerPoint and make a new slide to present information about the project time line.

9. Open the PowerPoint presentation file *ProposalSlideshow.pptx*. It already contains a *Project timeline* slide. Click on the *Project Timeline* slide.
10. Click the New Slide button on the Home tab. Make this slide a *Title only* slide.
11. Type *Project Timeline* in the title box. Click outside the title box to deselect it.

12. Go to Excel (*ProjectLog.xlsx*). Since this slide is only a sample of the journal-log, select the contents of the worksheet from cell A8 down to F12. Click the Copy button.

13. Go to the *Project Timeline* slide in PowerPoint. Click in the open area of the slide and click the Paste button. The table should appear (see Figure 9.26).

14. Extend the width of the table by clicking on the sizing handles and dragging to the left or right.

15. Place borders around the cells to separate them. Select the table by right-clicking inside it and choosing *Select Table* or click in the table and press Ctrl+A. With the table selected, click the Design tab (under Table Tools) and click the Borders button in the Table Styles group and select *Inside Borders* (see Figure 9.27). Alternatively, you can apply a Table style by selecting a style from the Table Styles group on the Design tab.

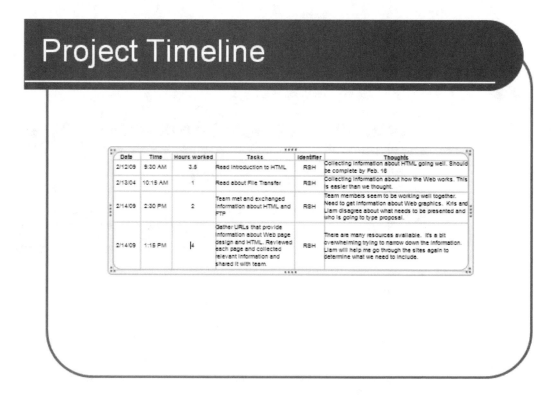

Figure 9.26
Select table

Figure 9.27
Borders

Figure 9.28
Alignment

Project Timeline

Date	Time	Hours worked	Tasks	Identifier	Thoughts
2/12/09	9:30 AM	3.5	Read introduction to HTML	RSH	Collecting information about HTML going well. Should be complete by Feb. 16
2/13/04	10:15 AM	1	Read about File Transfer	RSH	Collecting information about how the Web works. This is easier than we thought.
2/14/09	2:30 PM	2	Team met and exchanged information about HTML and FTP	RSH	Team members seem to be working well together. Need to get information about Web graphics. Kris and Liam disagree about what needs to be presented and who is going to type proposal.
2/14/09	1:15 PM	4	Gather URLs that provide information about Web page design and HTML. Reviewed each page and collected relevant information and shared it with team.	RSH	There are many resources available. It's a bit overwhelming trying to narrow down the information. Liam will help me go through the sites again to determine what we need to include.

Figure 9.29
Complete slide

16. With the table still selected, click the Layout tab and in the Alignment group click the Centered Vertically button (see Figure 9.28). In addition, click the Cell Margins button and select *Normal*. If portions of text wrap around the cells, you can enlarge a column by clicking on the column border and drag it left or right.

17. The finished slide should look like Figure 9.29.

Creating a Chart Illustrating the Time Members Have Spent on Project Tasks

This third section of Show Me presents the following:

- Creating and formatting an Excel chart
- Adding an Excel chart to Word
- Inserting a chart into PowerPoint from Excel

In the proposal as well as in the presentation, the members of team 1 think it is important to illustrate how they have spent their time on the project. You will create a chart that shows how they allocated their time to various tasks and place it in Word and in PowerPoint.

Adding an Excel Chart to Word

In column C of the project journal-log (*ProjectLog.xlsx*), the members recorded time on task (Hours Worked), and in column E they categorized specific tasks (Identifier).

Figure 9.30
Project journal-log

8	Date	Time	Hours worked	Tasks	Identifier
9	2/12/09	9:30 AM	3.5	Read introduction to HTML	RSH
10	2/13/04	10:15 AM	1	Read about File Transfer	RSH

Figure 9.31
Task identifiers

	G	H	I	J
8	RSH	DEV	ADM	OTH
9				

For instance, in Figure 9.30, cell C9 contains *3.5*, and cell E9 contains *RSH*. This indicates that members spent 3.5 hours on a research (RSH) task.

Figure 9.32
AutoSum

1. The members would like to chart the time they spent on all tasks so far. In Excel, create four column headings: RSH, DEV, ADM, and OTH (see Figure 9.31).
2. Click in the cell below the RSH heading and click the Sum button in the Editing group of the Home tab (see Figure 9.32). After clicking *Sum*, Excel waits for you to select the cells. Since you have labeled this column RSH, you want to select only the cells that correspond to the RSH (research) label. Click in cell C9 and drag down to cell C12 (see Figure 9.33). Doing this informs Excel that you want to sum the data in this range of cells. If you want to select nonadjacent cells, then hold down the Ctrl key while clicking, and you will be able to select cells that are not adjacent to one another.

8	Hours worked	Tasks	Identifier	Thoughts	RSH	DEV
9	3.5	Read introduction to HTML	RSH	Collecting information about HTML going well. Should be complete by Feb. 16	=SUM(C9:C12)	
10	1	Read about File Transfer	RSH	Collecting information about how the Web works. This is easier than we thought.	SUM(number1, [numb	
11	2	Team met and exchanged information about HTML and FTP	RSH	Team members seem to be working well together. Need to get information about Web graphics. Kris and Liam disagree about what needs to be presented and who is going to type proposal.		
12	4	Gather URLs that provide information about Web page design and HTML. Reviewed each page and collected relevant information and shared it with team.	RSH	There are many resources available. It's a bit overwhelming trying to narrow down the information. Liam will help me go through the sites again to determine what we need to include.		

Figure 9.33
Selected cells

3. Press the Enter key, and the value appears.
4. After you add the values for the RSH identifier, click in the cell below the DEV heading. Click *Sum* and select the cells in column C that correspond to DEV (development) tasks.
5. Repeat this procedure for the ADM and OTH identifiers (see Figure 9.34) so that you have summed the hours spent on all tasks.
6. To chart the data, click the left mouse button and drag across the data headings and the values. In this example, the headings and values are in cells G8 through J9. With the data selected, click the Pie chart on the Charts group of the Insert tab (see Figure 9.35).

RSH	DEV	ADM	OTH
10.5	13	2	1

Figure 9.34
Summed values

Figure 9.35
Charts group

7. From the Pie chart pallet, select *3-D Pie*, and a pie chart will appear (see Figure 9.36).

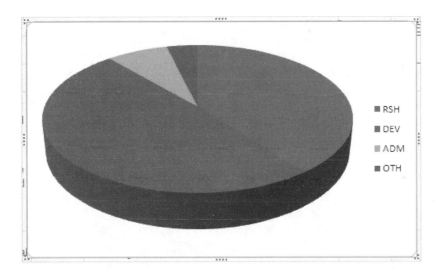

Figure 9.36
Pie chart

8. Click on the border of the chart. Under the Chart Tools tab, click *Design*. In the Chart Layouts group, choose *Layout 1*. Click on the chart title and type *Project Work Tasks*.
9. Click on the series labels (ADM, OTH, DEV, or RSH) to select them. Make the Home tab active, choose a font (Arial), set it to bold, and set the size to 10 points. You may have to reposition the series labels so they are readable. To move a label, click it and drag it to a new location. The completed chart should look similar to Figure 9.37.
10. In the worksheet, move/drag the chart to the right of column F so that it does not cover the worksheet content.
11. Click on the chart to select it and then click the Copy button (Home tab) or press Ctrl+C.
12. Go to Word and position the cursor where you would like to place the chart. In this example, you will place it in the *Project Timeline* section.
13. Since the team members may need to add more data to the chart, you will paste it as an Excel chart object. On the Home tab, Clipboard group, click the Paste button and then select *Paste Special*, and the *Paste Special* box appears (see Figure 9.38).

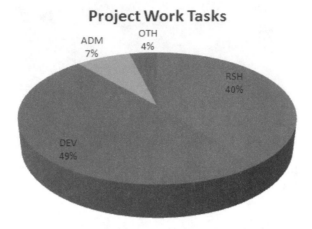

Figure 9.37
Complete chart

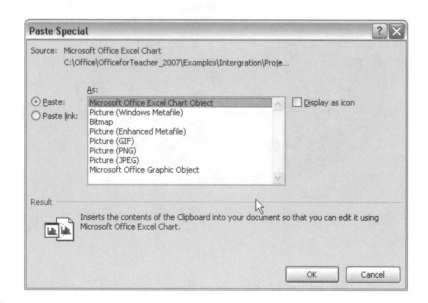

Figure 9.38
Paste Special box

14. Click the *Microsoft Office Excel Chart Object* option and click the Paste button.
15. Click *OK*, and the chart appears as a chart object in Word.
16. In this example, let us suppose that you need to increase the hours on the OTH tasks. To edit the chart, right-click on it and select *Edit* from the *Worksheet Object* item. In the edit mode, you have access to worksheets as well as the chart (see Figure 9.39).
17. Click the Sheet1 tab to view the data sheet.
18. Click in the cell that contains the value for the OTH category and type the number 5 (see Figure 9.40). Before exiting the edit mode, click the Chart1 tab and then click outside the Object area to exit the edit mode. If you exit the edit mode without clicking the Chart1 tab, then the worksheet and not

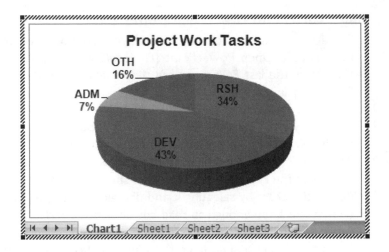

Figure 9.39
Edit mode

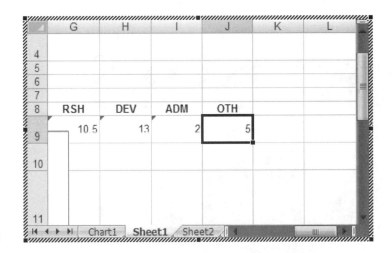

Figure 9.40
Edit mode—Sheet 1

the chart will display in Word. You may need to adjust the labels, and you can do so by clicking and dragging them to adjust their position.

19. The finished chart should look like Figure 9.41.

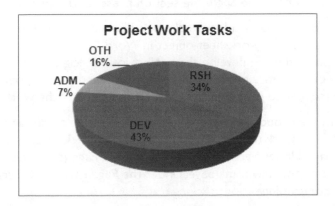

Figure 9.41
Complete chart

Inserting a Chart into PowerPoint from Excel

20. Since you made the chart in Excel, you do not need to re-create it in PowerPoint. Open PowerPoint (*ProposalSlideShow.pptx*) and insert a new slide after the last *Project timeline* slide. Make this slide Title Only and type *Project Timeline* in the title box.
21. Open the Project journal-log in Excel.
22. Previously, you created a pie chart, which should be in *Sheet1* of Excel. Click on the pie chart and then click the Copy button.
23. Return to PowerPoint and click in the *Project timeline* slide you created and then click the Paste button. The chart should appear.
24. Resize the chart by selecting it and dragging a sizing handle outward. Resize so that it is large enough to read but does not overlap the slide borders.
25. Click the chart to select it and then click the Design tab under the Chart Tools tab. Select a style from the Chart Styles group. In this example, you chose *Style 4*.
26. The chart should now look like Figure 9.42.

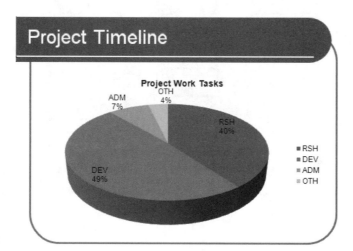

Figure 9.42
Chart in PowerPoint

Embedding an Excel Worksheet into a Word Document

This fourth segment of the Show Me section presents the following:

- Embedding a journal-log Excel worksheet as an object in Word
- Formatting the worksheet object in Word

Team 1 has taken time to develop the project journal-log, so the members intend to place a copy of the entire project journal-log at the end of the proposal (as an appendix) for the teacher to review. In this case, you will embed the worksheet object.

1. With the proposal opened in Word, position the cursor at the bottom of the last page. Click the Page Layout tab and then click *Breaks* and a list of options displays. Under Section Breaks, select *Next Page* (see Figure 9.43).
2. Click on the new blank page. Under the Page Layout tab, click *Orientation* and select *Landscape*.

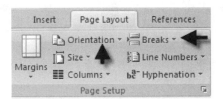

Figure 9.43
Layout

3. With the cursor positioned at the top of the new page, select *Object* from the Insert tab, and the *Object* box appears.
4. Click the Create from File tab. Click the Browse button, and the Browse window displays. Locate the Excel worksheet that you want to insert. In this example, you will insert a worksheet named *Project Log_Word.xlsx*. Click on the *Project Log_Word.xlsx* file to select it and then click the Insert button on the Browse window. Click *OK*.
5. In this example, you first need to make the object smaller. Right-click on the worksheet and select *Format Object*. When the *Format Object* box displays, click the Size tab (see Figure 9.44). Enter *6* for the height. If you have the *Lock aspect ratio* option selected, then the width changes automatically.

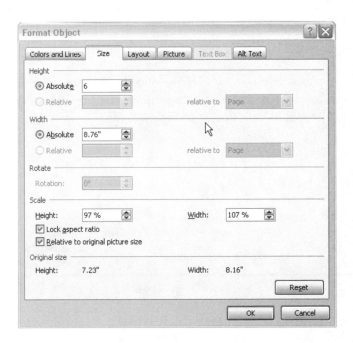

Figure 9.44
Format Object

6. Click *OK*, and the object should appear smaller.
7. If necessary, you can resize the object window. Right-click on the object and select *Edit* from the Worksheet Object menu item.
8. In the edit mode, you can resize the object window. Go to the bottom-right side of the object and position the cursor over the corner. The cursor changes to a double arrow (see Figure 9.45). While holding the left mouse button down, drag upward and to the left so that the empty rows and columns do not display (see Figure 9.46).

Figure 9.45
Cursor

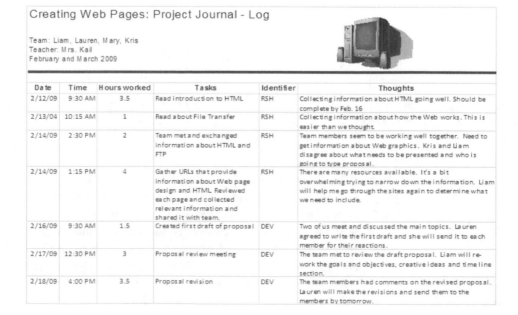

11	2/14/05	2:30 PM	2	information about HTML and FTP	RSH	Need to get information about Web graphics. Kris and Liam disagree about what needs to be presented and who is going to type proposal.
12	2/14/05	1:15 PM	4	Gather URLs that provide information about Web page design and HTML. Reviewed each page and collected relevant information and shared it	RSH	There are many resources available. It's a bit overwhelming trying to narrow down the information. Liam will help me go through the sites again to determine what we need to include.
13	2/16/05	9:30 AM	1.5	Created first draft of proposal	DEV	Two of us meet and discussed the main topics. Lauren agreed to write the first draft and she will send it to each member for their reactions.
14	2/17/05	12:30 PM	3	Proposal review meeting	DEV	The team met to review the draft proposal. Liam will re-work the goals and objectives, creative ideas and time line section.
15	2/18/05	4:00 PM	3.5	Proposal revision	DEV	The team members had comments on the revised proposal. Lauren will make the revisions and send them to the members by tomorrow.
16	2/19/05	2:15 PM	5	Project outline	DEV	The team met and reviewed the proposal. Liam and Kris will develop an outline of the project. Lauren and Mary will begin to prepare the text of the presentation and identify graphics

Figure 9.46
Oversize worksheet

9. Exit the edit mode by clicking outside the object area. You may need to increase the object's size using the *Format Object* box. When complete, the object should look similar to Figure 9.47.

Creating Web Pages: Project Journal - Log

Team: Liam, Lauren, Mary, Kris
Teacher: Mrs. Kail
February and March 2009

Date	Time	Hours worked	Tasks	Identifier	Thoughts
2/12/09	9:30 AM	3.5	Read introduction to HTML	RSH	Collecting information about HTML going well. Should be complete by Feb. 16
2/13/04	10:15 AM	1	Read about File Transfer	RSH	Collecting information about how the Web works. This is easier than we thought.
2/14/09	2:30 PM	2	Team met and exchanged information about HTML and FTP	RSH	Team members seem to be working well together. Need to get information about Web graphics. Kris and Liam disagree about what needs to be presented and who is going to type proposal.
2/14/09	1:15 PM	4	Gather URLs that provide information about Web page design and HTML. Reviewed each page and collected relevant information and shared it with team.	RSH	There are many resources available. It's a bit overwhelming trying to narrow down the information. Liam will help me go through the sites again to determine what we need to include.
2/16/09	9:30 AM	1.5	Created first draft of proposal	DEV	Two of us meet and discussed the main topics. Lauren agreed to write the first draft and she will send it to each member for their reactions.
2/17/09	12:30 PM	3	Proposal review meeting	DEV	The team met to review the draft proposal. Liam will re-work the goals and objectives, creative ideas and time line section.
2/18/09	4:00 PM	3.5	Proposal revision	DEV	The team members had comments on the revised proposal. Lauren will make the revisions and send them to the members by tomorrow.

Figure 9.47
Complete worksheet object

LET ME TRY

Suppose you want to create a multimedia team research report. You assign team members to research a topic of interest and collect text information, photographs, video, audio, and numerical data about the topic. We use Word to compile the text information; PowerPoint to assemble the photographs, video, and audio; and Excel to organize the numerical data.

Next, you define tasks for each team member. Assign a student to coordinate the project and integrate the slideshow and worksheet materials in Word. Assign at least one student to develop the PowerPoint slideshow and one student to prepare data and create data charts with Excel.

Linking PowerPoint Files and Excel Files to Word

1. Create a folder to store your files and name it *Team Project*.
2. Create a rough draft of the report in Word.
3. In addition, create drafts of the slideshow and Excel worksheet(s); save the files in the Team Project folder with descriptive names.
4. Link the PowerPoint slideshow and Excel worksheets to the Word document. From the Word Insert tab, select *Object*.
5. Click the Create from File tab and locate the PowerPoint slideshow.
6. Click the *Link to File* option and click OK.
7. Repeat these steps for the Excel worksheet.
8. Each team member then works on his or her part of the project. As members work on their respective tasks, they must remember to save their files with the same names as used earlier.
9. When the members have completed their tasks, copy the files to the Team Project folder. As long as the file names are identical to the names given earlier, the new (or most up-to-date) files will overwrite the existing (draft) files in the Team Project folder.
10. Open the report Word document, and the linked objects should be updated.

Creating a Credit Slide: Outlook and Access

This fifth segment of the Show Me section presents the following:

- Creating an e-mail contact in Outlook
- Exporting contacts to Access
- Copying and pasting data records from Access to PowerPoint

Suppose that for the duration of the project, the members of team 1 maintained an e-mail contact list in Microsoft Outlook of individuals who assisted them with the project proposal and presentation. As the list developed, they added information in addition to e-mail address, such as phone number, fax number, and address. They would now like to export the list to Access to create a database of experts that will be a valuable resource for them and their classmates. From the database, they will make a *Credits* slide to give those individuals credit for their assistance.

Creating a Contact in Outlook

1. Open Outlook. Select *Contacts* from the Go menu (Figure 9.48).
2. Select *New* from the File menu and then select *Contact* from the submenu (see Figure 9.49).

Figure 9.48
Outlook contacts

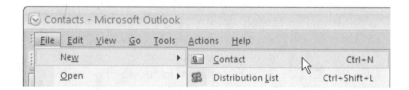

Figure 9.49
Create Outlook
contacts

3. An untitled contact box displays. Enter the contact information (see Figure 9.50).

4. Select *Save & Close* in the Actions group of the Contact tab. To add more contacts, select *New* and then *Contacts* from the File menu.

Export Contacts to Access

5. Select *Import and Export* from the File menu. The Import and Export Wizard displays. Choose the *Export to a file* option and click *Next* (see Figure 9.51).

6. The *Export to a File* box displays. Click the *Microsoft Access* option and then click *Next.*

7. On the next *Export to a File* screen, click *Contacts* under *Select folder to export from:* (see Figure 9.52). Click *Next.*

8. On the next *Export to a File* screen, give the file a name and specify a location in which to save it. For this example, you will name the file *Team1Contacts* and save it in the My Documents folder. Click *Next.* The next screen informs you of the action to be taken, and *Export "Contacts" from folder; "Contacts"* should be checked. Click *Finish.*

9. The contacts export to Access, and an .accdb file is created with the name you assigned. For example, you named the file *Team1Contacts*, so you will find a file in the My Documents folder named *Team1Contacts.accdb.*

10. Open Access. Click the Office button, select *Open*, and locate the *Team1Contacts.accdb* file. You can locate *Team1Contacts.accdb* on the CD. The *Team1Contacts:* database window displays (see Figure 9.53). On the left side of the window, double-click *Contacts table.*

11. From the Access View menu, select *Datasheet view*, and the data records display (see Figure 9.54).

Figure 9.50
Contact
information

Figure 9.51
Import and Export
Wizard

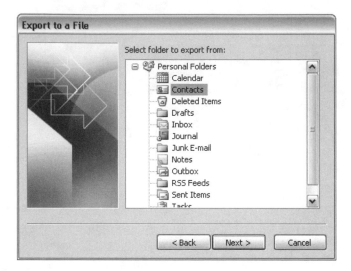

Figure 9.52
Export to a File

Figure 9.53
Team1 Contacts

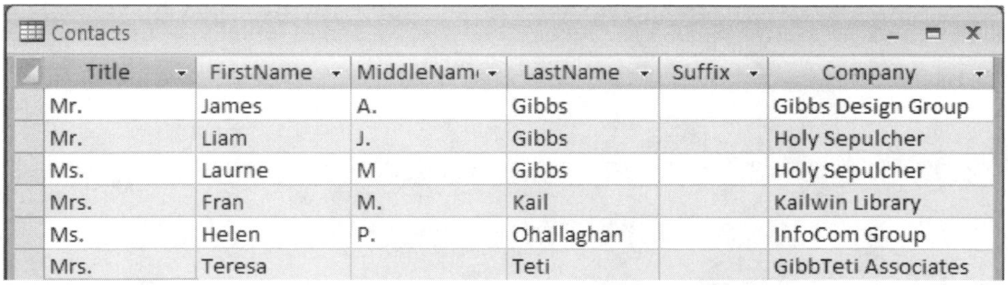

Title	FirstName	MiddleNam	LastName	Suffix	Company
Mr.	James	A.	Gibbs		Gibbs Design Group
Mr.	Liam	J.	Gibbs		Holy Sepulcher
Ms.	Laurne	M	Gibbs		Holy Sepulcher
Mrs.	Fran	M.	Kail		Kailwin Library
Ms.	Helen	P.	Ohallaghan		InfoCom Group
Mrs.	Teresa		Teti		GibbTeti Associates

Figure 9.54
Access datasheet view

Copying and Pasting Data Records from Access to PowerPoint

Now that you have created your database, let's copy some of the data records and paste them into PowerPoint to create the credits slide. For the credits slide, you will need only the person's name and company. However, the columns with this information are not adjacent, so you will move them.

↓ Company
Holy Sepulcher
Holy Sepulcher
Kailwin Library
Penn State
InfoCom Group
GibbTet Associ
Gibbs Design G

Figure 9.55
Field selector

1. From the Datasheet view, position the cursor over the field selector for the *Company* column, and the cursor changes to an inverted arrow (see Figure 9.55). Clicking anywhere in the gray title area selects the column.
2. Select the *Company* column and, while holding the left mouse button down, drag it to the right of the *LastName* column. The *Contacts: Table* should look like Figure 9.56.
3. Select the *Title, FirstName, MiddleName, LastName,* and *Company* columns by dragging the mouse over the field selector (gray area with column name) of each column.
4. Click the Copy button (in the Clipboard group on the Home tab).
5. Go to PowerPoint. Click the last side and then click the New Slide button.
6. Set the slide layout to Title Only. Type *Credits* in the Title box.
7. Click outside the Title box to deselect it.
8. Click the Paste button, and the Access data should display in the slide. Notice that the title (*Contacts*) of the data table also appears on the slide, which you can delete for this example by right-clicking in the row and selecting *Delete Rows*.
9. Resize the table so that it fits below the title and within the slide frame.
10. When first clicking on an object, its border changes to a dashed line, indicating that it can be modified. Clicking on the border a second time changes it from a dashed line to a solid line. The line indicates that the contents of the object are selected and that changes (e.g., font size or style) will affect the entire contents of the object.
11. Click inside the table and press Ctrl+A to select it. With the table selected, click the Layout tab under Table Tools. Set the text alignment to *Center* and *Center Vertically* (see Figure 9.57).

Figure 9.56
Contacts table

Contacts				
Title ▾	FirstName ▾	MiddleNam ▾	LastName ▾	Company ▾
Mr.	James	A.	Gibbs	Gibbs Design Group
Mr.	Liam	J.	Gibbs	Holy Sepulcher
Ms.	Lauren	M	Gibbs	Holy Sepulcher
Mrs.	Fran	M.	Kail	Kailwin Library
Ms.	Helen	P.	Ohallaghan	InfoCom Group
Mrs.	Teresa	M.	Teti	GibbTeti Associates

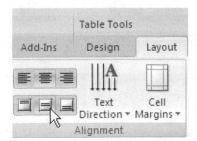

Figure 9.57
Center vertically

Contacts

Design	First Name	Middle Name	Last Name	Company
Mr.	James	A.	Gibbs	Gibbs Design Group
Mr.	Liam	J.	Gibbs	Holy Sepulcher
Ms.	Lauren	M	Gibbs	Holy Sepulcher
Mrs.	Fran	M.	Kail	Kailwin Library
Ms.	Helen	P.	Ohallaghan	InfoCom Group
Mrs.	Teresa	M.	Teti	GibbTeti Associates

Figure 9.58
Complete slide

12. Click the Design tab and (with the table still selected) select *Inside Borders* in the Table Styles group.
13. Click the Home tab and set the font to Arial and the size to 14 points and the style to bold.
14. When you are done, the slide should look similar to Figure 9.58.

LET ME TRY

In this Let Me Try, you will extend the game activity presented in chapter 4. Following the directions in chapter 4, you can quickly and easily create a PowerPoint Jeopardy game to use in classes. However, if you want to change questions, you have to modify them on each slide, which is time consuming. In this Let Me Try, you will use Excel to store questions. When you want to change a question, the change is made in Excel rather than PowerPoint, which will allow for more rapid updates. You can review a sample file (*Jeopardy.pptx*) on the CD in the Integration folder inside Examples. The *Jeopardy.pptx* file is linked to an Excel file (*JeopardyData.xlsx*) and simply serves as a menu that connects to other PowerPoint files. Inside *Jeopardy.pptx* there is one slide that has five buttons on it. Only the Multiplication button is active, and when clicked, it opens another PowerPoint file titled *Multiplication.pptx*. The button labels and questions in *Jeopardy.pptx* and *Multiplication.pptx* have been entered into the Excel file (*JeopardyData.xlsx*). The PowerPoint files are just set up to display them. As you change the labels or questions in Excel, the PowerPoint files reflect those changes. You can use these files to expand on the Jeopardy game.

1. Open *Jeopardy_Game_Linked.pptx* and *Jeopardy_Game_Linked.xlsx*.
2. Make the *Jeopardy_Game_Linked.pptx* active and click on *slide 2*.
3. Go to the *Jeopardy_Game_Linked.xlsx* file. Click in cell A2 and click the Copy button or press Ctrl+C.

4. Go to the *Jeopardy_Game_Linked.pptx* (PowerPoint) file. Click *slide 2* and from the Paste button select *Paste Special*.

5. Select *Paste link* and *Microsoft Office Excel Worksheet Object* in the *Paste special box* and click *OK*. The text *3 Times 4* should appear.

6. Click on *slide 3*.

7. Go to the *Jeopardy_Game_Linked.xlsx* file. Click in cell B2 and click the Copy button or press Ctrl+C.

8. Go to the *Jeopardy_Game_Linked.pptx* (PowerPoint) file. Click *slide 3* and from the Paste button select *Paste Special*.

9. Select *Paste link* and *Microsoft Office Excel Worksheet Object* in the *Paste Special box* and click *OK*. The text *What is 12?* should appear.

10. Now, go back to *Jeopardy_Game_Linked.xlsx* file and change the statement in cell A2 from *3 Times 4* to *4 Times 7* and change the question in cell B2 from *What is 12?* to *What is 28?* Save the Excel file. Go back to PowerPoint, and you should see the changes that you made in Excel.

11. Using this approach, you can add more questions and change the formatting (fonts, color, and so on) from Excel, leaving the PowerPoint slide to look the same with only the content changing.

A CHALLENGE INTEGRATING OFFICE

For those who would like a challenge beyond the instructions presented in this chapter, try the following exercises:

1. Create a multimedia research report. Research a topic of interest. In your research, collect text information, photographs, video, audio, and numerical data about the topic. Use Word to compile the text information, PowerPoint to assemble the photographs, video, and audio; and Excel to organize the numeric data. After you compile your research findings with the respective program, integrate your data and provide access to them through one program (e.g., Word). Assume that the reader of your research report will be able to view it on a computer. As the reader reads, he or she can click on illustrations (figures and tables) to view more in-depth information in either a PowerPoint slideshow or Excel.

2. Create a short PowerPoint presentation. Insert it into a Word document as an embedded object. Insert the same object as a linked object and compare the differences.

3. Insert an Excel worksheet object into a PowerPoint slide. Enter data and view it on the slide. Try saving the worksheet as a separate file.

4. Create a PowerPoint slideshow that links to two or more presentation objects. Assume that multiple students will each develop PowerPoint slideshows and present them to the class on the instructor's workstation, connected to a computer/video projector. Early in the development process, create a folder to store all the slideshows. Have students create drafts of their slideshows and name them descriptively. Place them in the folder. Create a master slideshow and link all (draft) files to it. Prior to the students' presentations, collect all the completed slideshows and place them in the folder overwriting the draft versions of the files, assuming the names are identical.

TYING IT ALL TOGETHER

In this chapter, you used the example of students preparing a multimedia project proposal and presentation. You modified materials in ways that caused you to integrate the Office products. You used several integration approaches, including copy and paste, drag and drop, and inserting objects by embedding them in files and by linking to them. In addition, you made a contact list in Outlook and exported it to Access. You then took data records from Access and placed them in PowerPoint. The examples presented in the chapter serve as an introduction to some of the many ways you can use and incorporate the Office programs to work more effectively and efficiently.

A WINDOWS

Windows Vista

You access Microsoft Office 2007 through the Windows operating system. This appendix provides a basic overview of the Windows Vista operating system. It presents fundamental features of Vista that can help you use Office 2007.

A Word About Windows

At the time of this writing, Vista is the current Windows operating system. Its visually rich and consistent graphical user interface is intended to help users experience programs, dialog boxes, and menus in a reliable and easy-to-use manner (Bowman, 2007). Before you open and work with any of the Microsoft Office products, it is useful to have a basic understanding of Vista. It is an operating system that helps you access, store, and organize information or data on your computer. There are several versions of Windows, such as Windows XP, Windows NT, Windows 98, Windows Me (Millennium edition), Windows 2000, and the latest version, Vista.

Vista offers many notable features, including a new visually rich interface named Windows Aero, which, with an appropriate hardware configuration, features transparent windows, 3D views of program windows (Flip 3D), and live taskbar thumbnails. There is a new desktop, instant search capabilities, and sidebar Gadgets that enable quick access to resources such as calendars, news, and weather. These items are but a few of the features included in the Vista operating system that aim to make your experience interacting with your computer easy, efficient, and fun.

As the name *Windows* implies, interaction with programs is facilitated through adjustable rectangular areas, or windows, that appear on your computer screen. Windows Vista, like earlier versions of the operating system, has a graphical user interface. It contains objects (e.g., buttons and icons) through which you access and work with files, folders, and programs. The interface makes working with the computer easy and efficient, and it eliminates the need to type commands that are often confusing.

The Desktop

When you turn your computer on, the desktop displays (see Figure A.1). The desktop is the work area where you place files and folders. The folders, programs, or files that you open display in rectangular windows on the desktop. Icons, such as Computer and Recycle Bin, may appear that represent applications, files, or system resources (e.g., scanner). To activate these objects, double-click them with the left mouse button.

The desktop usually contains the following features, although the configuration of your system may differ:

Gadgets: The Vista sidebar houses Gadgets, such as calendars, news and weather feeds, and clocks as shown in Figure A.1.

Computer: In early Windows versions, it was referred to as My Computer. The Computer object allows you to see the contents of your disk drives and to access your computer's

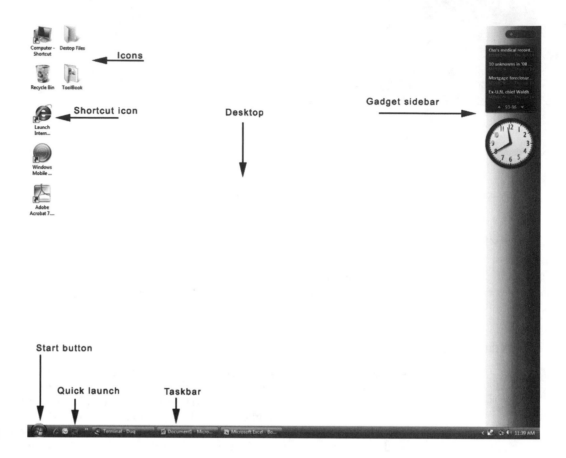

Figure A.1
Windows desktop

configuration settings. It contains the C: drive icon, the E: drive icon (and icons for any other disk drives you have connected to your computer), and the Control Panel. When the C: or E: drive icons are double-clicked, their contents display on the screen. For instance, double-clicking the C: drive icon displays a list of all the folders, directories, and files contained on the C: drive.

Recycle Bin: Temporarily stores deleted files. All files deleted from the C: drive go first to the Recycle Bin. Only when the Recycle Bin is emptied are the files removed from your computer. You can retrieve files from the Recycle Bin if you deleted them erroneously. If you do not empty the Recycle Bin, your deleted files still occupy disk space. Files deleted from external disk drives do not go to the Recycle Bin. They are removed from your computer as soon as you delete them. If you want to delete a file from the C: drive without sending it to the Recycle Bin, hold down the Shift key when you delete it.

Taskbar: The taskbar provides access to opened folders and files and makes switching between them convenient (see Figure A.2). It contains the Start button, on the left side of the taskbar, which is your beginning point to access programs and files. As you open items, a button representing each program displays on the taskbar. You can switch between programs by clicking the appropriate button. In Figure A.2, both Microsoft Word and Excel are open. Clicking either button makes the corresponding application active by bringing the application's window to the forefront on the desktop. Depending on the computer's configuration, icons appear in the Notification area on the right side of the taskbar, providing information and access to programs and resources. For instance, the icons on the right of the taskbar in Figure A.2 provide access to and

Figure A.2
Taskbar

Figure A.3
Shortcut icon

information about audio and network resources. In addition, you can place icons of frequently used programs in Quick Launch to access them easily and quickly. Quick Launch, located to the immediate right of the Start button, features an icon to the desktop that, when clicked, minimizes all open windows and displays the desktop.

Shortcuts: Instead of searching your computer each time you want to open a frequently used file or program, you can create a shortcut to it on the desktop. When you double-click the shortcut, the file or program opens. Each Shortcut icon has a small arrow at the bottom-left corner (see Figure A.3) to distinguish it from other icons.

The Mouse and Windows

The computer's mouse is integral to working with Windows. You use the mouse to scroll documents, select icons, make choices from dialog boxes and pull-down menus, and move and resize windows.

A typical computer mouse has at least two buttons (left and right) and a scroll wheel. You use the left mouse button to select and open objects and to resize and position windows. The right mouse button helps open shortcut menus that display commands for a particular object. The scroll wheel allows for efficient scrolling, especially for long documents.

Selecting an object with the mouse informs Windows that you are going to work with the object in some way, such as opening or moving it. Objects become highlighted when selected. Figure A.4 illustrates the Computer object as selected and not selected. The selected Computer object is on the right side of Figure A.4.

Figure A.4
Icons not selected and selected

Double-clicking the left mouse button on an object opens it in a window on the desktop. For example, double-click the left mouse button on the Computer object to open its contents (see Figure A.5).

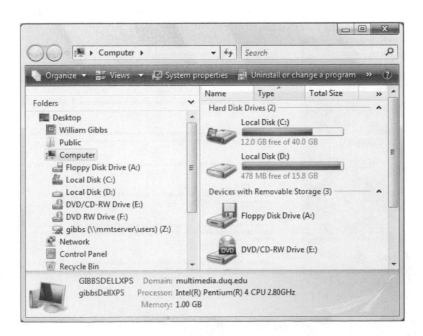

Figure A.5
Computer

Personalize Vista

You can personalize many features of Vista so that the operating system is tailored to your preferences and needs. To access the personalization options, right-click on the desktop to display the shortcut menu and click *Personalize* (see Figure A.6). The *Personalize* box appears (see Figure A.7) with which you can access options to alter Windows Vista features. For instance, clicking the first option, *Window Color and Appearance*, displays the *Window Color and Appearance* box, where you can set the color and styles of windows. In Figure A.8, the default is selected, and it will be applied to all windows. With the Desktop Background option, you can choose a background color or image for your desktop. When this option is selected, the *Choose a Desktop Background* box appears (see Figure A.9) with which you can select or browse for a desktop image. The remaining five items on the *Personalize* box afford similar access to options for customizing Vista features.

Figure A.6
Desktop shortcut menu

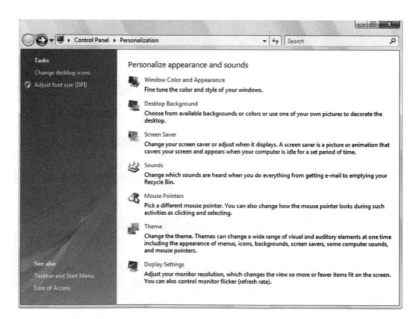

Figure A.7
Personalize box for personalizing Vista

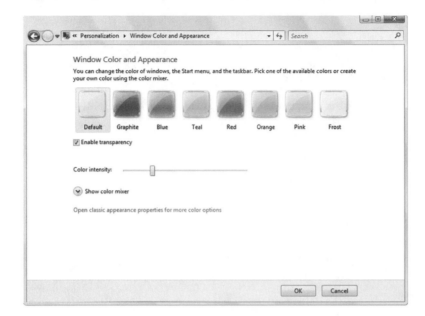

Figure A.8
Changing window color and appearance

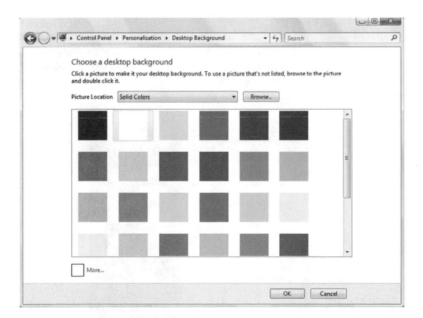

Figure A.9
Changing the desktop background

Shortcut Menus

Shortcut menus can be an efficient way to access files, programs, and system resources, among other things. By positioning your mouse on a folder, an object, the desktop, or the taskbar and then right-clicking, a shortcut menu appears displaying the commands for that object. Right-clicking on *Computer,* for example, displays its shortcut menu (see Figure A.10). As mentioned, position the mouse on the desktop and right-click, and the desktop shortcut menu appears (see Figure A.6).

Figure A.10
Computer shortcut
menu

Start Menu

Click the Start button on the taskbar, and the Start menu displays (see Figure A.11). The items on this menu contain most of the things you need to begin using Vista. An arrow to the right of a menu item indicates that more items or submenus are present. When you pass the mouse over the arrow, a submenu appears.

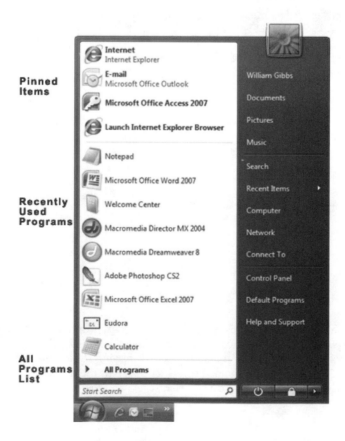

Figure A.11
Start menu

Some of the items on the Start menu are described next. The items on your Start menu may vary from those presented here because your computer is configured differently from the one used in this example. The Start menu items include the following:

All Programs: Displays a list of programs that can be opened. To open a program, click on *All Programs,* and a listing of all the programs displays. When you see the name of the program you want to open, click it.

Recent Items: Presents a list of recently opened documents. This item is useful for quickly opening a document without searching for it on your computer.

Search: Allows you to find files and folders located on your computer. You can also search the Internet using this option.

Help and Support: Opens Vista's Help and Support module, which provides information about Vista and many of its features and functions.

Shut Down/Turn Off Computer: Shuts down Windows and turns off the computer. It can also be used to restart the computer or to put it in Sleep mode. Shutdown options are located at the bottom right of the Start menu (see Figure A.12).

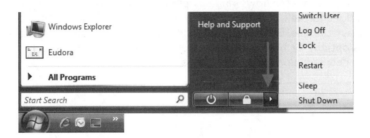

Figure A.12
Start menu: Shut
Down

Repositioning and Resizing Windows

As you work in Vista, you will likely open several files or programs at the same time and may need to reposition windows to work efficiently. All windows have an address bar (see Figure A.13) that displays breadcrumbs, or the current location of the file or folder. For instance, Figure A.13

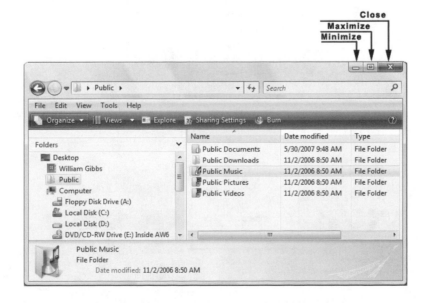

Figure A.13
Window

displays the Public folder in the address bar. You can reposition a window by clicking on the title bar (the area above the address bar) and, while holding the left mouse button down, dragging the window to a new location. You can also activate a window simply by clicking on the title bar.

Title bars contain three buttons on the upper-right side. The button on the left reduces, or minimizes, the window. The button in the center enlarges, or maximizes, a window to the full size of the desktop. When the window is enlarged to full screen, the Maximize button changes to the Restore Down button. Restore Down returns the window to its original size prior to maximizing it. The button on the right closes the window or program. When you have a program open (e.g., Word), clicking the Close/Quit program button exits the program. In addition, right-clicking on the title bar displays a pop-up menu with minimize, maximize, and close/quit options.

To make a window larger or smaller, move the mouse pointer to any one of the four sides of the window. The pointer will change to a double arrow. Drag the border to enlarge or reduce the window size. A box appears around the window as you resize it. Resizing from the bottom-right corner sizes the window proportionally. If you just want to adjust the width, place the cursor over the left or right side of the window and drag. Change the length by placing the cursor at the top or bottom of the window and drag.

You may also alter how windows present information. Clicking the Organize button provides options for adjusting the layout of windows (see Figure A.14). For example, clicking *Menu Bar* displays the File, Edit, View, Tools and Help menu options. Clicking *Views* (see Figure A.15) provides options for how the contents of the window get displayed. For instance, clicking *Details* presents detailed information about files.

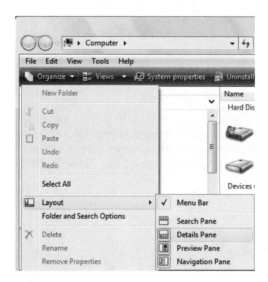

Figure A.14
Window layout options

Figure A.15
Window view options

Working with Programs and Files

Opening Programs

1. To open a program such as Microsoft Word, click the Start button on the taskbar. On the Start menu, click *All Programs* to display the Program list. Click *Microsoft Office* to display the Microsoft Office group (see Figure A.16).
2. Click *Microsoft Office Word 2007* to open it. Word opens with a blank untitled document. A button representing Word appears on the taskbar. Depending on how you installed Office 2007, the menu item for it may be located in various locations on the Start menu. In most cases, it can be found under All Programs or under All Programs within the Microsoft Office folder.

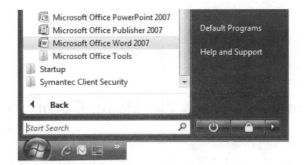

Figure A.16
Program list

Opening Files

There are multiple ways to open a file. In this section, we discuss three methods: (a) opening a file using the application that created it, (b) accessing and opening a file using Computer, and (c) opening a file using Recent Items on the Start menu.

Opening a File Using the Application That Created It

Using the Start menu, open the application with which you created the file. For example, open a file created with Microsoft Word.

1. Once Word is open, click the Office button and select *Open* (see Figure A.17). The Open dialog box appears (see Figure A.18).
2. Use the Open dialog box to locate the file you want to open. If you need to open a file in a different folder, click the down arrow in the address bar, then select the disk drive that contains the folder. Once you locate the file, select it by clicking on it one time, then click *Open*. In this example, the file to be opened is *Lecture_Week1.docx*, and it is in the *A_Week1* folder.

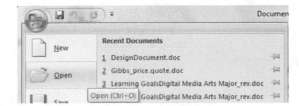

Figure A.17
Open file

Figure A.18
Open dialog box

Accessing and Opening a File Using Computer

1. For this example, access and open a file named *Lecture_Week1.doc* located on the local disk, or C: drive, in a folder named *A_Week1*. Double-click *Computer* on the desktop or select *Computer* from the Start menu (see Figure A.19), and the Computer window appears (see Figure A.20). Double-click the drive where the file is located. In this case, the drive is the local disk, or C: drive.

Figure A.19
Computer

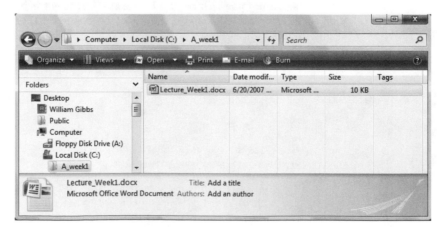

Figure A.20
Computer window

2. In the local disk (C:) window, locate and double-click the *A_Week1* folder (see Figure A.20) to open it and then double-click the file *Lecture_Week1.docx*. Notice the breadcrumbs or path (Computer>Local Disk(C:) > A_Week1) in the address bar.

Opening a File Using Recent Items

The Recent Items option on the Start menu presents a list of recently opened files. Keep in mind that the list changes as you open and close files. Using Recent Items, you can quickly open a file that you have been working on without searching for it on your computer or opening the application that created it. Both file and its application open when you open a file with Recent Items.

1. Click the Start button and then select *Recent Items,* and a submenu displays.
2. Click the name of the file that you want to open (see Figure A.21). This step assumes that you already have a file created and that you recently opened it. In this example, the Microsoft Word file *DesignDocument.doc* opens.

Figure A.21
Recent Items

Opening Multiple Programs

When using Windows, you can work with several files simultaneously, each of which opens in its own window. For example, you can open Microsoft Word and Excel files and copy and paste data between them. The following steps illustrate how to open multiple programs, switch between programs, reposition and resize program windows, and exchange data between programs.

Opening Programs

1. Click the Start button on the Windows taskbar. On the Start menu, click *All Programs,* and the Programs list appears. Click *Microsoft Office* to display the Microsoft Office group. Click *Microsoft Word* to open it. Word opens with one blank untitled document. Notice that a button representing Word appears on the taskbar.
2. Open Microsoft Excel, and Excel opens with one blank workbook. You now have two programs open, Word and Excel, and each of these programs has one blank file.

Switching Between Programs

1. The Word and Excel documents appear on the taskbar. If you are viewing the Excel document, switch to Word by clicking the Word button on the taskbar. Alternatively, you can switch between programs by pressing the Alt and Tab keys simultaneously

(see Figure A.22). Pressing the Tab key repeatedly (while holding the Alt key) changes the selection. Release the keys, and the selected program becomes active.

Figure A.22
Program switching
(Alt+Tab)

Repositioning and Resizing Program Windows.

In this example, you can resize the Word and Excel windows and then copy data from Excel into Word.

1. If Word and Excel are open to full screen, restore them to adjust the window size. Click the Restore Down button at the top right of the window on the Word file. Remember that when a window is full screen, the Restore Down button replaces the Maximize button.

2. Switch to Excel by clicking the button that corresponds to it on the taskbar. Click the Restore Down button at the top right of the Excel window. *Note:* If, when you restore the Word file, you see Excel in the background, click on Excel's window. This makes Excel active, and it is an alternative to switching between programs using the taskbar. Clicking on windows in the background brings them to the foreground and makes them active.

3. Make either the Word or Excel window active. Resize the window by positioning the mouse pointer at the bottom-right corner of the window. The pointer changes to a double arrow (see Figure A.23). While holding the left mouse button down, drag upward and to the left. The length and width of the window should change.

4. Resize the Word and Excel windows so that they are both visible (see Figure A.24). For this example, assume that you have data in an Excel worksheet and you will copy the

Figure A.23
Resize window

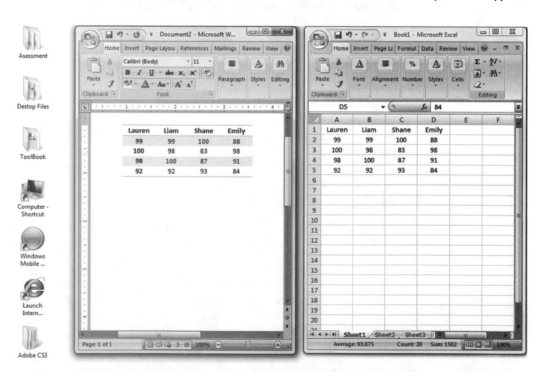

Figure A.24
Resize Word and
Excel windows

data to Word. Make the Excel window active by clicking its title bar or by selecting the Excel button on the taskbar. With the Excel window active, select the data in the spreadsheet and copy it.

5. Make the Word window active by clicking its title bar or by clicking the Word button on the taskbar. Now paste the data from Excel into the Word file. Notice in Figure A.24 that the Word window title bar is darker and that the Excel window title bar is a lighter shade. The darker title bar indicates that the Word window is active.

6. To reposition either window, click on the title bar and, while pressing the left mouse button, drag the window to a desired location.

Quitting a Program

Figure A.25
Close button

You can quit, or close, a program by clicking the Close/Quit button at the top-right corner of a window (see Figure A.25). The Close button also closes windows associated with folders. In addition, right-clicking on the title bar and selecting *Close* from the shortcut menu closes or quits the program (see Figure A.26).

When working in a program, you may have multiple documents open. In such cases, there is a main program window and within it individual document windows. Each window has a Close button, and each window may appear as a button on the taskbar. For example, in Figure A.27, the Excel program window has Minimize, Maximize, and Close buttons, as do the individual document (Book1 and Book2) windows. Note that Book2 buttons do not display until the book is active. Clicking the Close button on Excel's program window closes Excel and all open documents. Clicking the Close button on a document window closes that document only. Excel and all other documents remain open.

Figure A.26
Close program

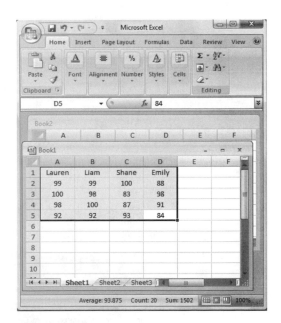

Figure A.27
Multiple document windows

Windows Explorer

Windows Explorer allows you to view and manage files and folders on your computer. When you open Windows Explorer, you get a detailed view of your computer's contents, such as the contents of disk drives, folders, and any connected network drives. You can also manage your files and folders using the Copy, Delete, and Move functions.

Opening Windows Explorer

To open Windows Explorer, click the Start menu, select *All Programs, Accessories* and then click *Windows Explorer.*

The Explorer Window

Once you open Windows Explorer, the Explorer window appears (see Figure A.28). The left pane of the window displays disk drives and folders on your computer. The right pane displays the contents of the item selected in the left pane. For example, if you single-click a folder on the left side of the screen, its contents display in the pane to the right. In Figure A.28, the Documents folder is selected, and the items contained in it display on the right. You can run a program or open a file by double-clicking it when it appears in the right pane.

The panels present a hierarchy with sub- or child folders indented under parent objects, such as disks and folders. Clicking disks or parent folders expands the list and displays the subfolders. You can collapse the list by clicking the parent item again or the small arrow that appears to the left of the item. In Figure A.29, the arrow to the left of the parent object Computer is selected, and items,

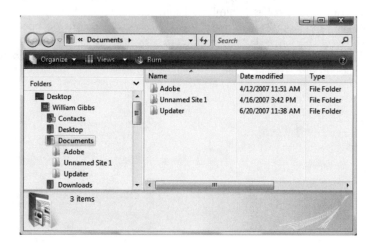

Figure A.28
Windows Explorer

Figure A.29
Window Explorer
folder list

such as Floppy Disk Drive (A:) and, Local Disk Drive (C:), display. Clicking the arrow or parent object (Computer) again collapses the list. In this example, Floppy Disk Drive (A:), Local Disk Drive (C:), and the other items are child objects of the parent Computer.

The Explorer Toolbar

The Windows Explorer toolbar makes working with files and folders easy. The Explorer toolbar (see Figure A.30) contains buttons to view and organize folders and to copy, move, and delete files, among other things.

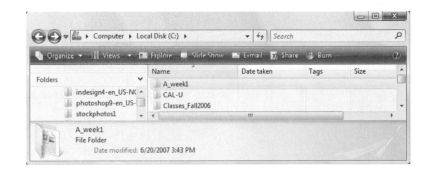

Figure A.30
Explorer toolbar

Figure A.31
Drop-down list

Back and Forward buttons: The back arrow at the top left of the window takes you back through the most recently visited folders. After going back through recently visited folders using the Back button, Forward takes you forward though these same folders. You may also navigate across folders using the drop-down list as show in Figure A.31.

Address bar: Provides the path (breadcrumbs) of the current folder. Click the down arrow to navigate to other locations on your computer. In Figure A.30, Computer > Local Disk (C:) is in the address bar.

Search: Allows you to type a search query in the search box to search the contents of your computer and all disks connected to it.

Organize: Provides options for how the information in the window displays. The Layout option under Organize provides the option for adding a toolbar on the window that includes File, Edit, View, Tools, and Help.

View: Provides alternative ways to view file and folders in the Window.

Slideshow: Presents a slideshow for viewing images within a folder.

E-mail: Provides options for e-mailing a file.

Burn: Provides an option for burning or placing your files on disk, such as CD or DVD.

Managing Files: Moving, Copying, Deleting, and Renaming Files

This section explains how to manage files using Windows Explorer.

Moving a File

When moving a file or folder, the object that you want to move is removed from one location (e.g., folder or disk) and placed in another location. Note that the Move command differs from Copy. Copy places a duplicate file in the location of your choice and leaves the original file unaltered.

1. To move a file or folder, open Windows Explorer.
2. Find the file or folder that you want to move and click on it one time to select it. For this example, move the file *Lecture_Week1.docx* from the *A_Week1* folder to *A_Week2*. One way to do this is to place a menu bar on the window using the Organize and Layout options. In Figure A.32, the Menu Bar option is selected by clicking the Organize

Figure A.32
Organize Layout options

button and then selecting *Layout* and *Menu Bar*. Browse to locate the file you want to move. In this example, the file is titled *Lecture_Week1.docx,* and it is in the *A_Week1* folder on the local disk drive (C:). When the *A_Week1* folder is located and selected, it displays in the left panel, and the file displays in the right panel. Select the file by clicking on it one time.

3. Select *Move To Folder* from the Edit menu (see Figure A.33), and the *Move Items* box displays (see Figure A.34). Select the folder where you want to move the file, which in this example is *A_Week2.* Click *Move,* and Windows Explorer moves *Lecture_Week1.docx* from *A_Week1* to *A_Week2.*

4. Alternatively, you can move files by dragging and dropping them. Using the same example as previously, move *Lecture_Week1.docx* from the *A_Week1* folder to *A_Week2* by dragging and dropping it.

5. Locate and select the *Lecture_Week1.docx* file. Click on it and, while holding the left mouse button down, drag it to the *A_Week2* folder. The *A_Week2* folder highlights as the mouse pointer approaches it. With the folder highlighted, release the mouse button, and the file moves to *A_Week2.*

6. A third method you can use to move a file or folder is to select the object you want to move by clicking it one time. From the Edit menu, select *Cut* or press Ctrl+X. Locate the new location where you want to place the file or folder. Select *Paste* from the Edit menu or press Ctrl+V. This cuts the object from its present location and places it in the new location.

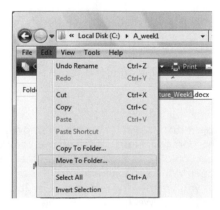

Figure A.33
Moving a file

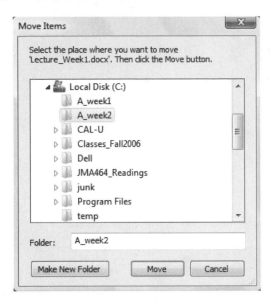

Figure A.34
Move Items box

Copying a File

1. The Copy function duplicates a file or folder. Find and select the file or folder that you want to copy. For this example, make a copy of the *Lecture_Week1.docx* file in the *A_Week1* folder and place the copy in *A_Week2*. Ensure that the menu bar displays in the window by clicking the Organize button and then select *Layout* and *Menu Bar*. In Figure A.35, the *A_Week1* folder is selected in the left pane. The contents of *A_Week1* display in the right pane, with *Lecture_Week1.docx* selected.

2. Select *Copy To Folder* from the Edit menu, and the *Copy Items* box displays (see Figure A.36). Locate and select the folder where you want to copy the file, which in this example is *A_Week2*. Click *OK*, and Windows Explorer copies *Lecture_Week1.docx* and places the copy in *A_Week2*. The original copy of *Lecture_Week1.docx* is still in the *A_Week1* folder.

3. Alternatively, you can copy files by dragging and dropping them. Using the previous example, you will copy the *Lecture_Week1.docx* file to *A_Week2*. Locate and select the *Lecture_Week1.docx* file. Press the Control (Ctrl) key and, while holding the left mouse button down, drag *Lecture_Week1.docx* onto the *A_Week2* folder. The *A_Week2* folder highlights as the mouse pointer approaches it. With the folder highlighted, release the mouse button, and the file is copied to *A_Week2*.

4. A third method you can use to copy a file or folder is to select the object you want to copy by clicking it one time. From the Edit menu, select *Copy* or press Ctrl+C. Browse

Figure A.35
Copy To Folder
option

Figure A.36
Copy Items box

to the new location where you want to place the copied file or folder. Select Paste from the Edit menu or press Ctrl+V. This copies the object and places a copy of it in the new location.

Deleting Files and Folders

There are several ways to delete files and folders, two of which are presented next: (a) using a shortcut menu and (b) using the Delete button.

Using a Shortcut Menu to Delete Files

Suppose you want to delete a file named *Lecture_Week1.docx* located in the *A_Week1* folder.
    1. Find and select *Lecture_Week1.docx* and right-click it. Right-clicking on a file or folder displays a shortcut menu (see Figure A.37).

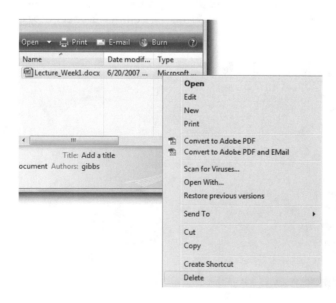

Figure A.37
Deleting files

2. Select *Delete,* and the *Confirm File Delete* box appears (see Figure A.38). Click *Yes* to send the file or folder to the Recycle Bin.

To remove a file or folder from your computer without sending it to the Recycle Bin, press the Shift key while selecting *Delete.*

Figure A.38
Delete file

Using the Delete Button to Delete Files or Folders

Another way to delete files or folders is to select the item to be deleted and press the Delete key. The *Delete File* box appears asking whether you want to send the file to the Recycle Bin. Click *Yes* if you want to remove the file from its current location and place it in the Recycle Bin.

Remember that files or folders in the Recycle Bin can be recovered. In addition, they take up disk storage space and remain on the computer until you empty the Recycle Bin.

Emptying the Recycle Bin

Windows sends all deleted files and folders to the Recycle Bin before removing them from your computer. Items on removable disks (e.g., floppy disk) are an exception to this fact. Windows removes files or folders on removable disks from your computer as soon as you issue the delete command. They are not sent to the Recycle Bin.

You must empty the Recycle Bin to remove deleted files or folders.
1. Right-click *Recycle Bin* on the desktop and then select *Empty Recycle Bin* from the short-cut menu (see Figure A.39). The *Delete File* box appears. Click *Yes* to remove the files or folders. Once you empty the Recycle Bin, deleted files are permanently removed from your computer.

Figure A.39
Empty Recycle Bin

Selecting Multiple Files

In the preceding discussion, the examples illustrate moving, copying, or deleting one file at a time. You can also select multiple items at one time to be moved, copied, or deleted.

1. To select multiple items that are adjacent, press the Shift key and click the first and last items. If, for example, you have 14 files that you want to select, press the Shift key and click items 1 and 14. This action selects all items between and including 1 and 14 (see Figure A.40).
2. When items to be selected are not adjacent, press the Control (Ctrl) key and click the files, folders, or programs that you want to select (see Figure A.41).
3. You can select numerous files and folders by clicking the left mouse button and, while holding it down, dragging across the items that you want selected.

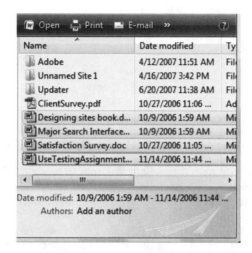

Figure A.40
Selecting adjacent items

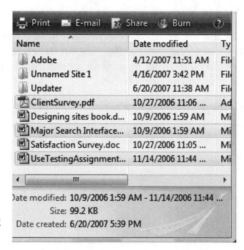

Figure A.41
Selecting nonadjacent items

Renaming a File

1. Right-click the file or folder that you want to rename and select *Rename* from the shortcut menu that appears (see, Figure A.42).
2. The file name becomes selected, and a blinking cursor appears in the name box. Type a new name and press Enter or click outside the name box.
3. Another way to change a file or folder name is to click on the item two times, pausing briefly between clicks. The first click selects the item, and the second click makes the name available for editing (see Figure A.43).

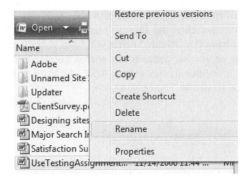

Figure A.42
Rename file

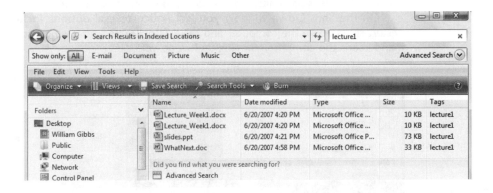

Figure A.43
Rename file, mouse
click

Searching for Files or Folders

Search is a useful tool for locating files or folders on your computer and information on the
Internet.

1. To locate a file or folder on your computer, click the Start button, then select *Search*.
    You may also begin a search by typing directly into the *Start Search* box.
2. The Search Results screen displays. Click *All* for the *Show only:* option, which will cause
    all items matching the search query to display (see Figure A.44).

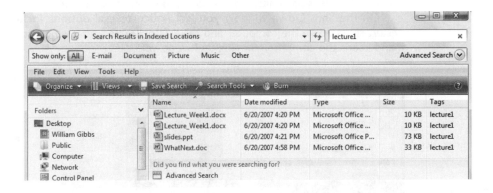

Figure A.44
Search

3. In the *Search* box at the top right, type the name of the file or folder that you want to
    locate. For example, typing *Lecture_Week1.docx* will locate files with this name in all
    locations on your computer.
4. Specify where to search for files or folders by clicking the down arrow on the right side
    of the Address Address box.
5. After typing the information, press Enter to begin the search. In Figure A.44, notice the
    word *lecture1* under the Tags column on the right side of the window. Suppose you
    have four files, each of which relates to the first lecture of the term (*lecture1*). You can

right-click each one of the four files and on the shortcut menu select *Properties*. When the Properties box displays, click the Details tab (see Figure A.45) and next to the Tags item type a word or phase (i.e., *lecture1*) that will help you identify the file. You can type multiple items as long as you separate them with a semicolon. Now when you search, you can type the tag identifier in the search box, and Vista will locate all the files with that tag such as those shown in Figure A.44.

Figure A.45
File Properties box

Shutting Down Your Computer

You should shut down your computer before turning it off. To exit Vista and turn off your computer, click the Start button and select *Shut Down* from the options. The shutdown options are located by clicking the small arrow to the right of the Computer Lock icon (see Figure A.46). The Windows session ends, and you can turn off your computer.

On the Shut Down window, you will notice several options, including *Restart* and *Sleep*. *Restart* shuts down the computer and restarts or starts a new windows session. The *Sleep* command keeps the computer running on low power.

Figure A.46
Shut Down

References

Bowman, B. (2007). Preview the Microsoft Windows Vista Interface and User Experience. Microsoft Corporation. Retrieved June 16, 2007 from http://www .microsoft.com/windowsxp/using/web/expert/bowman_vistapreview.mspx

APPENDIX

B MACINTOSH

Macintosh Overview

As of this writing, Microsoft Office 2004 is the most current Office version for Macintosh. You access the Microsoft Office products (Word, Excel, Entourage, and PowerPoint) through the Mac OS (operating system). This appendix, therefore, provides a basic overview of the Mac OS X operating system. It presents fundamental features of the OS and explains how to use them when working with Office 2004.

A Word About MAC OS X

Figure B.1
Microsoft Word file icon

If you purchased Microsoft Office, it may be useful to review a few fundamentals of Macintosh OS X to see how the OS works with Office. The Macintosh OS X helps you access Office applications and organize information or data on your computer. You interact with the applications and associated files through adjustable rectangular areas or windows that appear on your computer screen. The operating system has a graphical user interface. It contains objects (e.g., buttons and icons) through which you access and work with files, folders, and programs such as Figures B.1, B.2, and B.3, showing the different Microsoft Word file, folder, and Word application icons. The interface makes working with the computer easy and efficient, and it eliminates the need to type commands, which are often confusing.

The Desktop

Figure B.2
Folder icon

Typically, when you turn your computer on, the desktop displays (see Figure B.4). The desktop is the work area where you place files and folders. The folders, programs, or files that you open display in rectangular windows on the desktop. Several objects, such as Macintosh HD, appear on the desktop and represent disks, folders, applications, files, or system resources. To activate these items, double-click on them. For example, the Macintosh HD icon when double-clicked provides access to the contents of your computer.

Aliases

Figure B.3
Word application icon

A useful item for obtaining quick access to your computer contents is the alias. Aliases on the desktop provide easy access to files and programs. Instead of searching your computer each time you want to open a frequently used file or program, you can place an alias to it on the desktop. When you double-click the alias, the file, program, or disk opens.

Aliases look different from other desktop icons. The icon of each alias has a small arrow at the bottom-left corner, and the icon's text is italicized (see Figure B.5).

You can place an alias on the Desktop to access Office applications. For example, to make an alias, double-click *Macintosh HD* on the desktop and locate the Office applications icons. Click on the icon (e.g., Word) and press the Command key and the letter L at the same time. Once the alias is created, drag it to the desktop or to the Dock.

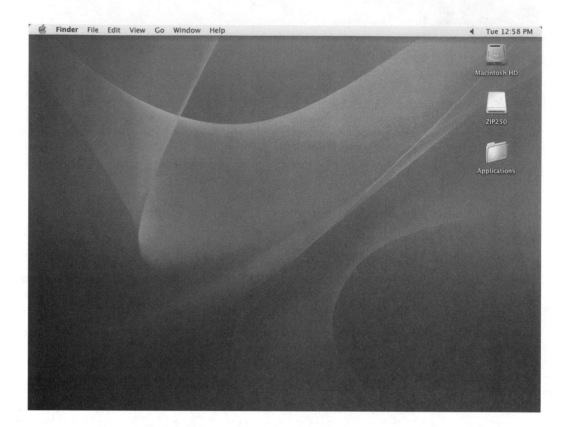

Figure B.4
The desktop

Items on the Desktop

Figure B.5
Alias icon

A typical desktop contains the following features:

Macintosh HD: Allows you to see the contents of your computer's hard drive. For instance, double-clicking the Macintosh HD icon opens the Macintosh HD window that displays all the folders or directories and files contained on your computer. You can change the name of the Macintosh HD icon by clicking the icon's name and typing.

Trash: Temporarily stores files that you want to delete. A Trash icon can be found on the Dock. All files that you intend to delete get sent first to the Trash, and only when the Trash is emptied are the files removed from your computer permanently. You can retrieve files from the Trash as long as you have not emptied it.

The Dock: Gives access to frequently used items. Click an item in the Dock, and it opens. Minimized documents contract to the Dock. You can add to it by dragging an item over the Dock and dropping it. The Dock is located at the bottom of the screen but can be moved or resized. The Trash icon is found on the Dock.

Desktop menu: The desktop contains several menu items that help you work with your computer and its files. The items include Apple, Finder, File, Edit, View, Go, Window, and Help. The desktop menu is located at the top of the screen (see Figure B.6).

Finder File Edit View Go Window Help ◀ Tue 12:52 PM

Figure B.6
Desktop menu bar

Desktop Menu Items

When working with the Microsoft Office 2004 applications, you will use the desktop menu often. For this reason, each menu item found is reviewed in the next section.

Apple: Allows quick access to system preferences. You can shut down, restart, or put your computer to sleep. Clicking the Apple on the desktop menu bar displays the Apple menu (see Figure B.7). An arrow to the right of a menu item indicates that more items, or submenus, are available. When you pass the mouse over the arrow, a submenu appears.

File: Allows you to perform operations with disks, files, folders, windows, and applications. You can also use the File menu to search the contents of the hard drive and other disks.

Edit: Use the Edit menu to copy and paste when working on the desktop, to select items, or to set desktop preferences.

View: Use the View menu to change the way files, programs, folders, and information about them display on your computer screen.

Go: Use Go to access folders, drives, files, and applications on your computer.

Window: Use the Window menu to close or activate windows opened on the desktop.

Help: Use Help to get information about your computer and how to use it. This menu option opens the Help module, which provides information about the Macintosh operating system and many of its features and functions.

The Dock: Located on the bottom of the desktop, the Dock allows you to alternate among all open applications. As you open applications, their icons appear in the Dock. You switch among them by clicking the Applications menu and selecting the item you need. In Figure B.8, both Microsoft Word and Excel are open. Clicking *Microsoft Word* makes it active.

Figure B.7
Apple menu

Figure B.8
Dock

Selecting Icons

The mouse is an integral component of your computer, and it enables you to work with applications such as Office. You can use the mouse to select icons, make choices from dialog boxes and pull-down menus, and move and resize windows.

You select items by clicking on them one time with the mouse, and you open items by double-clicking on them. Selecting an item signals the computer that you are going to work with the selected object in some way, such as opening or moving it. Icons highlight when they are selected. For instance, Figure B.9 illustrates the Macintosh HD icon as not selected or highlighted, whereas Figure B.10 shows it selected and highlighted.

Double-clicking an object or icon opens it in a window on the desktop. For example, double-clicking *Macintosh HD* opens its contents (see Figure B.11).

Figure B.12 illustrates three Word document icons with three different states of selection: not selected, selected, and selected for renaming. The first item is an unselected icon of a

Figure B.9
Icon not selected

Figure B.10
Icon selected

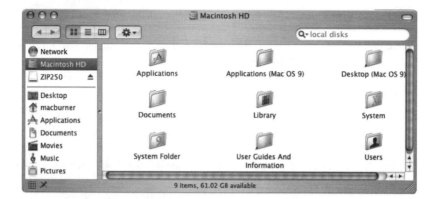

Figure B.11
Macintosh HD
window

Figure B.12
Word icons

document named *Liam.doc*. The second item is an icon of a selected document named *Lauren.doc;* it was selected by clicking the mouse pointer on the icon. The third item is an icon of a document named *Lauren.doc* with its name selected for renaming. If you want to change the name of a file, you could do so by clicking on the icon name, then typing the new name. To select the icon's name, click on the file name rather than the document's icon.

Contextual Menus

Contextual menus can be an efficient way to access and work with files, folders, and windows, among other things. By clicking the mouse pointer on a folder, a file, a window's title, or the desktop and holding the Control (Ctrl) key down, a menu appears displaying the commands for that item (see Figure B.13).

Figure B.13
Contextual menu

Repositioning and Resizing Windows

Often you will have several files or programs open at the same time. To work efficiently, you may want to reposition the document windows. All windows have a title bar (see Figure B.14) that displays the name. You can reposition a window by clicking on the title bar and, while holding the mouse button down, dragging the window to a new location. You can also activate a window by clicking on the title bar or any location within the window.

Figure B.14
Window title bar

Title bars contain three buttons. *Close* closes the active window. *Minimize* makes the window larger or reduces the window to its previous size once it has been enlarged. *Collapse* collapses the window so that only the title bar is visible.

Scroll horizontally in a window by clicking the scroll arrows at the bottom of the window. Scroll vertically by clicking the arrows to the right of the window. You may also move quickly across or up and down a window by dragging the scroll bar.

To make a window larger or smaller, move the mouse pointer over the resize box at the window's bottom-right corner. Drag the border to enlarge or reduce the size of the window. A box appears around the window as you resize it. When resizing a window, dragging diagonally resizes the window proportionally.

Working with Programs and Files

Opening Programs

1. There are several ways to open an application such as Microsoft Word. If you have the application's icon (e.g., Word) on the Dock, click it (see Figure B.15), and the application opens. In Figure B.15, the Word icon is the fifth item from the right on the Dock.
2. Another way to open an application (e.g., Word) is to double-click the Macintosh HD icon on the desktop, locate the Applications folder, and double-click it. Within *Applications,* double-click the Microsoft Office 2004 folder and then double-click the application's icon.

Figure B.15
The Dock

Opening Files

There are multiple ways to open a file. In this section, we discuss three methods of opening a file: (a) opening a file using the application that created it, (b) accessing and opening a file using the Macintosh HD, and (c) opening a file using Recent Documents from the Apple menu.

Opening a File Using the Application That Created It

1. Open the application with which you created the file. For this example, open a file created with Microsoft Word.
2. Once Word is open, click *File* and select *Open* (see Figure B.16). The Open dialog box appears (see Figure B.17).

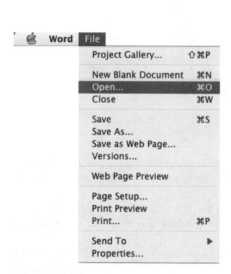

Figure B.16
Open file

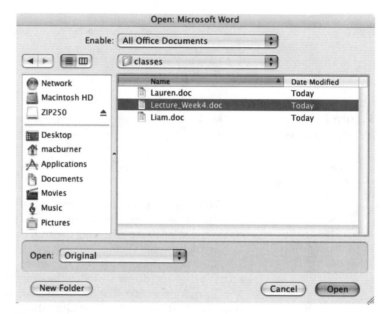

Figure B.17
Open dialogue box

3. Use the Open dialog box to locate the folder or file you want to open. If you need to open a file in a different folder, click the double arrows on the location box (in Figure B.17 the location box has *classes* selected as the current folder), then select the disk drive or folder that contains the item. Once you locate the file, select it by clicking on it one time, then click *Open*. In this example, the file to be opened is *Lecture_Week4.doc,* and it is in the Classes folder. Once it is selected, click the Open button to open the file.

Accessing and Opening a File Using the Macintosh HD

The Macintosh HD can be used to access and open a file named *Lecture_Week4.doc* located on the computer's hard drive in a folder named Classes.

1. Double-click the Macintosh HD icon on the desktop, and its window appears.
2. Double-click the folder that contains the file you want to open. In this example, open the file *Lecture_Week4.doc* located in the Classes folder. In the Macintosh HD window, locate and double-click the Classes folder (see Figure B.18), which opens the Classes window.
3. In the Classes window, locate the file *Lecture_Week4.doc* and double-click it to open the file.

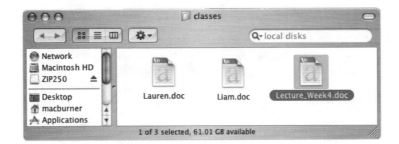

Figure B.18
Open folder

Opening a File Using Recent Items

Recent Items on the Apple menu presents a list of recently opened files and applications. Using Recent Items, you can quickly open a file that you have been working on without searching for it on your computer or opening the application that created it. The Recent Items option opens both the file and its application. Keep in mind that the Recent Items list changes as you open and close files.

1. Click *Apple* and then select *Recent Items*. The Recent Items submenu displays.
2. Click the name of the file that you want to open (see Figure B.19). This step assumes that you already have a file created and that you recently opened it. In this example, the Microsoft Word file *Lecture_Week4.doc* opens.

Figure B.19
Recent Items

Opening Multiple Programs

You can work with several files simultaneously, with each file opened in its own window. For instance, you might open Microsoft Word and Excel files and copy and paste data between them. The following steps illustrate how to open multiple programs, switch between programs, and reposition and resize program windows.

Opening Programs

1. Open Word by clicking its icon on the Dock or by accessing it through the Macintosh HD. The Project Gallery appears (see Figure B.20). Click *OK*, and Word opens with one blank untitled document.

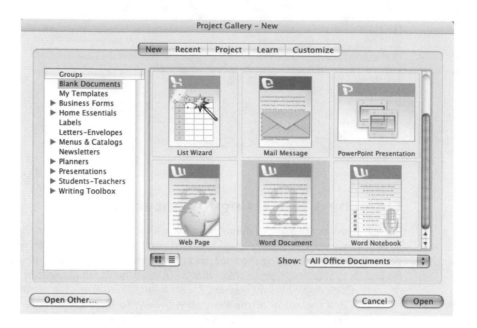

Figure B.20
Project Gallery

2. Repeat the process (step 1) for Excel. You now have two programs open, Word and Excel, and each program displays one blank document. Both program icons display on the Dock.

Switching Between Programs

Use the Dock to switch between Word and Excel (see Figure B.21). If you are viewing the Excel document, switch to Word by clicking the Word icon on the Dock. Alternatively, you can switch between applications by pressing the Command and Tab keys simultaneously. When you press Command and Tab, program icons display on screen indicating the active program (see Figure B.22). In Figure B.22, Word is the active program or the program to be selected. Repeatedly pressing the Tab key changes the selection. Release the key, and the selected program becomes active.

Figure B.21
The Dock: Switching
between applications

Figure B.22
The Command + Tab:
Switching between
applications

Repositioning and Resizing Program Windows

In this example, you can resize the Word and Excel windows and then copy data from Excel into Word.

1. If Word and Excel are open to full screen, restore them to adjust the window size. Click the Zoom (expand/contract) button at the top-left corner of the window on the Word file.

2. Switch to Excel by selecting it on the Dock and, if it is full screen, reduce it. *Note:* If you are in Word and see Excel in the background, click on Excel's window. This makes Excel

Figure B.23
Resizing windows

active; it is an alternative to switching between programs using the Dock. When programs are visible, clicking on them in the background brings them to the foreground and makes them active.

3. Resize document windows. Make either the Word or Excel window active. Position the mouse cursor at the bottom-right corner of the window. The cursor changes to an arrow (see Figure B.23). While holding the mouse button down, drag upward and to the left. A shadowed box displays around the window as it resizes.

   Resize the Word and Excel windows so that are both visible (see Figure B.24). If you need to reposition either window, click on the title bar and, while pressing the mouse button, drag the window to the desired location.

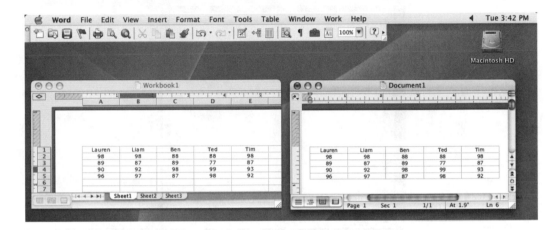

Figure B.24
Resized Word and
Excel windows

4. For this example, suppose you have a data set entered into Excel. Make the Excel window active by clicking its title bar or by selecting the Excel icon on the Dock. With the Excel window active, select the data in the spreadsheet and copy it.

5. Make the Word window active by clicking its title bar or by selecting the Word icon on the Dock. Now paste the data from Excel into the Word file. The data appear in a table within Word. Notice in Figure B.24 that the Word window is darker than Excel's window. The darker shaded window indicates the active program.

Closing a File

1. Clicking the Close button at the top-left corner of a window closes the file. In addition, the Close button closes windows associated with folders.

2. You can also close a file by selecting *Close* from the application's File menu (see Figure B.25). When you close a file, only the active file is closed. The program and any other files remain open.

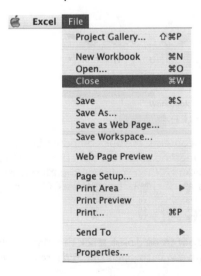

Figure B.25
Close file

3. When working in a program, you may have multiple documents open. In such cases, each document has a window, and each window has a Close button. For example, in Figure B.26, Word has two documents open (Document1 and Document2). Clicking the Close button on Document2 closes only the Document2 file. The Document1 file remains open.

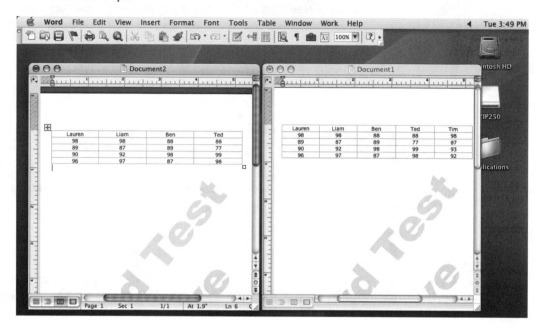

Figure B.26
Multiple document windows

Quitting an Application

To quit a program, select *Quit* from the program's menu (see Figure B.27) or press the Command and Q keys. Quitting a program closes the application (e.g., Word or Excel) and all open files.

Figure B.27
Quitting an application

Viewing the Contents of Your Computer

There are several ways to view the contents of your computer. Double-clicking the Macintosh HD icon on the desktop is an easy method to access the contents of your computer. It allows you to view and manage files and folders. When you open the Macintosh HD, you get a detailed view of your computer's contents, such as the folder contents, files, and programs.

Opening the Macintosh HD

Figure B.28
Macintosh HD

To open Macintosh HD and view its contents, double-click the Macintosh HD icon on the desktop (see Figure B.28). As an alternative way to open the Macintosh HD from the desktop, you could press the Tab key until the Macintosh HD is selected, then press the Command and the letter O keys.

The Macintosh HD Window

Once you open the Macintosh HD window, you will see the programs, files, and folders contained on your computer's hard drive as well as devices (disk drives) connected to your computer. You can view these items in a variety of ways, including as lists (see Figure B.29), icons (see Figure B.30), or columns (see Figure B.31).

Figure B.29
List view

Figure B.30
Icon view

Figure B.31
Column view

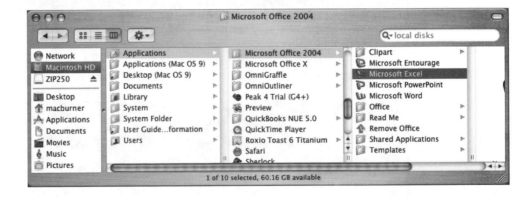

You can alter the view (e.g., icon, list, and columns) of window contents by selecting *as Icons*, *as List*, or *as Columns* from the View menu on the desktop (see Figure B.32).

Double-click a folder to view its content or, when in the List view, click the arrow to the left of the folder to expand or collapse it. For example, in Figure B.33, the Applications folder was expanded by clicking the arrow to its left. The arrow turns to a downward position. The contents of the Applications folder appear indented under it. In this case, *Applications* contains folders named *AppleScript* and *Art Directors Toolkit 3* as well as other items that are visible in the Macintosh HD window.

From the Macintosh HD window, you can also open files and programs by double-clicking their icons.

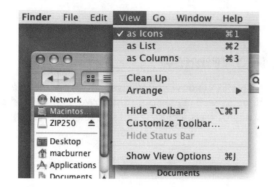

Figure B.32
View menu

Figure B.33
Macintosh HD
window

Managing Files: Moving, Copying, Deleting, and Renaming Files

This section explains how to manage files with the Macintosh operating system.

Moving a File

When moving a file or folder, you move it from one location (e.g., folder or disk) to another. If, for example, you have a file titled *MyLesson.doc* in a folder titled *Week1*, when you move *MyLesson.doc* from the Week1 folder to another folder, *MyLesson.doc* is no longer in the Week1 folder. The Move command differs from copy. Copy places a duplicate file in the location of your choice. It leaves the original file in place and unaltered.

1. You can move files by dragging and dropping them. To move a file or folder open Macintosh HD by double-clicking its icon on the desktop.
2. Find the file or folder that you want to move and click it one time to select it (see Figure B.34). Figure B.34 shows the List view with *Lecture_Week4.doc* selected.

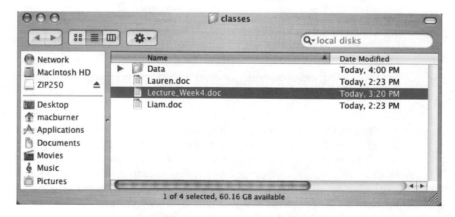

Figure B.34
Moving files

3. In Figure B.34, the Classes folder is open, and its contents are displayed beneath it.
4. Move the *Lecture_Week4.doc* file into *Data* by dragging and dropping it. Click *Lecture_Week4.doc* one time to select it and, while holding the left mouse button down,

drag it onto the Data folder. The Data folder highlights as the mouse pointer approaches it. With the folder highlighted, release the mouse button, and the file moves to *Data*.

Copying a File

The Copy function duplicates a file or folder. Find and select the file or folder that you want to copy. For this example, make a copy of the *Lecture_Week4.doc* file in the Classes folder and place a copy of it in *Data*. In Figure B.35, the *Lecture_Week4.doc* file is selected. From the desktop File menu, select *Duplicate* (or press the Command and the D keys), and a copy of the file appears in the Classes folder. Notice that the duplicate file, *Lecture_Week4copy.doc,* appears below the original file in Figure B.35. Now move the duplicate file to *Data* by dragging it on top of the Data folder and dropping it.

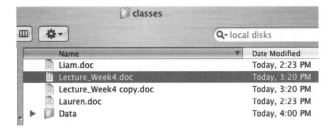

Figure B.35
Copy files

Alternatively, to copy *Lecture_Week4.doc* to the Data folder, you can drag and drop it onto the Data folder while holding the Option key down. This duplicates the file and places the copy inside the Data folder. With this method, *copy* is not appended to the file name.

Deleting Files and Folders

There are several ways to delete files and folders (see Figure B.36), two of which are presented: using the *Move To Trash* option and dragging and dropping files to the Trash.

Figure B.36
Deleting files

Using the Move to Trash Option to Delete Files or Folders

Suppose you want to delete a file named *Lecture_Week4.doc* located in the Data folder. Find and select *Lecture_Week4.doc* and then select *Move To Trash* on the Desktop File menu (see Figure B.36). This command removes the file from its current location and places it in the Trash. Alternatively, once you select the file, you can send it to the Trash by pressing the Command and Delete keys.

Remember that files or folders in the Trash can be recovered or retrieved. In addition, files or folders in the Trash take up disk storage space, and only after emptying the Trash are they removed from your computer permanently.

Dragging and Dropping Files to the Trash

Locate the file that you want to delete. Click it once to select it and, while holding the mouse button down, drag the file to the Trash can on the Dock. As the mouse pointer approaches the

Trash icon on the Dock, the icon highlights (see Figure B.37). With the Trash icon highlighted, release the mouse and the file is moved to the Trash.

Figure B.37
Trash icon on Dock

Emptying the Trash

All deleted files and folders are sent to the Trash before they are removed from your computer.

1. You must empty the Trash to permanently remove deleted files or folders. Empty the Trash by selecting *Empty Trash* from the Finder menu (see Figure B.38). You can also empty the Trash by pressing the Command, Shift, and Delete keys simultaneously. Another way to empty the Trash is by pressing the Control key while clicking the Trash icon on the Dock.

Figure B.38
Empty Trash

2. An alert box appears asking if you want to remove the items from the Trash (see Figure B.39). Clicking *OK* removes the items.

Figure B.39
Empty Trash alert

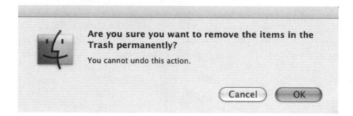

Selecting Multiple Files

In the preceding discussion, the examples illustrate moving, copying, or deleting one file at a time. You can also select multiple items at one time to be moved, copied, or deleted.

1. To select multiple items that are adjacent, click the mouse button and, while holding it down, drag across the items that you want to select. After highlighting all the items that you want selected, release the mouse button (see Figure B.40).

Figure B.40
Selecting
adjacent items

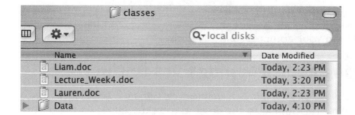

2. When items to be selected are not adjacent, press the Command key and click the files, folders, or programs that you want to select (see Figure B.41).

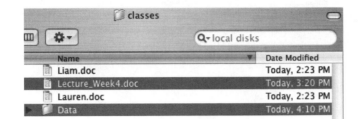

Figure B.41
Selecting nonadjacent items

Renaming a File

Figure B.42
Rename file

Click the file or folder that you want to rename. Click on the item's name rather than on the icon. Clicking the name selects the text. Figure B.42 shows an icon with the text selected. With the text selected, you can edit it or type a new name.

Searching for Files or Folders

Search is a useful tool for locating files, folders, or applications on your computer and information on the Internet.

1. To locate a file or folder on your computer, click the File menu on the Desktop and select *Find*.
2. The *Find* box appears (see Figure B.43).

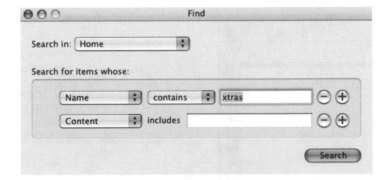

Figure B.43
Search

3. In the *Search in* box, type the name of the file or folder that you want to locate. You can search for items by file name or by content.
4. Specify where to search for files or folders by selecting the location with the *Search in* box option.
5. Begin the search by clicking the Search button, and the Search Results screen displays. You can stop the search at any time by closing the Search Results screen.

Shutting Down Your Computer

You should shut down your computer before turning it off. To exit the Mac OS system and turn off your computer, click the Apple menu on the desktop and select *Shut Down* (see Figure B.44).

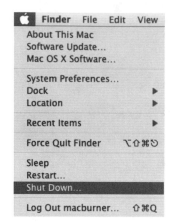

Figure B.44
Shut Down

On the Apple menu, you will notice several options, including Restart and Sleep. Restart shuts down and restarts the computer or starts a new session. Sleep keeps the computer running on low power, but it maintains the contents of memory. While in the Sleep mode, touching a key wakes the computer.

The Microsoft Office 2004 and Office 2007 Workspaces

As of this writing, Microsoft Office 2004 is the most current version of Office for the Macintosh. Microsoft Office 2004 for Macintosh includes Word, Excel, Entourage, and PowerPoint. The database program Access is not included. Generally, there is much commonality between the Microsoft Office 2004 applications and the Windows version. The following screens illustrate the workspaces of three of the Office applications: Word (see Figures B.45 and B.46), Excel (see Figures B.47 and B.48), and PowerPoint (see Figures B.49 and B.50). For each application, two sets of screens are presented, one for the Macintosh Microsoft Office 2004 version and the other for Windows Office 2007. Notice that overall the menu items, toolbars, and workspaces between these versions are similar and that both versions offer many of the same options and features.

Figure B.45
Office 2004—Word

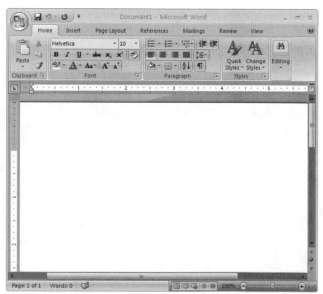

Figure B.46
Windows Office 2007—Word

Figure B.47
Office 2004—Excel

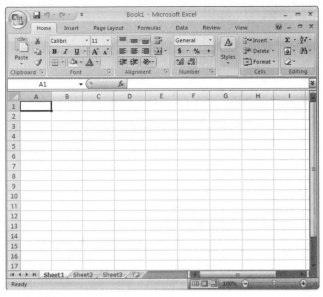

Figure B.48
Windows Office 2007—Excel

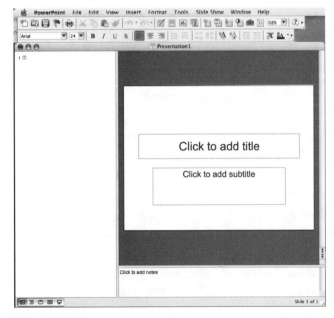

Figure B.49
Office 2004—PowerPoint

Figure B.50
Windows Office 2007—PowerPoint

In many instances, Microsoft Office 2004 and Microsoft Office 2007 offer a variety of methods for accomplishing similar tasks. An understanding of the Mac OS X operating system components, such as the desktop, and knowledge of the varied approaches that it offers for opening and managing files and programs will be beneficial to you when using Microsoft Office 2004.

GLOSSARY

Acceptable Use Policies: A set of rules for students, teachers, staff, and administrators that govern the use of school or school district computers, networks, and the Internet.

Alias: A file that provides quick access to frequently used items, such as programs, folders, documents, or disks. An alias is equivalent to a shortcut on the Windows platform.

Application: A software program that performs a specific function or purpose. For example, Word is an application that helps you compose a letter or a report, and Excel is an application that helps you analyze data. Word, Excel, and PowerPoint are all applications.

Attachment: A file sent along with an e-mail message. Documents, pictures, and multimedia objects may be sent; the receiving computer must have the software installed to read the attached file.

AutoCorrection: Word has an AutoCorrect options button that allows you to undo automatic corrections or select a different AutoCorrect option.

Calendar: An Outlook folder that keeps track of appointments.

CC, or Courtesy Copy: An option used to send a copy of an e-mail message to one or more persons.

Cell: A unit in an Excel worksheet column that holds information, such as text and numerical data.

Clip Art: Professionally prepared art stored as files that may be inserted in Office applications.

Commands: Tasks that are performed in an Office program, such as Open and Save, and are found in the Office menu bars.

Contacts: An outlook folder that maintains an address book.

Copyright: Laws that regulate and describe the manner in which materials may be used and copied.

Design Templates: Predefined colors, layout formats, and font styles that give PowerPoint presentations and Word documents a specific look.

Desktop: A work area on the computer where you place files and folders. The desktop is the screen that typically displays when you first turn on the computer.

Document Object: A Word document that has been inserted into a file.

Drafts: An outlook folder that stores unsent e-mail messages.

Drag and Drop: A method of moving objects by dragging them with the mouse and dropping them in a desired location by releasing the mouse button.

Dragging: A method of moving objects by dragging them with the computer mouse.

Embed: A method of inserting an object in an Office application file whereby the object embeds or becomes part of the file.

Expanded Menu: A menu format that displays all the commands in a pull-down list.

Field: In a database, a specific category or location to store information. For example, a field called *first name* could store students' first names.

File: A unit of information produced by a program (e.g., Microsoft Word). For example, a Word document, PowerPoint presentations, and Excel workbooks are files. To organize files, put them in folders.

Floating Toolbars: Toolbars that can be detached from the application window's border, moved, and resized.

Folder: Often referred to as a directory. Computer files or directories are places to store digital work files. Placing work files into folders or directories keeps them organized.

Form: A database object that presents display boxes where information may be displayed or entered. A form usually displays one record at a time.

Formatting: Refers to characteristics (e.g., bold, italic, color, size, type, and so on) applied to text, tables, lists, and documents. In a document, it allows for paragraph formatting or changing columns.

Formula: An Excel expression in the form of a series of numbers or cell references that produces a new value. The formula $= (A1 + B1)$ when placed in cell C1 adds the contents of cells A1 and B1 and places the results in C1. All formulas must start with an equals sign $(=)$.

Frames: A space in Publisher that contains pictures. Pictures may be clip art, a circle, an arrow, a line, or AutoShapes as well as a variety of graphic files such as GIF (Graphics Interchange Format), JPEG (Joint Photographic Experts Group), or scanned photographs taken with a digital camera.

Function: Formulas built into Excel (see Formula).

Home Page: The first Web document the user sees when entering a Web site.

HTML (HyperText Markup Language): The computer language used to format Web documents. You can save your Word documents, PowerPoint presentations, and Excel worksheets as HTML documents and put them on the Web.

Hyperlink: Creates a connection between a word or phrase in a document to another document on the computer or to the Internet.

Hypertext Links: Often associated with Web documents but may also be in other files, such as PowerPoint presentations. Hypertext links are text and/or pictures that can be clicked to take the user to another screen, Web document, or media object (e.g., video or audio). These screens, documents, and objects may be within the same file, the same Web site, or at a Web site around the world. They are often referred to as hyperlinks.

Inbox: An Outlook folder that stores incoming (received) e-mail messages.

Independent Design Elements: In Publisher, text and picture portions of a publication that act as independent entities when designing publications.

Insert Object: A method of placing an object or a portion of an object into an Office application file. For example, when a PowerPoint slide is placed or inserted into Word, it is referred to as a slide object.

Internet: A large, worldwide network of computers (computing hardware and software) in which the computers communicate with one another.

ISTE (International Society for Technology in Education): An international organization of educators that develop teaching standards for students and teachers.

Link to File: A method of inserting an object in an Office application file whereby the object is linked to the file. The object does not embed or become a part of the file.

Mac OS: The Macintosh operating system (Mac OS X).

NCATE (National Council for Accreditation of Teacher Education): A council that developed a set of standards for the accreditation of teachers. NCATE also accredits teacher education organizations.

Objects: A Word document, PowerPoint slide or presentation, Excel worksheet, image, sound, video, and so on are some examples of the files or objects that can be embedded or linked to Office application files. When a file created by a separate application is placed into the Office file, it is referred to as an object.

Office Button: Office 2007 provides the Office button located at the top left of the application window. When clicked, it displays a menu of file commands, such as New, Open, and, Save As, as well as a listing of recently opened documents. In many ways, it takes the place of the File menu item in previous Office versions.

Outline Tab: One of several view options available for viewing a PowerPoint presentation while it is being developed. The Outline tab presents slides in text outline form.

Outlook Today: Outlook function that displays a summary of the current day's activities.

Presentation Object: A PowerPoint presentation that has been inserted into a file.

Publication Types: A set of business publications created in Publisher that contains consistent color and font schemes and designs.

Queries: Searches in Access that allow users to find specific information in a database, such as who lives in a particular ZIP code area.

Quick Access Toolbar: Displays quick access buttons such as undo and save commands. It is located at the top of the application window on the right side of the Office button.

Record: A collection of information about a thing or person (e.g., name, address, phone number, e-mail address, and so on) in a table of an Access database.

Relative Cell Reference: In Excel, a reference to a cell (e.g., C1) that, when used in a formula, changes when the formula is copied to another cell. If cell E1 contains the formula $= (C1 + D1)$ and E1 is copied to E2, then E2's formula changes to $= (C2 + D2)$.

Report: Summarizes Access database information in a document format.

Ribbon: The Office 2007 interface presents the Ribbon, which displays groups of related commands in tabs across the top (it can be moved) of the application window. Tabs provide access to major program functions and features.

Right-click: On Windows computers, pressing the right mouse button. The computer mouse often has two buttons: a left button and a right button. In most instances, the left button is used for selecting menu options, moving objects, and dragging and dropping. When the right mouse button is clicked, menu choices associated with the selected object appear.

Shortcut Menus: Menus that appear on the screen when you right-click an item and that display the most frequently used commands.

Shortcuts: Provide quick access to frequently used files and programs. You can place shortcuts on the desktop or in folders. Instead of searching the computer for a file or program, you can create a shortcut to it that opens the file or program.

Slide: A screen that may contain text and content such as pictures, clip art, graphs, tables, diagrams, video, and audio. Several slides make up a presentation.

Slide Object: A single PowerPoint slide that has been inserted into a file.

Slide Show: A PowerPoint view that presents the finished slides of a presentation. In this mode, slides cannot be edited.

Slide Sorter: One of several PowerPoint view options that presents small images of each slide in the presentation. It is useful for seeing the order of all slides. You can copy, paste, delete, and rearrange slides in the Slide Sorter.

Slides Tab: One of several view options available for viewing a presentation while it is being developed. The Slides view presents miniature slides of the presentation.

Start Button: Appears to the left of the taskbar. Clicking *Start* displays the Start menu and provides access to programs, files, help, and search facilities, among other things.

Table: (a) Allows you to display information in a table format in the word processed document. (b) A collection of information in an Access database about a specific topic (e.g., student information, class materials inventory, and so on). A table consists of fields and records. Those may be more than one table in a database.

Task Pane: A window that allows users to work with common tasks, such as opening a new document and formatting text.

Taskbar: Contains buttons that provide access to opened folders and files and make switching between them convenient. Although you can position the taskbar at the top of sides of the screen, it typically appears at the bottom.

Tasks: An Outlook folder that allows the creation of lists of activities.

Text Box: A space that acts as a container for text and can be arranged, reshaped, and created within a publication.

URL: Uniform Resource Locator. Frequently referred to as the address or Web address, such as http://www.duq.edu.

Web Browser: A software application used to view Web content. Some popular Web browsers include Internet Explorer, Netscape, and Mozilla Firefox.

Web Page: A singe Web document that may contain images, text, graphics, video, and audio.

Web Site: A collection of Web documents that may contain images, text, graphics, video, and audio.

Windows Vista: The current Windows operating system. Windows XP, 98, NT, and 95 are earlier versions of the Windows operating system.

Workbook: An Excel spreadsheet file comprised of one or more worksheets. Excel identifies worksheets as Sheet1, Sheet2, Sheet3, and so on. A single workbook may contain numerous worksheets.

Worksheet: A screen in an Excel workbook made up of columns, rows, and cells. Each worksheet may contain as many as 256 columns and 65,536 rows.

Worksheet Object: An Excel worksheet that has been inserted into a file.

World Wide Web: Often referred to as the Web. A collection of information viewed with a Web browser that is available though computing networks.

INDEX